Joyful Revolution

Joyful Revolution
Poverty, Social Justice, and the Story of Mary Rabagliati

Diana Skelton

Edited by Kate Evans

The Lutterworth Press

The Lutterworth Press

P.O. Box 60
Cambridge
CB1 2NT
United Kingdom

www.lutterworth.com
publishing@lutterworth.com

Paperback ISBN: 978 0 7188 9830 4
PDF ISBN: 978 0 7188 9832 8
ePub ISBN: 978 0 7188 9831 1

British Library Cataloguing in Publication Data

A record is available from the British Library

Published by The Lutterworth Press, 2025

Copyright © Diana Skelton, 2025

All rights reserved. No part of this edition may be reproduced, stored electronically or in any retrieval system, or transmitted in any form or by any means, electronic, mechanical, photocopying, recording, or otherwise, or used for artificial intelligence training without prior written permission from the Publisher (permissions@lutterworth.com).

Contents

Part I. An Unusual Life Choice   1

   1. First Encounters: 'My Life Was Shallow'   3

   2. Origins: Worlds Colliding   18

   3. 'The Road just Stopped and No One Else Gave a Damn'   35

   4. Laundry and 'Creating Atmosphere'   43

   5. Joyfulness and a Spirit of Inquiry   54

Part II. Social Change and Racism: 'Our Blood is the Price We Have to Pay for Change'   67

   6. Choosing between Freedom or Safety: On the Front Lines of the War on Poverty   69

   7. Racism, César Chávez, and Dolores Huerta   82

   8. 'Immense but Hidden Potential' in Apartheid South Africa   92

   9. Solidarity in the Face of Racism   106

Part III. 'Women Always Seem to Get the Short End of the Stick'   113

   10. Violence against Women, and the Intersection of Poverty and Gender   115

11. Bedbugs in Birmingham and a Prison Visit in Pontoise	121
12. Losing Custody of Children in Family Court	130

Part IV. Founding a UK team: 'The Best and Worst of Humanity and of Myself' — 141

13. Frimhurst Family Centre: 'The Threat of Violence Is Always in the Air'	143
14. 'Kicking Myself for My Temper'	154
15. Dreamers and Lunatics? Changing Minds	162
16. 'Providing a Megaphone' while 'Everybody Else Had Their Clipboards'	170
17. A Westminster Abbey Exhibition and Being a Rottweiler	179
18. An Alliance with Social Workers to Denounce a Culture of Risk	193

Part V. Bringing the World on Board — 201

19. The United Nations: Women's Conferences in Mexico, Copenhagen, and Nairobi	203
20. Travelling in Africa: 'She Missed the Memo!'	215
21. A Meaningful Foundation for Friendship in Sierra Leone	235
22. Palestine, Israel, and Sunrise over Mount Tabor: A Fractured and Disharmonious Land	251

Part VI. Forging Legacies — 269

23. Upheaval	271
24. Dissonance and the Black Forest	277
25. Doubt, Religion, and Beliefs	293

26. 'Faith in Life; Faith in People'	302
27. Some of my Best Friends are Journalists	313
Conclusion: 'Mary Helped Us to Discover our Strengths'	326
Acknowledgements	333
Notes	335
Index	359

Part I

An Unusual Life Choice

Chapter 1

First Encounters: 'My Life Was Shallow'

'You can't leave the house like that! Go use the pressing iron in that cupboard.' Barely 21 years old, I was being scolded about my only slightly rumpled Indian-print wrap-around skirt by a woman I'd met just a few weeks earlier. Mary Rabagliati was one of the bossiest women I'd ever met, so I meekly complied, not wanting to end up on her bad side; but also slightly offended that she was applying her own high standards for personal appearance to me as part of my training for the International Volunteer Corps of All Together in Dignity/ATD Fourth World.

Mary Rabagliati

Provided courtesy of Paul de St Croix

It didn't occur to me then that when she first joined this anti-poverty movement in the 1960s people struggling with homelessness and stigmatisation had no wish to be seen with middle-class hippies choosing to drop out of society and 'slum it'. Conditions were harsh in the emergency housing camp where Mary lived when she was 21. Assigned a bunk in the barracks for female volunteers, every morning she joined hundreds of other camp residents to queue at a pump for a bucket of water, and to 'slop out' her chamber pot at the very edge of camp, where a reeking latrine pit stood amid a rat-infested moat. Mary agreed with ATD's founder Father Joseph Wresinski that volunteers should defy these unhygienic conditions and be well groomed – washing from a bucket of water behind the curtain around their bunk bed – because appearances are essential for being taken seriously. And their intentions were very serious indeed: to gain societal recognition of the expertise of people in poverty.

The emergency housing camp where ATD Fourth World was founded

© *Reprinted from April 1966 issue of "Igloo" Magazine, ATD Fourth World*

Later Mary recalled, 'In that terrible place, we got up every day and dressed respectably. Being presentable was a way of showing respect to the families around us.' Wresinski used to tell new volunteers: 'If you want to look a mess, go home. In the middle of miserable poverty, you should look so handsome that people are glad to see you.' I'm sure this message appealed greatly to Mary because the idea of her ever having *wanted* to 'look a mess' is beyond the realms of imagination. Slender and neat, she was always dressed to draw attention not only to her good looks but to the magnetism that made you want to hear what was on her mind.

Although Mary had a commandingly abrasive side, she charmed me from the start. I had been sent from my country, the United States, to spend two years in France at ATD's international centre. Four of us new trainees moved into a group house where Mary was the senior of six Volunteer Corps members already there. On our first evening, we all crowded around the heavy oak dinner table – a cast-off gift from a donor redecorating her second home. As we dined our way through potatoes, chicken, and home-made béchamel sauce (which seemed impossibly fancy to me as an American, but turned out to be the thrifty French housewife's trick to make any meal stretch farther), Mary led us in a round of introductions and an orientation to housework and cooking rotas. I was still trying to remember the French vocabulary for mopping – a convoluted phrase about 'passing a rag' over the floor (which is more or less what they do, not having squeezy sponge-mop technology) – when suddenly Mary decided to ask everyone's birthday. She soon got to me, but I was reluctant to answer, and just said, 'It's in the fall.'

'When in the fall?' Her British tones sounded imperiously posh as she pressed me for a more specific answer.

First Encounters: 'My Life Was Shallow'

'September.'

'But it's September now! Which date?'

As everyone stared, I felt incredibly awkward because my birthday was the very next day. In childhood, my birthday fell at the beginning of the school year when friend groups often hadn't formed yet. Between this and my extreme skittishness about calling attention to myself, I had never enjoyed my own birthdays. When I moved in with Mary, I had just travelled 4,000 miles from home. The last thing I wanted was to become the focus of a sudden social obligation for this group of total strangers.

And yet Mary made my 21st birthday a delightful one! When I awoke the next morning, in addition to a breakfast treat of croissants, I found a gift. This was puzzling, given that the bakery was the only shop open at that early hour. But when I shyly unwrapped the small package, I discovered that Mary had generously decided to offer me one of her own possessions, brought back from her recent trip to Kenya. In between meeting with an eccentric philanthropist at the High Commissariat for Refugees and visiting a dynamic community organiser, befriended during the Nairobi World Conference on Women, Mary had made time to shop, price haggling in a crowded marketplace. This was how she got the object she now offered me: a square of batik cloth the colour of amber and sandstone depicting five women in conversation together. (When I look at it now, in the entryway of my flat, the grace and energy of the central woman makes me think of Mary.) After work that evening, Mary invited two English-speaking friends over for dinner, followed by a sing-along. Although I wasn't yet familiar with Irish songs like 'Molly Malone', my family has always loved singing together, so Mary found the best possible way to allay my homesickness.

I met Mary in 1986, and lost her when she died in 1992. In those six years, our conversations made a lasting impact on my own life choices. Later on, I missed her, and often wondered what she would have gone

Me, shortly after I first met Mary, trying to figure out how to be useful during an ATD Fourth World construction project

© *Patrice Le Ridant, ATD Fourth World / Joseph Wresinski Centre* on to accomplish if she hadn't succumbed to cancer at the age of 50. What I didn't realise was that much of what she actually *did* accomplish was hidden from view. I was astounded in 2016 when I visited ATD's archives and began reading Mary's correspondence, interviews, and reports. I had known that she spent a great deal of time and energy editing or translating other people's writing; but I had no idea that she also made time to do so much writing of her own.

Year in and year out, she wrote volumes, usually late at night after a long day of work, and often in French where she sometimes struggled to find an apt translation for an English turn of phrase, such as when she tried to refer to the 'baby boom' by writing about 'le bombardement de bébés'! As I plodded through cardboard archive boxes, opening folders made of reused scrap paper and noting rust stains radiating from staples, I was rewarded with Mary's wit and obstinacy crackling off the page. Reading her correspondence, my jaw dropped as implausible stories unfolded of run-ins with authority figures and her deft ways of resolving them (at least on most occasions). Using a third-hand typewriter in an unheated shed, she recorded hard-hitting descriptions of dire poverty along with her own insights. For example, she recalled her first arrival at an emergency housing camp in Noisy-le-Grand, where Wresinski was just beginning to develop the anti-poverty movement that would become ATD Fourth World:

> On a dark misty February evening, I got off the bus and walked down the tarmac road. Suddenly the tarmac

Daily life in the emergency housing camp in 1966

Provided courtesy of Margaret Bourgein

became only a dusty potholed path. The nearest bus stop was hundreds of metres away from the camp. The road stopped, and you had to walk in the dust – or the mud – to a place where everything was filthy. There were rats all over. People were *living* there! I was really shocked. The conditions were indescribably terrible. These people made me realise that my life was shallow, empty, and futile.

Mary's description makes me think of my own shock at deep poverty. I grew up in the 1970s, on a dead-end street three houses long in working-class Oxon Hill, Maryland, just outside Southeast Washington, DC, where every spring the drabness is sprigged with the mustard yellow of rampant forsythia bushes. With the population about 75% Black, I was in the minority as a white kid (occasionally called a 'honky'). A mile from home, not far from the liquor store, was my elementary school. Grandly named Barnaby Manor, the school emblem was an eagle, emblazoned on small sweatshirts. Some of us were white; most of us were Black; and our school colours were blue and gold. All teachers were white except for one.

'One nation under God, indivisible, with liberty and justice for all.' Every morning, the pledge of allegiance was fluently reeled off by the same childish voices that stumbled awkwardly over read-aloud English lessons, Dick-and-Jane irrelevancies about Johnny Appleseed and Daniel Boone. Until the five days a year of Martin Luther King Week when suddenly brown faces appeared on our mimeographed history hand-outs and we all scrambled for the Burnt Sienna crayon in the Crayola box to copy King's photo while the white teacher retold the story of the Underground Railroad. Just one week; then attention snapped back to 'regular' history as we memorised the order of the Presidents and turned back to the peach-coloured crayon labelled 'Flesh'. At recess, the shout ringing out from the monkey bars was often: 'It's a fight, it's a fight, between a blackie and a white!' That was Barnaby Manor, with no thread of black in the red-white-and-blue we saluted.

When I was 15, concern about racism led me to volunteer in a part of down-town DC that was 100% Black and much poorer than Oxon Hill. All summer, I went every day to a children's soup kitchen called Martha's Table at the intersection of 14th and W Streets. At the time, that was the headlined 'heart of the drug district', abutting the red light district. Commuting about seven miles from my home meant transferring twice, each time to a filthier bus, lumbering towards seedy strip clubs and peep shows.

Disembarking each morning, I wince at the sudden stench of sewage and desolation. From the bus stop, past the windowless purple-and-black store-front marked 'Black Chen's Soul Kitchen', I thread my way past bleary men with bloodshot eyes who ask: 'Hey, Blue Eyes, how much you want?' My eyes are green, but that's not where they're looking. Then past 'Jewel's Beauty Salon' comes the vacant lot where four elderly gentlemen sit in folding chairs playing spades. One with yellowed teeth tips a battered hat towards me. From the shroud of a doorway scampers a 5-year-old calling out, 'Hi Danny!', his childish distortion of Diana.

'Hi Tyrell', I smile. Gleefully, he skedaddles ahead, into Martha's Table where he plops down to chomp his way through a grilled cheese sandwich and a storybook. All day long, kids flock in, fishing pennies out of their shoes for the nominal meal fee and wolfing down peanut-butter-and-jelly as fast as I slap sandwiches together. They turn up their noses at donated croissants, not because they are going stale, but because they are unfamiliar. Then at 6 o'clock, I whip out Lysol to clean up and leave, back past hock shops, liquor stores, and a Woolworth's where the windows wear chain mail.

As smudges of dusk approach, the children trickle homeward, and the gentle spades players go inside to watch from barred and broken windows the gradual massing of teens on the street corner. Regularly police cars skid up onto the side-walk shouting 'Sasquatch!' to scatter the teens – for a few moments until they drift back together a bit further on.

Excitement one night: as I await my bus – fingers taut against my purse, clutching a strand of home as much as warding off purse-snatchers – just in front of me a police car tears screaming up, in hot pursuit of a red Jaguar, only to crash into a creaky Dodge Dart that was too sluggish to give way to the siren in time. The police aren't hurt – but they are suddenly immobilised in hostile territory. Within seconds, throngs of people materialise to jeer the police. As the first bottle is tossed, the air flares with more sirens. Fire ambulances; police reinforcements; an unmarked sedan that has improbably sprouted a siren – all converge on my corner to take some of the unruly crowd into custody. For me, the event ends as a hulking red-white-and-blue Metrobus arrives to carry me homeward, unscathed.

That's the memory that floods back when I read Mary's words: 'These people made me realise that my life was shallow, empty, and futile.' That path of 'shallow futility' was exactly what I feared in an ordinary job, and avoiding it drew me to ATD. Ours is an unusual organisation with a unique approach that can be hard to explain. This was a challenge for Mary too. In 1964, she fumed in a letter home: 'It's very difficult to make these journalists understand anything if they think some other story will sell their paper better!' Her fury was sparked by the first line of a *Daily Mail* profile of her: 'The drunkards and derelict families of the Paris shanty town know her as "our little English friend Mary".' The entire article was meant to compliment her. But the author's paternalistic tang echoed centuries of social engineering designed to 'save the deserving poor' – while damning those considered 'undeserving' with bigotry. As Mary later told another journalist: 'Nothing is said about what the victims of extreme poverty are doing for themselves under impossibly hard conditions. I was struck by their courage and resourcefulness and just what they have to do to simply survive.'

At the age of 20, Mary quit her job as a secretary in an architectural firm to volunteer in the emergency housing camp in Noisy-le-Grand

Most of the camp's Nissen huts housed two families each.

© ATD Fourth World / Joseph Wresinski Centre

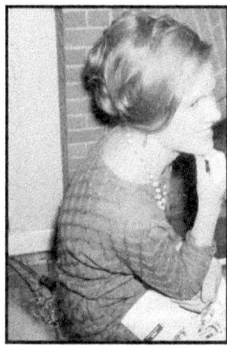

Mary in the 1960s
© Photo by Peter Akehurst

where 280 families lived in bleak squalor. What struck Mary most powerfully was the lives of teenage girls and young mothers. In the mud and without indoor plumbing, chores filled every waking hour, particularly if a girl had younger brothers and sisters. Early marriage, motherhood, and violence further curtailed these girls' horizons. The girls challenged Mary and amused themselves by playing tricks on her – but they also won her lifelong dedication.

The project that led me to Mary's archives was nominally connected to preparing ATD's 60th anniversary, marking the journey of a

The barracks where volunteers slept in bunk beds
Provided courtesy of Margaret Bourgein

group that began with only a French name, the Association 'Aide à Toute Détresse' and eventually became ATD Fourth World, with the original letters reassigned to mean All Together in Dignity. But once I began sifting through Mary's carefully filled notebooks and carbon-copies of her reports on brittle onion-skin paper, it struck me that I was 50, exactly Mary's age when she died. Outliving her made me feel a responsibility to tell her story to those who never met her. At first, the project was straightforward. Hitting on the idea of a draw-my-life video format, I drafted nine scripts and prevailed on an artistic teammate to film his hands painting watercolour backdrops for the narration of Mary's life journey.

First Encounters: 'My Life Was Shallow'

Paul Maréchal created all the artwork
for the draw-my-life video series.

© Paul Maréchal

© Paul Maréchal

However, by the time we posted the final video to YouTube two years later, the project felt incomplete. It wasn't that I had spare time on my hands. Living in London, my days were endlessly busy with ATD's Giving Poverty a Voice programme and also my three daughters. My then 15 and 24 year olds were both studying and living at home, and my 27 year old was a short bus-ride away. But in between work, family meals, or traipsing to the library to help print out the kids' homework, memories of Mary kept tugging at me. For instance, this journal entry of hers, on a rainy day walking through the camp, composed of hundreds of repurposed Quonset-hut army barracks (nicknamed 'igloos' by residents because of their shape):

> *24 November 1964*: I hear only faint noises: a child's raised voice; someone chopping wood; a chicken clucking, perhaps

© Paul Maréchal

© Paul Maréchal

roaming the street. Otherwise, no music, no voices, no shouting, as though everyone left. Only one child is outdoors: a boy who ought to be in school, playing with a dog while wearing shoes twice as big as his feet.

It's hard to explain the feeling of another world, filthy and chaotic – but the atmosphere feels somehow soothing.

Every igloo has a makeshift fence cobbled from planks or cardboard, plastered with posters, pictures of movie stars missing heads, announcements disappearing behind the next cardboard slab. Draped over clotheslines and fences is laundry, grey and threadbare. How hopeless to hang it up in perpetual damp cold, as though there were any chance of it drying!

First Encounters: 'My Life Was Shallow'

> Every yard and garden is different in the summer; but in the winter, they look alike: firewood stacked in flowerbeds; always chickens, maybe a duck; miserable dogs; always junked cars, one flipped upside down mid-road. There might be a refrigerator or a bathtub. Occasionally, there's a surprise: a pretty yard in perfect order; a well-tended rose garden, with a statue of an angel or a cupid. Perhaps a memory or a dream?

I had many conversations with people who found Mary unforgettable. While creating the videos, I contacted: her brother Paul de St Croix in Wales; her cousins in London, Kenya, and the United States; and members of ATD in Surrey, Oxford, the Netherlands, France, the Central African Republic, and elsewhere. Those exchanges spiralled into more dialogues, with more people, and finally into interviews, like one with Anneke Van Elderen, chain-smoking on a bench in spring twilight:

> Mary could be quite fierce. If you didn't have a strong personality as well, you couldn't really connect with her. Sweet gentle people were sometimes afraid of her – but she didn't actually *want* to intimidate people. And she was also so much fun – we used to turn the tables on blokes by whistling, just to provoke them![1]

Although Mary faced challenges, in childhood and as part of ATD Fourth World, it was her strong sense of joy that captivated me. With the privations of the camp, she was eager to offer young people there something thrilling. She got her chance when a new volunteer, Christopher Mason, started a project for teenage boys. Mary was delighted with way the project flourished. She said:

Mary with Anneke van Elderen, at left, and Stuart Williams
© *ATD Fourth World / Joseph Wresinski Centre*

> The camp had a rotten reputation. But once Christopher started, we built a fantastic youth club. To raise money, he organised the boys to collect dustbins, charging a few centimes for each. Collecting rubbish was a useful community project – although rain discouraged the boys, so then it was just Christopher and me pushing the dust cart through the mud. But the youth club was beautiful.

Mary also recalled the influence of Wresinski (who she usually referred to as 'Père Joseph', 'père' being the French word for father):

> One volunteer played guitar, so Père Joseph asked him to form a dance band. It was right when bands were starting, so all the local kids came, even from outside the camp. Some already danced well, and Père Joseph found someone to teach dancing to others.[2]

Father Joseph Wresinski with Mary

© ATD Fourth World / Joseph Wresinski Centre

Mary Rabagliati played a crucial role in developing ATD Fourth World into the international anti-poverty human rights organisation it is today with the ear of some governments and international organisations. She also founded the UK branch and embedded it into the lives of those who live in deep poverty in this country as well as profoundly affecting the approach of many professionals, politicians, academics, and others.

Looking for ways to influence public policy, Mary developed ATD Fourth World's archive and research institute. She spent a year in the United States at the invitation of the Ford Foundation to evaluate the work being done by the War on Poverty. She also spent that year – 1966 – volunteering with the civil rights movement. On her return to Europe, she and Wresinski drew on both the civil rights movement and the War on Poverty to shape ATD Fourth World. They were inspired by the passionate engagement of many diverse people and groups; however, seeing many organisations working at cross purposes made them determined to avoid the pitfall of a lack of cohesive strategy.

First Encounters: 'My Life Was Shallow'   15

During Mary's years founding the British branch of ATD Fourth World, she also pioneered some of our initiatives at the United Nations, bearing witness to the plight of women and girls in poverty, particularly at the first three UN World Conferences on Women. Outspoken and dynamic, Mary never hesitated to speak to ministers or members of Parliament. She often went to the Speakers' Corner in Hyde Park, where she was usually the only woman standing on a box in a sea of male speakers. At the same time, she was fond of 'the all-stops-out … roll-up-your-sleeves-and-do-everything jobs',[3] including all kinds of manual work.

Over her years with ATD, Mary lived alongside families in deep poverty in France, the US, and her native Great Britain. She made a long series of study visits, first to South Africa, and later to Ghana, Israel, Kenya, Lesotho, Palestine, Sierra Leone, Tanzania, and Uganda. She fell foul of police or military authorities on three continents; but everywhere, she inspired people with her message that:

> When you're stuck in the misery of poverty, joy matters even more. All of us should find something to celebrate: a reason to go out together, or plan a journey, or just dance. This is not 'in spite of poverty'; it is so that people who are excluded from society can finally join in everything that makes the world extraordinary![4]

That was the message Mary drummed into me when I joined ATD's full-time Volunteer Corps in 1986 and first met her. Preparations were under way for ATD's thirtieth anniversary. Despite three decades of efforts, poverty remained a cruel fact of life. I found it perplexing that a celebration was considered appropriate. Exasperated by my question, Mary told me in no uncertain terms how much joy *does* matter. Eventually I came to understand the truth of her words.

Among the events planned for that anniversary on 17 October 1987 was the unveiling of a stone to commemorate the lives of people in deep poverty, a sign that they matter to communities and nations. In the years that followed, people around the world gathered every 17 October to demand an end to poverty. Then in 1992, this World Day for Overcoming Poverty was officially recognised by the United Nations. As Mary and Wresinski dreamed, 17 October is now marked each year on every continent as people draw inspiration from one another and renew our personal and collective commitment to end poverty.

Mary addressing a crowd at Speakers' Corner in Hyde Park
© *ATD Fourth World / Joseph Wresinski Centre*

First Encounters: 'My Life Was Shallow' 17

© ATD Fourth World / Joseph Wresinski Centre

Thanks to the work Mary initiated by developing ATD Fourth World's archives in the 1960s, her own daily writings are now collected at the Joseph Wresinski Centre of Archives and Research in Baillet-en-France. She wrote most often in French, so that Wresinski could read her reports and letters. As we prepare to mark the fortieth anniversary in 2027 of the World Day for Overcoming Poverty, this book is the first opportunity for Mary's distinctive voice to be heard in her native language.

Discovering Mary's bygone sayings and doings, what strikes me is how relevant they are to my life today. From her staunch feminism to doubts and musings about secularism and religious faith – and particularly her work to build and sustain an anti-poverty movement that avoids the pitfalls of Victorian philanthropy – I'm riveted by Mary's approach and how it unsettled many around her. Researching her life has become a gift I am offering to my 21-year-old self, who had so little time with Mary, but was nevertheless in the thrall of her force field.

Chapter 2

Origins: Worlds Colliding

The deep poverty of Wresinski's childhood convinced him that social justice could be achieved only by transforming relationships, specifically creating opportunities for some of the most disadvantaged people to think together with world leaders like the Secretary-General of the United Nations. A strength that made Mary a significant asset to ATD Fourth World was her ease at navigating very different social contexts. She drew this from mixed origins, with a bricklayer on her mother's

Mary as a baby with her parents
Provided courtesy of Duncan Rabagliati

Origins: Worlds Colliding

side of the family and a member of Parliament on her father's. Anneke recalls: 'Mary's accent was so posh that meeting her mother was a big surprise for me. You could tell she had to struggle a lot. I think Mary didn't talk about her mother for the same reason that it's hard for me to talk about my father. He was from a lower class than my mum.'[1]

Mary's father, Alexander Coultate Rabagliati, was a flight commander in the Royal Air Force. In 1940, the Battle of Britain raged for three months as the RAF tried to fend off large-scale attacks by Nazi Germany's *Luftwaffe*. Two days after the battle ended, he eloped with a chambermaid, Rhoda Bourgein (always called Sandra after her marriage). After hurried wedding vows, Alexander (nicknamed Sandy) had to rush back to duty. This left Sandra alone to travel into war-damaged London, summoned to meet her new mother-in-law for afternoon tea at one of the world's most luxurious hotels. The anxious bride arrived first to wait awkwardly among imposing marble columns. When Julia Rabagliati made her entrance, tea was served. Keen to make a good impression, Sandra immediately offered to pour, reaching for the milk. More than 70 years later, Margaret Rabagliati Wood, a niece of Sandra, recalls vividly how she recounted the occasion: 'There was an audible gasp, and my grandmother told her sharply, "Milk *after* tea". Aunt Sandy always told this story with much hilarity, laughing at having made such a lower-class error.'[2]

As an American, at this point, I needed explanation. In *Watching the English: The Hidden Rules of English Behaviour*, we read: 'Putting the milk into the cup first is a lower-class habit.'[3] I still couldn't understand the issue until I discovered in the *Dorchester Collection Magazine*: 'It became a sign of wealth to pour the milk in after the tea, as it demonstrated to guests that you could afford the best teacups.'[4] Margaret continued:

Mary's grandmother, Julia Rabagliati
© *Aimé Dupont*

> Uncle Sandy was a family wild card, so no one was surprised he had gone and married someone considered 'other'. But Aunt Sandy was always very dignified under verbal assault or teasing, and she was also so sweet, funny, and wonderfully

Mary's mother, Rhoda 'Sandra' Bourgein

Provided courtesy of Paul de St Croix

Mary's great great grandmother, Priscilla Bright McLaren

Provided courtesy of Duncan Rabagliati

warm that she won them all over. Everyone loved her, including my grandmother Julia. But at that afternoon tea, the potential was clearly there for total rejection.[5]

In Britain, even today, 'more often than not it matters crucially not only to whom one has been born, but where and in what circumstances one has grown up'.[6] Seventy years ago, when those class distinctions were more rigidly entrenched, Mary's childhood was shaped by having family on both sides of the class divide. Among her Rabagliati ancestors were the renowned Scottish suffragist Priscilla Bright McLaren,[7] Liberal parliamentarian Duncan McLaren, social reformers, prominent advocates of abolishing slavery, and pioneering medical practitioners. On the Bourgein side are a bankrupt shoemaker whose widow was forced to work as a laundress to support their children, a gardener whose wife also took in laundry, and a bricklayer turned shop-keeper and then coal hawker.

The bricklayer – Sandra's father – finally did well enough to purchase a back-street premises in Walthamstow and set himself up as a coal merchant. However, by the time Sandra was old enough to remember, her father was absent, fighting in the First World War. Her earliest years were spent in a single-parent household with her mother running the coal business and looking after five children. After the war ended in 1918, years passed with no sign of Sandra's father. Her eldest brother believed his education was cut short because their father abandoned his family. In later years, Sandra wrote: 'I scarcely remember my father, who deserted us when I was very young. [We] were all brought up on this "let's hate dad" campaign, especially the girls, who were instructed that all men are evil liars and rotters only out to have their way with women before leaving them.'⁸

Although life was tough, Sandra won a scholarship to the prestigious Walthamstow High School for full payment of fees and – as the daughter of an absent father – a maintenance grant. For perhaps for the first time in her life, Sandra mixed with daughters of the middle classes and learned to hold her own among them. When the Second World War broke out, she was 26 and working as a chambermaid at Ye Olde Thatched House in Epping. This happened to be the drinking den of choice for nearby RAF airmen like Sandy Rabagliati, who had already been awarded the Distinguished Flying Cross.

Sandra's father, Joseph Bourgein, with his second wife Louisa

Provided courtesy of Raymond Bourgein

Shortly after their elopement, Sandy was given full command of 46 Squadron, which was soon assigned to the Middle East. With no idea when they would reunite, he and Sandra said their goodbyes. Although pilots and aircraft set sail for Egypt, plans had changed, as recorded the following day in Winston Churchill's war diary: 'The 24 Hurricanes should have departed today for Egypt along with fifteen others. However, Squadron Leader Sandy Rabagliati DFC has been informed that 46 is to remain in Malta to strengthen the island's fighter force.'⁹ Not long after Sandy's departure, Sandra found that she was expecting a child. Their daughter, Mary Catherine Rabagliati, was born in Guildford, on 12 January 1942. During Sandy's year in the Mediterranean, his squadron destroyed eleven enemy aircraft and damaged seventeen more.¹⁰ On 31 October 1941 he was awarded a medal bar. At last in March 1942 came his long-awaited recall to Britain where he met his infant daughter for the first time. There followed several months of tactical work at HQ Fighter Command, after which he was appointed station commander

Mary's father, Alexander "Sandy" Rabagliati

Provided courtesy of Duncan Rabagliati

Sandy, sitting in the deck chair, at the RAF Hornchurch Station
Provided courtesy of Duncan Rabagliati

Sandy

Provided courtesy of Duncan Rabagliati

at RAF Fairwood Common in Wales, where Sandra and Mary joined him to begin life together as a family. In May 1943, Sandy was appointed wing leader at RAF Coltishall and the family relocated to Norfolk. Two months later on 6 July 1943, Sandy flew out of RAF Ludham, leading seven Typhoons on a shipping strike. Sixty miles from home he reported mechanical problems. He was seen to be climbing, smoke streaming from the engine, before descending and crashing into the sea. A massive search was launched, monitored by Sandy's brother Francis Rabagliati, also based at Coltishall with an air-sea rescue squadron. But no trace was found. Alexander Rabagliati's death, at age 29, is commemorated on the Runnymede Air Forces Memorial, near Egham in Surrey.

When he was declared 'missing presumed killed', Sandra was left with an 18-month-old daughter, a small pension, and no fixed abode, having moved from airfield to airfield. Friends and Rabagliati relatives rallied round; but Sandra was uncomfortable with imposing too long upon their generosity. Margaret Bourgein, a niece of Sandra's (who called her by her birth name, Rhoda) reflects on the vast class differences between the Bourgeins and the Rabagliatis.

Mary with her father
Provided courtesy of Duncan Rabagliati

Remembering childhood visits to her grandmother (Sandra's mother), Margaret writes:

> Her demeanour was that of a poor old woman, like a character in a Grimms' story. Our visits seemed like a duty, to deliver coal, food and money, which I am sure was for rent. Maybe the disparities of social class had a huge bearing on family relationships. I empathise with Rhoda; it must have been difficult to reconcile her home life and

Sandra with Mary and Sandy
Provided courtesy of Paul de St Croix

Mary with her father
Provided courtesy of Paul de St Croix

Sandra's mother, Marion Bourgein née Willson
Provided courtesy of Peter Akehurst

family circumstances, with that 'outside'; trying to keep the two separate. This in turn must have affected Mary. I think my father too, was both at the same time, trying to leave his 'working class' roots behind and become something better, as he saw it. On reflection, my brother and I feel as though we lived in a precarious kind of parallel universe, our 'home' and the world outside.[11]

To remain independent of her in-laws, Sandra looked for a child-friendly residential position. A friend urged her to apply for a job that was about to become vacant: the position of custodian at Chequers, the country seat of the Prime Minister. Although still numb with grief, she allowed herself to be persuaded and was invited for a weekend that included being vetted over sherry by Churchill's daughters. Sandra was also summoned by the great man himself for a viewing of 'The Four Feathers'. By then, however, she had decided that Chequers was not a suitable environment for her to raise her small child, so she was not disappointed to hear the next day that she would not be offered the position because 'I

Sandra
Provided courtesy of Paul de St Croix

was too young, too attractive – and also my foreign name, Rabagliati, could rouse suspicion among the natives!'¹²

Sandra eventually found a more suitable position at the Central Hotel in Royal Tunbridge Wells, a spa town in Kent. As for Mary, described as a child with 'lovely red-gold hair',¹³ while her mother was working, she spent hours on end 'helping' in the hotel kitchen or being 'kept an eye on' by off-duty staff – and becoming thoroughly spoilt in the process. Mary recalled:

> Once Mummy went up to London for a day and I was left in the charge of a girl called Bertha. I told Bertha I was going downstairs to stir the soup, as the staff allowed me to 'help'. But instead, I walked out the front door and virtually 'ran away' for a few hours. I walked a couple hundred yards away from the hotel until I found a taxi-man. I asked him to take me for a ride, which to my disappointment he refused to do, as I had no money. Whilst I was pleading, a lady came up and offered to take me to her home for tea. I accepted, and off we went. Luckily, the lady's kindness was genuine and I was not kidnapped or suffered any ill treatment – as I could quite easily have. Instead, I was given a wonderful tea, and afterwards she took me round her garden and gave me a strawberry plant, which afterwards gave at least three strawberries.
>
> All this time, poor Bertha must have been driven nearly mad with worry over her charge who had completely forgotten her. When I was finally brought home, we found Bertha in the act of ringing the police. Her relief must have been enormous, for she was hardly cross with me at all.¹⁴

Mary

Provided courtesy of Paul de St Croix

When the time came for Mary to attend primary school, she found it hard to adapt to the unfamiliar world of structure and rules. Looking back, Mary freely acknowledged that she had been a problem child; but she also retained troubling memories of 'dreadful scenes' and

Mary

Provided courtesy of Paul de St Croix

Sandra

Provided courtesy of Paul de St Croix

frightening punishments, such as being locked in a shed for straying into a forbidden part of the garden. 'I have never forgotten it, for I was so frightened that I would never see my family again and would be forgotten forever.'[15]

Mary's hatred of the local school only increased with time, and she was also becoming finicky about her food. Sandy's aunt Catherine Rabagliati, known as Catrine, grew concerned, and offered to pay for boarding school. Because of their lack of a proper home and her long working hours, Sandra reluctantly accepted the offer, and Catrine organised a place for Mary at Moira House School in Eastbourne.[16] Looking back, Mary wrote, 'At first I was terribly unhappy at having to leave Mummy, and Mummy was probably quite worried about me too. But boarding school did me a world of good.' Mary also spent more time with her Rabagliati relatives during school holidays, especially her great-aunt Catrine, who was a politician. When Mary was 12, Catrine was elected mayor of the Metropolitan Borough of Paddington, making her the first female mayor of a London borough.

Sandra, meanwhile, joined Tunbridge Wells Squash Club where she met Victor de St Croix, a manager for British Belting and Asbestos. They married on 25 August 1950 and moved to Guildford. Victor had two sons from a previous marriage, 13-year-old John and 12-year-old

Tim. The following year, Sandra gave birth to a baby named Paul. So overnight Mary's single-parent family grew to include a loving step-father and three brothers.

Mary continued her education at Moira House and three schoolfriends have shared their memories of her time there. Moira House was a progressive boarding school with self-governance inspired by the order of chivalry in King Arthur's court.[17] Pupils and teachers voted for their fellow pupils to be promoted up the ladder from page to knight, but Judith Stone recalls that: '"Ragbags", as we called her, never advanced beyond the lowly status of a page. She was always popular with the other pupils and they will certainly have voted for her – but the teachers probably did not because Mary was seen as a naughty girl.' Julie Jarman said, 'She

Mary, age 7, in a school photo taken at Moira House

Provided courtesy of Judith Stone

Mary is in the middle of the front row; Judith Stone is the middle of the back row.

Provided courtesy of Judith Stone

Mary

Provided courtesy of Paul de St Croix

Mary

Provided courtesy of Judith Stone

always seemed to be up to something naughty, but never anything malicious, just fun.' Despite Mary's frequent misbehaviour as a tomboy and a rebel, she was also serious about her studies. And she had more valuable other qualities even then. 'She was quick to take under her wing anyone she thought was treated unfairly. Juliet Salaman remembers Mary coming to her in tears at some injustice suffered by another child.'[18] Despite Mary's frequent misbehaviour, she was always popular with peers, another of whom remembered her as 'a real tomboy and a rebel'.

Eventually however, the head teacher, Mona Swann grew exasperated with Mary. Following yet another infringement of the rules, when ringleader 15-year-old Mary led three friends to leave school grounds without permission, Swann wrote to Sandra:

Provided courtesy of Paul de St Croix

'Latterly, Mary has taken the attitude to the staff when she has broken rules: "Well, what can you do about it now?" So she must see that something *can* be done. When *will* she learn to behave?'[19] The punishment meted out – dismissing Mary from school a day before the end of the spring term with no chance to say goodbye to her friends – led Sandra to refer to this as 'practically an expulsion'.

That summer, Sandra decided that, instead of continuing at Moira House, Mary should return

Provided courtesy of Paul de St Croix

Provided courtesy of Paul de St Croix

Origins: Worlds Colliding

home to prepare A-Level exams at Guildford Technical College. In September 1957, Mary began studying for A-Levels in history, literature, and French, while also learning shorthand and typing. She loved sports, particularly tennis, and also cared about beauty, good taste, and the arts. At the Tech, this interest led Mary to 'hang out with beatnik art students'.[20] When she completed her exams at 17, Mary was sent to the Sorbonne for six months, ostensibly to improve

Mary with her brother Paul de St Croix
© Peter Akehurst

Mary and Paul at their home in Farnham
Provided courtesy of Paul de St Croix

Mary, age 23, with her brother, mother and stepfather, Victor de St Croix
© Peter Akehurst

Mary and her niece Tania (Paul's daughter), at a family gathering in May 1987. Tania has spent her life pursuing social and environmental justice as an activist and youth worker. Now at King's College London, she developed an innovative social sciences module that involves regular collaboration with ATD.
Provided courtesy of Paul de St Croix

Victor and Sandra on their 40th wedding anniversary in 1990
Provided courtesy of Paul de St Croix

her knowledge of French language and civilisation. However, Sandra later divulged that her real aim was to 'divert Mary from a disastrous friendship with an art student' via the chaperoning of a strict Parisian landlady.[21] In 1960, Mary returned to London to complete a one-year secretarial course before being hired in an architect's office. It was not long, however, before Mary began to feel restless, leading her to depart for Noisy-le-Grand where fighting poverty became her life's work.

In an interview Mary paid this tribute to Sandra: 'What influenced me was my mother's example. She was from a poor background. She taught me the pride that poor people have, and how to stand up for the little people.'[22] Mary's brother Paul recalls: 'Mum always proudly used the term "working class" to describe her own background and was often outspoken in her defence of the underprivileged, and her disdain for what she saw as the ignorance and paternalism of the rich and privileged.'[23] Mary had witnessed Sandra's dignity and self-respect throughout the hardships and humiliations of early widowhood: the effort to keep the two of them decently clothed and well presented; the unremitting daily grind of poorly paid hotel work to keep a roof over their heads; and generally being treated as a nobody by guests with an overblown sense of entitlement. As for the second lesson Mary mentioned, she was referring to her mother's instinctive empathy and support for anyone excluded or belittled in any way. Sandra knew only too well what it felt like to be 'othered' and made to feel small. At Walthamstow High School, her status as a scholarship holder made her immediately stand out as living in poverty and also fatherless. In later years, during the brief period she spent among the wives of her husband's fellow officers, not everyone would have been as accepting of her humble background as her Rabagliati in-laws.

Mary, too, lost her father very early, which drew pity. A child thrust into this position develops coping strategies, and Mary's rebelliousness and rule-breaking at school may have been her way of gaining acceptance and popularity. Even within a family, tensions may arise if a child feels stifled by attention. Listening to her cousin Margaret, it sounded to me as though perhaps Mary's rebelliousness was to show that she was doing just fine and didn't need sympathy. Margaret said:

> It can't have been easy for her to be Uncle Sandy's daughter. There was so much emotional family trauma around him

Mary's great-aunt 'Catrine', Catherine Priscilla Rabagliati MBE

Provided courtesy of Duncan Rabagliati

Statue of Millicent Fawcett in Parliament Square, London

© *Diana Skelton*

Priscilla Bright McLaren's inscription on the plinth of the Fawcett statue

© *Diana Skelton*

– having died so very young, and as a war hero – that it stuck to Mary and her mother like a level of static. There was always extra attention focused on Mary.[24]

Mary's great-aunt Catrine, who never married, took a great interest in all her great-nephews and nieces, 'especially those at boarding school with parents abroad'.[25] In spite of her busy public life, she always felt a particular responsibility towards Mary. In addition to being a mayor, Catrine was also an enthusiastic family historian who ensured that the whole family drew pride from the life and achievements of her extraordinary suffragist grandmother, Priscilla Bright McLaren, revered as 'an early Scottish Emmeline Pankhurst'.[26] McLaren's lifetime of work for women's suffrage was recognised in 2018 with the inscription of her name among those of fifty prominent activists on the plinth of the newly erected statue of Millicent Fawcett in Parliament Square.

Priscilla was also a fervent supporter of abolishing slavery, and was the first person to petition the Home Secretary to protect women from physical violence, including from their husbands.[27] Her passionate dedication to these causes inspired other women in her family to embrace women's rights and to pursue achievement. Priscilla's niece

Origins: Worlds Colliding

Mary's great grandmother, Helen Rabagliati née McLaren

Provided courtesy of Duncan Rabagliati

Helen Bright supported the independence of formerly enslaved people; her step-daughter Agnes McLaren – the tenth woman in the UK to qualify as a doctor – pioneered training female healthcare assistants in India;[28] and Priscilla's daughter Helen worked in a variety of health and welfare initiatives in Yorkshire, for which she was awarded Membership of the Order of the British Empire.[29]

It's worth dwelling on Helen Rabagliati née McLaren (Mary's great-grandmother) because of the strong resemblance in their characters. Helen had five children with Dr Andrea Rabagliati, the house surgeon at Bradford Royal Infirmary. Her charitable work began by providing after-care at that infirmary, and then broadened to: organising the Bradford Girls School, a partly feminist initiative; co-founding a hospice, St Catherine's Home for Cancer[30]; and supporting St Monica's Home for unmarried mothers, considered 'fallen women'. In the 1890s, Helen's family moved north of Bradford to Ben Rhydding, where she designed a new family home, Whinbrae.[31] During the First World War, she used Whinbrae to shelter Belgian refugees, a service for which the King of the Belgians awarded her the Médaille de la Reine Elisabeth in 1918.[32] Helen also spent 28 years as president of the Ben Rhydding Women's Unionist Association.

Assessing Helen's character, historian Jo Stanley writes: 'Used to leadership, she was very determined, to the point of bossiness. At the same time, she could be sweet. She was very bright, well-mannered, hospitable, and generous.'[33] A century later, this describes Mary to a tee. Helen's 1934 obituary said:

> Dignified … she was a speaker who always held the attention of her audience. She never trimmed her sails to popularity. Holding very firm views … she advocated them in the most outspoken manner. Her conversation never dwindled. Her sincerity won for her the respect even of those who were most violently opposed to her opinions.

She had little patience with those who were self-seeking or praise-looking or slack or undecided. She had the power of commanding devotion and inspiring energy.³⁴

Again, this description applies word-for-word to Mary.

When Mary was growing up, Catrine hoped that the proud legacy of the exceptional women in their family tree might arouse a sense of purpose in her rebellious great-niece. But the family did not overlook the exploits and achievements of the male Rabagliatis. When Ian Fleming published *Goldfinger* in 1959, 17-year-old Mary was thrilled to learn that the famous scene where James Bond emerges from the water and unzips his diving suit to reveal a perfectly pressed dinner jacket – a scene later immortalised by Sean Connery in the 1964 film – was based on a real-life Second World War exploit devised by her great-uncle, Catrine's youngest brother and MI6 agent Euan Rabagliati.³⁵

Mary Rabagliati's childhood was complicated and in some respects challenging. But as she matured, her vibrant personality and the positive elements she drew from her upbringing – her mother's example and being the proud descendant of extraordinary women – gave Mary an unmistakeable charisma. Her cousin Margaret describes it as 'a kind of electricity'. There was also a fearlessness about Mary that was rooted in her female-centric family. In her early years she saw her mother manage alone. When her mother remarried, Mary was studying at a single-sex boarding school where the teaching staff was mostly female and unmarried, like her great-aunt Catrine. While her friends were looking for a husband to support them, Mary knew full well that women could accomplish things without men. Her next steps showed just how fearless and independent-minded she could be.

MI6 agent Euan Rabagliati

Provided courtesy of Duncan Rabagliati

Chapter 3

'The Road Just Stopped and No One Else Gave a Damn'

Mary began her life's work by making an unusual choice in 1962. Her job typing out advertisements bored her. As she said later: 'When I was 19, the main choices in life for women like me were to go to university or get married. Neither appealed to me.' Her friend and teammate Huguette Bossot Redegeld, recalls: 'Of course, Mary had boyfriends and strong friendships with men. She was someone who aroused passion.'[1] Reflecting on the constraints that can arise from marriage and motherhood, Anneke adds: 'Mary considered getting married at times; but there was still this current of "men are nothing and who needs men". And she never wanted children because they would have been in her way. She was strong on her own and didn't need men. And she was picky too!'[2]

Mary said:

> My friends were desperately seeking a husband. I didn't judge them; but that didn't seem like a goal that should define me as a person. I wanted something else – but what? I know what it is to earn money, go home, and do your own thing. It didn't suit me. I thought it was a waste of time helping to get somebody else rich and then going out spending your salary. I was looking for something meaningful to do.[3]

Mary scoured the telephone directory, searching for an organisation that worked with children. She hit on one that helped children in refugee camps in Europe. Although Mary had no relevant experience or qualifications, she recalled, 'They were nice and didn't laugh at me, as they could have done.' Instead, they referred her to someone who worked with homeless families: Joseph Wresinski in Noisy-le-Grand, France. Mary wrote offering to help for three months. Her letter received a prompt reply saying that was too short and she should plan to stay a year.

A French journalist described Mary as:

> brown-eyed, with a thick blonde chignon pinned up … and in search of the sunshine of human intellect … in Noisy-le-Grand, this town at the end of a dirt track which seems to go into the dead of night. Twelve hundred people vegetate here, owning nothing, housed in sinister huts of corrugated steel in a place of colossal struggle for hope against despair.[4]

Postal delivery, rubbish collection, and all other municipal services stopped at the edge of the tarmac. Some 280 families – about 12,000 people – lived in one square kilometre without running water, gas, electricity, or toilets.[5] Some had jobs – setting up market stalls, doing circus work, or washing metro stations. Most had no regular work and scavenged for used items to sell for a pittance. Mary said:

Some 12,000 people lived in the Noisy-le-Grand emergency housing camp.
© *ATD Fourth World / Joseph Wresinski Centre*

> Beyond the shock I felt, Père Joseph made me realise immediately that I could do something. ... I had apparently no particular talent or use; but I could nevertheless do *something*. He told me that the families there needed me to meet them and begin to understand who they were as people.[6]

This camp was created in 1954. Because that winter was terribly cold, a priest named Abbé Pierre gave a radio address requesting donations for his organisation, Emmaüs, to help homeless men in Paris. A national outpouring of generosity followed. However, his appeal was heard not only by donors but also by homeless families who hoped he could help them too. Hundreds of families rushed to Paris from across France. Mary said:

> Mothers, fathers, children, all desperately poor, seemed to appear from nowhere. They had been sleeping under bridges. A few were originally from Algeria, Spain, Portugal, or Traveller communities, but the vast majority were French. That shocked French society. Many people thought there was no homelessness in France. They were scandalised to see all these people together.

Emmaüs responded by setting up a makeshift housing camp, intended to be temporary. Mathilde Aparicio, whose family lived there from 1954 on, recalls it as 'a field of mud by the woods where there were wild boars. The land was given to Abbé Pierre but none of us wanted to live there because there was nothing at all. And the adjacent town

Provided courtesy of Paul de St Croix

The only water came from outdoor hand pumps where women and children queued up to fill buckets and jugs.

© Reprinted from April 1966 issue of "Igloo" Magazine, ATD Fourth World.

'We collected scrap metal ... [to] try to sell it.'

© ATD Fourth World / Joseph Wresinski Centre

of Noisy-le-Grand was very middle-class, so of course they didn't want the camp.'[7] Families were allotted Nissen huts made of corrugated asbestos, used at air bases during the war. The huts were nicknamed 'igloos' because of their semi-circular shape – 'like a big barrel cut in half', as described by Bernard Jahrling, who grew up in one.[8]

Many igloos were crowded with families of nine or more in a one-room space of 16 by 26 feet. Smaller families shared a single igloo, with one family on each side of a divider. On the dirt roads, pitted with holes, handfuls of straw were scattered in efforts to absorb mud. A single latrine pit was made of light concrete blocks. Laundry was hung outdoors to dry, mildew, or freeze, depending on the weather. The only water was cold and came from four outdoor hand pumps where women and children queued up to fill buckets and pitchers. With no rubbish collection, scrap heaps stood outside each home. There were only six street lamps and two grocery stores, with any other shop situated two miles away.[9]

Every winter, Bernard recalls:

> Our only evening light came from candles. Everything froze: water, coffee, even oil when we could get it. My mother used to stay awake all night trying to keep the stove standpipe open; but it still froze. We collected scrap metal at the dump. We'd carry it away in baby prams and then try to sell it. For food, trucks would dump filthy leftovers from the market. The cheese was maggoty, but the

women fought rats and crows to get it. It was like a prison camp, or a place that time forgot.[10]

© ATD Fourth World / Joseph Wresinski Centre

About Bernard and other children, Mary recalls:

> On the way to school, the children's shoes got caked with mud. They'd hide their muddy shoes on the side of the road and put on clean ones; otherwise they'd get reprimanded for arriving in such a dirty state. Many homes were in a very bad state. So were the children; so were their clothes. Yet the children had to go to school. When they appeared in dirty, ragged clothes, they were treated as though their family was no good. One boy told me his teachers made nasty remarks about the camp that made him cry.

© Gérald Bloncourt, ATD Fourth World / Joseph Wresinski Centre

Wresinski's bishop assigned him to the camp parish in 1956, while reassuring him that no priest was expected to stick it out there for long. However, the camp reminded Wresinski of his own boyhood. He decided to create a movement with these families to overcome poverty once and for all. One his first changes was to dismiss charities that distributed soup. He had always hated the way his mother was patronised by charities that tried to dictate her behaviour – even instructing her to send him to an orphanage to have fewer mouths to feed. In Noisy-le-Grand, Mathilde Aparicio recalled, 'The soup kitchen degraded us even more. It was dreadful to go cry for a bowl of soup.'

Instead, Wresinski insisted on dignity, urging parents to figure out other ways to get by. He convinced a local factory to open a packaging workshop in the camp to provide jobs. To widen families' horizons, he invited volunteers to run a nursery school and an after-school programme. Because of the ugliness of the camp, Wresinski looked for ways to create beauty, opening a library and an art workshop. He gave the anonymous pathways names such as 'Daffodil Street' and 'Anemone Way'. Jahrling remembers joyous times: dances held to the music on a transistor radio, and outings Wresinski arranged to admire the radiance of Paris by night. Just ten miles west of the camp, they could gaze at the sophisticated city of lights.

For Mary, Noisy-le-Grand was a massive contrast to her Sorbonne studies in Paris. She and seven other volunteers were housed in box-shaped barracks. The women's dormitory could house up to eight women in four bunk beds. Although each bunk had a curtain for privacy, the women had to be wary of peeping toms at their windows.[11] Washing oneself behind the curtain was particularly challenging in the winter when the water froze. Next to each bunk was one stool and a chamber pot. During the day, volunteers could use an outhouse near the refectory, but at night they used the chamber pots. Like all camp residents, volunteers went to 'slop out' their chamber pots every morning. Mary said, 'That was really the worst for the families: having to live with a communal slopping-out place. It was always disgusting.'

© ATD Fourth World /
Joseph Wresinski Centre

Although the camp was meant to be temporary, families lived there for 20 years. Mary said: 'Children spent their whole childhood and adolescence there. They lived and died there.' During the winter before Mary's arrival in the camp, eighteen babies died.[12] Mary said, 'The families were dumped at the edge of French society. Social exclusion is a situation where everything just stops and people are

Because there was no postal delivery in the camp, Joseph Wresinski
recruited community helpers to bring mail to residents.
© ATD Fourth World / Joseph Wresinski Centre

left alone on the other side. The families were abandoned. No one else gave a damn about them.'

Mary's French visa listed her occupation as 'housemaid'. However, Wresinski described the volunteers as 'community helpers'. It was important that they live on site to take part in daily life. But they also worked regular hours: 8 a.m. to 6 p.m. every day. This was because families in poverty often lacked a regular rhythm of life. Unsure when they might manage to provide a meal, living by the clock was a challenge. There were often emergencies in the middle of the night: fistfights, health crises, women thrown out of their homes. The volunteers' regular hours provided a model to help parents be mindful of school schedules. With the volunteers working so hard, Mary recalled:

> Père Joseph stuck up for us so families in the camp would understand that we made a choice to join them and were paying a price for it. Sometimes families shouted at me to go back where I came from; but Père Joseph did not tolerate that. He imposed respect by shouting and arguing. When he caught a child skipping school, he would shout, 'Do you want to spend your whole life in ignorance?' He was really haunted by ignorance. He wanted everyone to use their mind.

Wresinski's stress on learning applied to volunteers as well. He wanted them to learn as much as possible about culture, science, and the world in order to build bridges with society. He invited many

Father Joseph Wresinski with Mary during a visit to her family's home in Farnham, England

Provided courtesy of Paul de St Croix

experts to the shanty town to speak to volunteers. The subjects were varied, as Mary recalled:

> We were taught literature, history, biology – anything, so that poverty didn't have to mean ignorance. Once when he met a maths teacher, we were given a maths test. Our average score was that of an 11-year-old child, so we were taught maths as well for a while. Père Joseph always wanted to open minds, give people a chance to think, and enable everyone to express themselves. At that point, the question of my work in the camp was secondary. Just living there was a shock. I was just starting out in life, and completely unprepared. I came from a completely different world. I never imagined such poverty could exist. What the families were going through was a brutal fact, not something to debate.

Although Mary's initial idea was to help out for three months, discovering the shock of deep poverty and also the creativity of Wresinski's approach caught her imagination. As disorienting as it was, she felt she might finally be on her way to doing something meaningful.

Mary in the camp

© Daniel Gingras, ATD Fourth World / Joseph Wresinski Centre

Chapter 4

Laundry and 'Creating Atmosphere'

Mary's first work assignment in the camp was addressing hundreds of envelopes. The periodical being mailed out explained what life in the camp was like and invited people to support Wresinski's work. Mary recalled an additional task as well:

> Just two weeks after my arrival, Père Joseph asked me to speak to visitors. My French was rudimentary and I knew nothing at all ... in terms of my lack of understanding of the families,[1] ... but I was to explain ATD Fourth World to them. I was a bit panicked, but I don't think that mattered to him. He offered me so much trust.[2]

The new women's centre had three washing machines.

© *ATD Fourth World / Joseph Wresinski Centre*

Three weeks after Mary's arrival, Wresinski set her a bigger challenge: to run the recently built women's centre, which included a laundry room. All washing had been done by hand with water from the pump. So Wresinski had convinced donors to buy three washing machines and electric irons. Volunteers built the centre with indoor plumbing. Unlike the curved metal igloos, the centre had upright stone walls and tiled floors. Large basins and ironing boards stood alongside the washing machines. Wresinski also wanted the centre to be far more than a functional laundrette. In the front of the room were a sewing machine, a nursery, four tables, and chairs for 20 people at a time to chat over coffee.[3] Floor-to-ceiling drapes matched the tablecloths. When Wresinski requested donations of art, major artists agreed: Joan Miró, Jean René Bazaine, and Georges Braque. All this made the centre cosy and inviting.

Outsiders often criticised Wresinski for his insistence on beauty and art. They told him: 'The more you help, the more people will want to continue living as they do. The women's centre is too fancy for them.' This infuriated him, as he explained:

> This camp was slapped together by people who refused to offer anything beautiful or solid to the poor. Because no one believes in the poor, they wasted money on prefabricated housing which can't last. This camp humiliates its residents. … All around us are barbed wire and rubbish heaps. … It's terrible that underprivileged families are considered parasites. All our projects show this is false. … The more we enable families to live surrounded by dignity and beauty, the more they will want to leave because they have tasted

A comfortable place for chatting
© *ATD Fourth World / Joseph Wresinski Centre*

Laundry and 'Creating Atmosphere'

Donations of artwork made the centre cosy and inviting.
© *ATD Fourth World / Joseph Wresinski Centre*

something better. That's why we made the women's centre so beautiful.[4]

The women's centre also had hair-washing sinks and hair-dryer hoods. Both female volunteers and mothers living in the camp were invited to shampoo their hair there once a week – however Gabrielle Erpicum, a volunteer who had arrived before Mary, remembers:

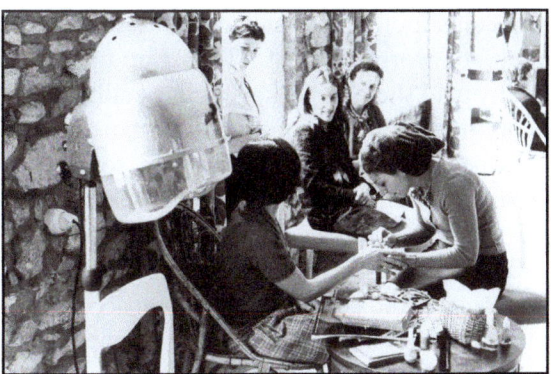

'It is fantastic what a boost make-up gives a woman when she feels down and out.'
© *ATD Fourth World / Joseph Wresinski Centre*

Most mothers were reluctant to do it because they didn't want to admit that they couldn't manage washing their hair at home. So Père Joseph invited a beautician. She came regularly to offer affordable haircuts, styling, and make-up tips. Once she told women that a fresh shampoo made hair-dos look better, everyone was convinced.[5]

Mary loved this project, saying: 'It is fantastic what a boost make-up gives a woman when she feels down and out.' On her arrival, however, Mary was daunted at being put in charge of the project:

> There I was, hardly speaking any French, and Père Joseph said, 'Look after the women's centre'. Families insulted me all day long: 'What are you doing here? We didn't ask you to come.' I was supposed to ask women for money to use the machines. For the sake of people's own honour, Père Joseph forbade us to give anything away. But these families had nothing so they ended up cheating and stealing. I had to be severe, while still understanding the importance of their dignity.

Like at least two of Mary's fore-mothers, women who struggled the most had sometimes earned money as washerwomen for better-off neighbours, who then treated them like servants. To change this dynamic, the women's centre required that each woman wash only her own family's laundry. This way, all women could get to know one another on an equal footing. At the same time, for those who needed to earn money, at a workshop that ATD set up in the camp, the 3M Scotch company paid them to package rolls of adhesive tape.

Mary spent nine months running the women's centre. Just as Wresinski stopped the distributions of free soup, he wanted the women's centre to break the cycle of used clothing distributions. Doing laundry by hand was so difficult that many families simply threw away torn or soiled garments. However clothing donated to the camp was also ragged and could not be chosen according to taste and fit. Mary called this a 'cycle of ugliness that no one was proud of'.[6] In the new centre, women could wash, mend, and iron clothing. Donated clothing was now put in a thrift shop where women could trade in washed and mended clothing for something that suited their family's dignity.

On Mary's first day on the job, when she was still trying to figure out how the up-to-date spin-drying machines worked, teenage girls came and stole the money box, used to collect a nominal fee of 30 centimes per kilo of laundry.[7] She recalled:

> I'm proud to say I got it back, which felt like quite an achievement when you consider that they were obviously seeing what they could get away with in front of a new person who didn't speak their language or know what was going on! But it was mainly the girls whom I found a thousand times more difficult and scary than their mothers.

Although Mary felt quite lost at the beginning, the mothers tried to make her comfortable, even while keeping watch to see whether they could trust Mary. Little by little, the situation became reversed. Finally, she was accepted as having authority and became the one helping to make the women comfortable. As Mary settled in, she was particularly struck by how hard the teenagers worked. They were often in charge of their family's laundry and caring for younger siblings. She said: 'Their laundry was startling, with their poverty written all over it. What shocked me even more was what little choice the girls had. All they could do was help their mothers and live in this muddy, dark place. Plus, they had to deal with me.'

Mary's own schedule was chock-a-block with tasks as shown in this chart:

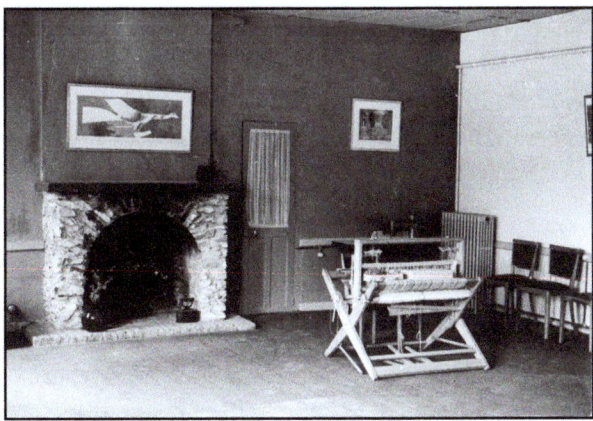

© ATD Fourth World / Joseph Wresinski Centre

Morning: Finish cleaning if no time last night; welcome women to iron, sew, etc.; teach machine-sewing, rethread machines, help cut fabric; make tea and wash up; straighten up for the afternoon; if someone else can staff the centre, visit families; if time, write reports.

Afternoon: Be constantly present; help women with their chores (but not too much); keep conversation going; serve biscuits and wash up; if not too many women come, there's always something to sew, mend, or invent (but no time when the centre's full).

Evening: Washing up; from 5:30 to 6:00, cleaning; stop by Miss Annique's to buy fabric or sell things made by the sewing class; get orders for sewn items; restock tea and biscuits; repair sewing machines.

Also: organise outings and visit women who are hospitalised.[8]

Mary tried to make the centre 'a place where each woman could express her personality'.

© *ATD Fourth World / Joseph Wresinski Centre*

'Keep conversation going' was described to Mary as her responsibility to create a welcoming, positive atmosphere. This did not come naturally to her. Soon after her arrival, another volunteer criticised her lack of chit-chat. She was furious.

Consciously trying to 'create atmosphere' paralyses me. Some people find it as easy as laying a table, but I want to flee to the other side of the earth. I find it foolish to chatter as a way of filling silence. There can be as much good atmosphere in silence as in conversation – sometimes more. That doesn't mean hours in silence; it means using good judgement and being relaxed. Always trying to think of something to say won't work. I'm not merry from sun-up to sundown. But I tried to create a place where each woman could express her personality.

Laundry and 'Creating Atmosphere'

The women's centre was a place to get away from the unpleasant igloos. In Mary's view, atmosphere came from the women and their moods. 'Each day the adventure was to discover what might be behind the moods of one of them, and sometimes of the whole group. I found that much more interesting than self-consciously trying to "create atmosphere".' Mary also experienced something that remains common to virtually all of us in ATD: people in poverty who have a long experience with a project often remain nostalgic for however it was run before our arrival! Mary said:

> It got on my nerves that women constantly said how much better things were when Anne-Marie ran the centre: it was more fun, they felt more at home, more women came, and on and on. But despite my tears of impatience, I never wanted to run away. Sometimes I *tried* to want to leave, but I couldn't manage!

'Their laundry was startling, with their poverty written all over it.'

© *ATD Fourth World / Joseph Wresinski Centre*

Wresinski's insistence on 'a welcoming atmosphere' was for a person to feel welcome even when their laundry was the filthiest. Mary did not encourage too many women to use the centre at the same time because she wanted to feel available to each one. However, she tried to make sure that as many women as possible developed the habit of coming once a week, instead of the same few women monopolising it every day.

Although the conditions of the camp were difficult for everyone, some struggled more to manage. Mary recalled, 'Some came with beautiful, white sheets and clean clothes; others came with filthy sheets and clothes crawling with bugs'. Her goal was for the laundry room to be especially welcoming for those with the dirtiest, most infested items. She wanted each woman to know that no others were better or had more rights.

Giving the inadvertent impression of favouritism and losing trust is a hundred times easier than winning it back. But from the beginning, this is what ATD Fourth World was about: welcoming the most and judging the least those who have the most difficult time, because they are judged by everybody. Better-off people should not despise very poor families or move away as soon as they can because in fact these are the people who can help the others.[9]

In Mary's personal journal, she recorded notes about her role offering a friendly ear to women having the most difficult time.[10]

> *19 November 1962:* Today, I travelled to Paris with Mrs Tessier[11] to help her get a certificate of past employment that would enable her to claim welfare benefits from the

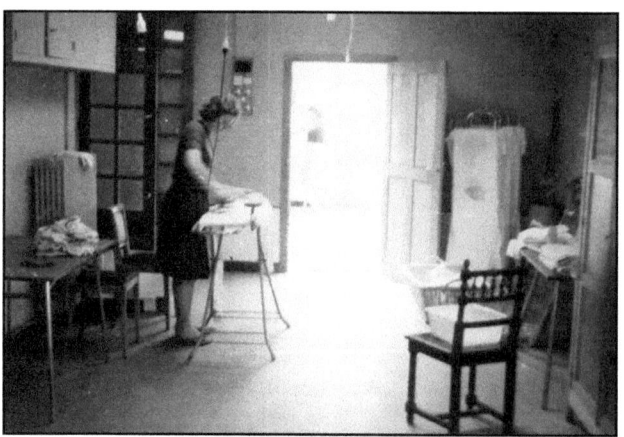

Mary's goal was for the laundry room to feel especially welcoming for those with the dirtiest items.
© *ATD Fourth World / Joseph Wresinski Centre*

> company that fired her husband. Mrs Fleury came along because she wanted to talk to me about her social worker, whom Mrs Fleury called a 'bitch'. Now she must apologise or risk having her children removed into state care. Mrs Fleury says everyone is terrified of this social worker. I asked, 'What if you're assigned to an even worse social worker?' She says no one could possibly be worse.

Having family courts remove children into state care, which continues to be one of the key issues ATD works on today, was an ever-present concern in the camp.

> *27 November:* Time for an outing! To Christmas shop in Paris, I invited all the mothers working in the Scotch workshop. Some were reluctant. One spent her earnings already and has nothing left for gifts. Mrs Barthélemy needed to borrow a pair of proper shoes. Then I knocked at the Fabres' igloo. It was very dim with only one petrol lamp lit. They're completely out of coal, so it was quite cold. Mrs. Fabre was in bed with cardboard boxes around her for a bit of warmth. I asked, 'Don't you remember? We're going shopping in Paris today!'
>
> 'But I can't afford the bus. And I'd get lost.'
>
> 'Don't worry. ATD is paying for the transportation, and I'll navigate.'
>
> 'But my coat is ratty. I can't be seen like that.'
>
> 'Please, come to make me happy. It will give you a change of ideas.'
>
> Her husband interjected: 'What ideas does she have? I know what you think, Missy, you're staring at how ugly our igloo is. We have nothing!'
>
> I had only been staring at their cat. Then Mr Fabre went over to a photo of their daughter's first communion, held a year ago, before she was removed by social services. I asked, 'Does she write to you?'
>
> 'Yes', Mrs. Fabre said.
>
> 'No, never', her husband contradicted.
>
> Mrs Fabre gave a deep sigh. 'Well, not at the moment.'
>
> Mr Fabre picked up the lamp to illuminate the photo. Now, he was crying, 'My little girl! I'll never see you again.' His wife tried to console him. Finally Mr Fabre said, 'I'm off rag-picking'.
>
> Seeing that I didn't understand the French expression, Mrs Fabre showed me the wheelbarrow he uses to collect old fabric to resell. As she explained, he kept apologising, as if ashamed. So I said, 'That's work as good as any other.'

*© Reprinted from April 1966 issue of
"Igloo" Magazine, ATD Fourth World.*

Lacking coal was a common concern in the camp. Mary wrote in one letter: 'The winter weather struck early. It's terribly cold and families need coal desperately, but we have no cash in hand. Could you fund-raise for coal? Even if you can't raise much, we're not too proud to accept the very smallest donation.'[12] In these harsh conditions, Mary made many hospital visits, some to new mothers; others to women whose children were stillborn; still others to women who had been injured, either in accidents or due to domestic violence. She once went to the hospital to accompany a woman told that her tuberculosis would require residential treatment – but 'when we asked about the date, the nurse said, "Tell her not to come back" and gave no more information'. A doctor conducting research about attitudes towards health professionals told Mary that not one woman in the camp was in good health.[13]

Mary worried constantly about the challenges faced by these women and their families. Although she had learned to make the most disadvantaged women feel the most welcome, she was looking for ways to make more of a difference in their lives. She was ready for a change.

Mary with Huguette Bossot Redegeld
© *ATD Fourth World / Joseph Wresinski Centre*

Chapter 5

Joyfulness and a Spirit of Inquiry

In 1963, Mary left the women's centre to begin developing an archive and engage in research with the aim of affecting public policy. That winter, Wresinski made notes for ATD Fourth World's mission statement: 'Ending extreme poverty means being constantly present among people in deep poverty and organising systematic action. ... It means working on all fronts: cultural, religious, social, and professional, [and] consolidating efforts by policy-makers with those of private charities and social movements.'[1]

Mary continued visiting mothers; but newer volunteers took over the women's centre. As the camp gradually acquired the reputation of a place where outsiders could learn about poverty, the number of volunteers grew, from seven when Mary arrived to 45 two years later. Half were French; others came from Belgium, England, Finland, Germany, Holland, Japan, Portugal, Spain, Switzerland, and the United States. Most were in their twenties and stayed only briefly, for a vacation. A few stayed for six months, a year or two. When the dormitory for volunteers overflowed, Mary moved into a trailer along with Huguette, a young woman who was also motivated to remain long term. She recalls that, even in the trailer, conditions were harsh, with 'water frozen every single day in the winter'.[2]

One of the short-term volunteers who passed through was Mary's cousin, Margaret Bourgein. They had rarely met as children but were close in age. Having recently begun college, Margaret's newfound independence made her curious to reconnect, so she asked to volunteer in Noisy-le-Grand during her Easter holidays. She recalls: 'Although I don't remember communicating about my arrival with Mary, I called her from the last Metro station, and she came to pick me up. (I did get into trouble for having given no warning!!! as you can imagine!!)'

This rocky start grew worse:

> My time there was not fulfilling in terms of getting to know Mary, her work there, or engaging with the refugees. I spent my days sending begging letters to wealthy French elites for

© ATD Fourth World / Joseph Wresinski Centre

> donations. Mary made no effort to seek me out; I hardly saw her; and we volunteers were forbidden to enter the fenced-off camp. Failure to make meaningful contact was disconcerting, and I managed to blame myself. Had I been an unacceptable cousin and volunteer? I now see that I was probably an irritating invasion into their lives, at that particular time, with all that Mary was dealing with. But being so sensitive, I misread the situation.[3]

Whatever irritation Mary might have felt at the time, the rule that kept Margaret away from those she imagined were 'refugees' was applied strictly to all newcomers. Before Wresinski's arrival, it was common for outsiders to make voyeuristic trips to gawk as if at a freak show. Camp residents felt they lived in a zoo. To end the rubbernecking, Wresinski imposed an iron-clad waiting period before trusting anyone to enter the camp. Wresinski was also concerned that no one take advantage of the trust of camp residents now accustomed to confiding in his close team of long-term Volunteer Corps members. As he explained in a morning meeting:

> A stranger who arrives as one of our volunteers will be welcomed like an old friend. … People here speak freely to our volunteers, saying things they would never tell a neighbour. … This is why we are slow and cautious when you arrive. … If your relationships go wrong, the relationships of our team with the entire camp will suffer.[4]

Wresinski saw the trend of post-war volunteerism fed by 'awareness that Europe needed to heal its wounds and an aspiration of the privileged to develop new ways of sharing with the disadvantaged'.[5] Unlike Huguette, who grew up in poverty, most volunteers grew up middle-class. Their parents were teachers, farmers, craftspeople, or office workers. One of the exceptions was a volunteer from a family of factory workers. The camp led her to reflect on her background. In a letter that Mary archived, she wrote:

> It was at birth that I became a factory worker. I was a girl, so my family knew I'd earn more. Boys are luckier because once they leave for military service the family won't ask them for money any more. Girls like me all knew that at 14 we would work in the factory. It was only boys who were encouraged to continue school. Girls work to pay for their brothers' studies; but brothers tell them: 'You left school because you weren't smart enough.' At work, girls who can't keep up become scapegoats. They can't possibly join others asking for more rights. They'd be told, 'You're not even qualified.' … Some women in the factory stand up for themselves. Others stick together. But still others don't know how to defend themselves, and have no one to defend them.[6]

Although her family was not as badly off as the residents of the camp, her explanation of gender differences reinforced what Mary saw among the teenage girls around them. This volunteer's words about

Joyfulness and a Spirit of Inquiry

'girls who can't keep up' bring to mind Mary's concern for the women whose laundry was always the filthiest. The same volunteer reflected:

> Factory workers live by the production-line clock. Every hour I worked in the factory over ten years is etched inside me, every day the same as every other, steeped in noise and filth. If only we could think – but so many avenues are closed with no chance of discovering them. Little by little, you forget the few things taught in school. Unlucky girls cannot join in discussion or put into words what they see in a painting. There's no future in the work; so to make herself feel better a girl has to find something of value. Workers can be manipulated because we believe promises so easily. After a long day, she'll go to a bleak home, overcrowded with children, more burden than comfort. Then she'll feel more lonely even than when at the machines. Watch-making work damaged my vision; it happens to half the women. For years now, I've had to stop reading after a short time. … For ten years, I expressed myself only with my hands. I was told to become a machine, and I did.[7]

The research done in the camp also looked at the situation of boys who struggled with not seeing a future for themselves. When Wresinski asked Christopher to start a project for teenage boys, Christopher interviewed the boys about their aspirations and obstacles. One said, 'I'm working now. But I won't get rich. Just look at the men here. Some kill themselves working their whole life but have nothing to show for it. My dad's really someone. He knows everything. But not in this country, because he never got working papers.' Christopher's project addressed this by teaching skills. He taught mechanics by taking apart motorbikes and old cars. He organised them to turn a vacant lot into a football field. Christopher also organised educational outings: to swim, to watch a reservoir being constructed, and to study railway-junction switches.

But beyond skills, Mary also saw the importance for the young people of joy and acceptance by society. Once the dance band formed at their new youth club, this started to make a crucial difference. Although dances were also held outside the camp in the town of Noisy-le-Grand, those dance halls had entry requirements: a male escort for girls; and a shirt and tie for boys. The camp's youth club was open to all and had a bar. It quickly became the best club in the area, attracting young people from outside the camp. Hosting the best Saturday night dance immediately changed the idea that the camp was no good. It gave a completely new image of what the young people had to offer. They were proud, and this offered a way to meet other young people.

Mary agreed wholeheartedly with Wresinski's view of celebrations as important to overcoming poverty:

> Père Joseph was profoundly joyful. He said that the most important thing for volunteers to do was to be happy. 'You cannot liberate the poor while you are sad.' People who have nothing can maintain joy when they realise they can change something. If you know you are capable of changing *something*, even when things are at their worst, you can overcome sadness.[8]

Joy matters so much! At the same time, fighting poverty requires the discipline of reflective practice and constant learning. Every morning and evening, Wresinski met with all the volunteers to react to events of the previous day and share his vision. In May 1962, for instance, he told volunteers:

> It's not our job to solve these families' problems; we are here to restore to them the privileges that are their right. ... Society blames the situation of these families on psychological problems without realising the economic and historical root causes. ... Deep poverty means life without regular rhythm, constancy, or traditions. This leads to cultural exclusion, a lack of knowledge, and a lack of control. To survive, people in poverty are ... obliged to adapt to the unbearable. ... The absence of rights causes disorder; and that disorder prevents people from accessing rights. Only after learning this can we, cautiously and hesitantly, try to speak about solutions.[9]

This view of human rights as vital to the question of poverty – groundbreaking in the 1960s – became central to Mary's view and remains at the heart of ATD's efforts today.

In daily meetings, Wresinski made clear his expectations of volunteers and swiftly denounced anything patronising or lacking

Joyfulness and a Spirit of Inquiry

© ATD Fourth World / Joseph Wresinski Centre

in rigour. He encouraged writing on the principle that systematic activity reports would create records to study in developing thinking about poverty. In Mary's reports, she recorded conversations and observations of families in poverty not as 'cases' but as complex human beings. Mary found writing rewarding. Each night, she felt she was reliving the day by thinking it over. She said:

> Even if what I wrote was foolish, writing became an important way for me to listen. I would think back to what was said by a person to whom I hadn't paid enough attention. Writing developed a spirit of inquiry: not just to write at night, but to be interested and ask questions during the day, to get to know people better.

© ATD Fourth World / Joseph Wresinski Centre

> We lived by the principle of understanding that families had something to say about their conditions. Instead of being judged and analysed by others, they needed to tell us about their experience and what they wanted from life. This is ATD's research: right from the beginning, people were writing.

A few months after Mary's arrival, Wresinski spoke of his determination to offer meaningful projects to women in particular through the women's centre: the jobs in packaging, the thrift shop, and several activities where mothers could drop off their young children. He said:

> Our efforts contribute to helping women feel less exhausted and unhappy. Faced with deep poverty, men are overwhelmed. Women are the last line of resistance. … Their inner strength resists despite everything. Every mother here has endured incredible hardship. … I am not saying women can solve poverty. But if they gain the upper hand, the household can stay afloat and breathe again.[10]

Wresinski was also concerned that women not be taken advantage of emotionally by volunteers passing briefly through the camp. In another meeting, he said:

> Many of these women have not experienced affectionate, trusting family relationships. Some grew up in orphanages or foster care. Many never met their father, or had several stepfathers. They've felt the weight of being distrusted … and they have lacked friends. … In this context, we must not create something that *seems* like friendship but that might prevent them from moving forward in their own lives. … True friendship is incredibly demanding.[11]

This was another aspect of the approach that makes ATD unusual to this day: we have a strong emphasis on relationships between people in poverty and people from other backgrounds, and on finding ways for them to go beyond superficiality and to be on equal footing. Wresinski developed this conviction further in a letter to a short-term volunteer who was upset when he spoke harshly to a family:

Joyfulness and a Spirit of Inquiry

© *ATD Fourth World / Joseph Wresinski Centre*

You're right to offer them your friendship. But you should simply shed light on *their* path, giving them strength to move forward independently. Otherwise, when you leave, they will feel even more lonely, miserable, and incapable than ever. Your mistake was in not understanding that it is not you *personally* who is developing a relationship with them; instead, it is through you that they should be able to develop a relationship with the world.[12]

For Mary, who disdained light chit-chat, this deep approach made sense. She also grew passionate about her new research responsibilities. In a 1962 report,[13] Mary wrote about differences between dynamic families and others in more dire situations. She described this second group as:

- defensive and ill-at-ease;
- fatalistic with no future plans;
- unable to manage, and dependent on charities, neighbours, and social services that may punish them. Their neighbours are just as badly off, straining trust. People deny having anything in common with neighbours (perhaps because of their own sense of failure?);
- judged by society, which says: 'No one needs them'; 'Their failures are their fault'; and 'Watch out for them or you'll catch something'. Others are allowed to intervene in

their personal lives and judge them according to different values.

In the 1960s and 1970s, sociologists and psychologists commonly spoke of 'problem families', defining poverty as a problem of 'maladjustment'. For instance, the British Secretary of State for Social Services wrote: 'Much deprivation and maladjustment persists from generation to generation through what I have called a "cycle of deprivation". Parents who themselves were deprived … in childhood, become parents of another generation of deprived children.'[14] Mary's report concluded by wondering:

> Are these families maladjusted to society? I'm really stuck. Why *wouldn't* they be considered 'maladjusted'? Being 'adjusted' to society requires participating in it; or at least being accepted as a group with its own values, even if they are not those of other people … as in the case of certain minorities who are recognised as belonging to a specific group. So should these families be integrated into society (if possible); or should public opinion be changed in order to value them?[15]

Mary remained passionate about her research responsibilities, as she described in a letter home on 20 November 1964:

> Darling Mama and Vic,
> I've been on a course in Paris about interviewing and analysing content. It left no time for thought outside. We were sixteen students told to work everything out for ourselves, having been given the course programme and object. Three psycho-sociologists were present but not to lead. They simply measured the situation from time to time. We were not taught interview techniques but rather led to discover our personal ways of communicating. In the last meeting, all participants expressed thoughts against the facilitators who remained deaf and dumb until the end – or rather, dumb, as I am sure they gained as much as we did.
> I took the course with another girl from Noisy-le-Grand. It was very tiring having no official lead during the

Joyfulness and a Spirit of Inquiry 63

> discussions. Now we have to communicate what we learned to the other volunteers, which may be even more difficult!
>
> The weather has turned warmer, which brings rain, dampness, and inches of mud. We go nowhere without boots. ... I hope very much to come home for Christmas this year, as quite a few volunteers are staying on. [...]
>
> Must rush as usual, this time to eat – otherwise there will be nothing left!
>
> Lots of love, Mary[16]

Mary seemed to have been quite at ease with the juxtaposition of psycho-sociological training with the continued challenges of life in the camp. However, she did have suspicions about one aspect of Wresinski's approach. She said:

> Each of us made an individual choice to come to the camp, without consulting anyone, and without deciding in advance to stay for the long term. When Père Joseph began speaking about a 'Volunteer Corps', we worried he wanted to found a convent! We also had mixed reactions to his plans for training us. No one wanted to be forced to study – and in the beginning some of the subjects were far-fetched. ... It was an original approach, considered dangerous by our families and friends. Even Catholic clergy told us it was impossible to live as we did. Once two nuns tried to join us but they brought an entire truckload of belongings and supplies – their personal bunker. They didn't last long.[17]

Mary's mother, Sandra, was also suspicious. A former classmate from Guildford Technical College remembers: 'Mary's mother rang me, very worried. She was afraid that Mary was "becoming a nun in some organisation near Paris!"'[18]

Eventually, however, Mary was convinced that the ATD Volunteer Corps was nothing like a religious order, and that it was a useful approach for working over the long term. She said: 'At first, I didn't see the need for a Volunteer Corps. But it takes so long to make real change, and there are no small solutions to extreme poverty. So we did need some people to stay and build something new.'[19]

In shaping the Volunteer Corps, Wresinski emphasised studying, reflecting, and discovering new things. He asked Mary's help to consider: 'How can our volunteers become capable of responding to the

Provided courtesy of Margaret Bourgein

needs of people in poverty? How can we become a corps that fights poverty in Europe, India, or America?'[20]

Availability also became a defining characteristic of the Volunteer Corps. In addition to availability of time and place, it means that, regardless of education or experience, we all pitch in with chores, and we all train for new responsibilities. Another defining characteristic is minimal salaries. Regardless of seniority or responsibility, we all receive the same stipends. As funding for ATD has grown, it's no longer necessary for us to sleep in barracks and eat all together as Mary and others did in the 1960s; but to this day we retain the original ethos by keeping this stipend equal for all.

In an October 1963 meeting, Wresinski explained the rationale behind this choice. He described volunteers as 'crossing borders' between the 'world of the poor and the world of the rich'. In each world, volunteers need to belong and be able to speak on behalf of others so as 'to convince the rich to meet the poor and to introduce the poor into the world of the rich'. Wresinski saw this as stemming from the values behind our choice, with a modest income as 'a sign of our sincerity'.[21]

At the same time, even though in ATD's Volunteer Corps our stipends are low, we are not living in deep poverty. Wresinski noted: 'There is no value in *extreme* poverty, the last stage before a spiral of despair.' A young man who grew up in the camp described to Mary the difference between his peers and her fellow volunteers:

> There will always be a bit of a wall between you and us. People who didn't grow up here would need to study for

> a long time before understanding. Before the igloos, we slept in tents where children froze to death. The rest of us survived; but you weren't here then and you would never have stayed. People notice us everywhere we go. When they see mud on our shoes, or a hole in our trousers, they know we're from Abbé Pierre's camp. Applying for a job is the worst. The minute they hear our address, it's: 'Don't call us; we'll call you'; except of course they won't. When I was 13, I saw a neighbour come back from applying for a job. He was crying. A grown man, crying. It was terrible to see; I'll never forget it.

Mary asked if he or others had friends outside the camp. He was silent for a while, and then said: 'It's complicated. I can't explain it.'
'What if you invited them to the bar here?'

> But then they'd see the rest of the camp – and they'd be afraid someone would strip their car while we had a drink. It's not that people don't like us; it's us who don't like them. It's weird, but that's how it is. And we don't talk properly. We say 'shit' when we shouldn't, and they get mad. They're right because we don't know how to talk to them.

Years later, when Mary gave a speech in Wales, she introduced her role as part of the Volunteer Corps by saying:

> The term 'volunteer' means we chose freely to accept the demands of working with ATD Fourth World. One is to receive only a minimum wage, funds permitting. ... ATD Fourth World exists to bring together, freely, all those who wish to overcome the exclusion of the weakest people in our society, ... families pushed outside the mainstream of society, excluded and rejected. They experience social exclusion in its worst forms because they are destroyed and dispossessed of the means to exist in our society.[22]

Still later, looking back on the earliest years, Mary recalled Wresinski's efforts to forge a Volunteer Corps that would endure over time. He was haunted by the need for volunteers to continue for the long term, being present to people suffering in poverty. This meant fostering teamwork and building a sense of community that would make it possible for new volunteers to join them. Mary wrote:

> It didn't matter so much which of us might work with children, or with adults, or in offices – the main thing was staying true to being guided by those in the worst situations. Poor Père Joseph! He must have really suffered because we all had so many considerations that had nothing to do with that goal. But of course we had worries, because dedicating our lives to these families is very challenging.[23]

Wresinski described volunteers as 'human relationship counsellors', building community at the heart of low-income neighbourhoods, as well as bringing together society: every social background, political persuasion, religion, race, culture, and nationality. Mary said:

> This wasn't based on ideology; it grew out of Père Joseph's daily habit of investing time with each person. That time took precedence over any project. He asked us to always look at the big picture instead of becoming specialists. … He didn't want some of us to focus only on grass-roots action while others focused only on policy work. The idea was that none of us categorise ourselves. Being aware of the big picture would give any of us the means to change roles.[24]

Mary's first year in Noisy-le-Grand plunged her into the challenges of direct action while her daily journal became a basis for future policy work. Living and working conditions were hard; but she drew motivation from feeling part of a useful effort, friendship and laughter with other volunteers – and dancing at the best club every Saturday night. Although her original plan was for a short stay, she had become very attached to her work. She said: 'I didn't arrive in Noisy-le-Grand with big ideas about justice or a very charitable soul or anything like that. And I never made a decision to stay for a long time because I don't think in those terms. But our work was interesting, useful and meaningful. I liked being there. So I saw no reason to leave.'[25]

Mary's immersion in the misery of Noisy-le-Grand started her on the path she continued, grappling theoretically and practically with poverty, 'maladjustment', and building a movement to effect social change. She would soon leave Europe to learn how these challenges were taken up elsewhere.

Part II

Social Change and Racism: 'Our Blood is the Price we Have to Pay for Change'

Chapter 6

Choosing between Freedom or Safety: On the Front Lines of the War on Poverty

In 1965, Mary got a crash course in different approaches to social change when Wresinski asked her to spend a year in the United States as part of its War on Poverty. The invitation originated with an ATD Fourth World seminar held at UNESCO. Professor S.M. Miller, an attendee from the prestigious Ford Foundation, was struck by the creativity of ATD's action amidst Noisy-le-Grand's squalor. Miller invited ATD to work with an organisation in New York City called Mobilization for Youth (MFY). In Miller's view:

> The MFY work was an action play-book for work on juvenile delinquency by Richard Cloward and Lloyd Ohlin. Their ideas were … derived from applying sociological theories about 'deviance' to poverty. They emphasised the importance of job opportunity in changing the outlook and actions of low-income youth to more productive activities and away from crime. Training was key.[1]

Previously, Mary had been asked to move to India for ATD and said no. But she felt differently about this new request: 'I was frightened of moving to India. But if you have a shred of youth in your heart, you want to discover America. And I've always liked doing and discovering new things if they're meaningful.'[2] She was also ready for a change

Mary (at right) in New York working
with Mobilization for Youth
© ATD Fourth World / Joseph Wresinski Centre

of pace. In Noisy-le-Grand, she said, 'We lived in an atmosphere of frequent arguments, which was not at all peaceful; if a middle-class person volunteered but complained about the training and structure, Wresinski would say, "We don't need you; go home."'

However, New York's Lower East Side was even less peaceful. Known for 'persistent poverty, crime, drugs, and abandoned housing',[3] the tenement district was a mixture of Black, Jewish, and Puerto Rican residents, with a sprinkling of white hippies. Mary recalled violence, rampant police brutality, and drug addiction, even among some children, with some addicts passed out on the pavements. She said,

The sign on the building says: 'Puerto
Ricans of Lower Manhattan United'.
© ATD Fourth World / Joseph Wresinski Centre

'The neighbourhood was very poor and full of life.' The constant noise was inescapable, as were bedbugs. In Mary's first four months, her flat was broken into twice.[4]

> First, someone took my typewriter, radio, and electric fan. The second time, they left me with nothing: no clothes and no food. So I put bars on the window to the fire escape. I felt I was putting myself in a cage; but it was freedom or safety. I had to push myself to step outdoors. It was hard, but you can't just curl up in a corner alone.

© ATD Fourth World / Joseph Wresinski Centre

The Mobilization for Youth housing clinic and tenants association
© ATD Fourth World / Joseph Wresinski Centre

Vincent Fanelli, a native New Yorker who was then teaching at a secondary school on the Lower East Side, described it as 'one of the poorest neighbourhoods in the city'. Years later, he wrote to Mary:

> Like the families in your building, you knew what it was to be afraid, surrounded by destruction, to see young men idle [with] no work and young teenagers lured into drug use. You knew [the fear] in the night of that dreaded cry 'Fire! Fire!', ready to flee into the streets, if you were lucky, with only the clothes on your back. You lived that – not as long as [your neighbours] but enough to know their courage to [not] give up.[5]

Although I imagine that Mary sometimes regretted moving to New York, she stuck it out.

Since 1962, MFY offered 'help to anyone in need',[6] starting with support to navigate welfare bureaucracy. In 1964, MFY led a rent strike antagonising 'important powers' who retaliated with allegations of Communist infiltration.[7] By 1965, MFY had shaken off these attacks and begun expanding. Mary described her work there: 'I followed co-workers around with a notebook all day long asking questions. For the first time since the Depression, organisers were bringing people in poverty together to speak out. But they were trying to evaluate a project that had not been planned in advance.' Daniel Kronenfeld worked at Henry Street Settlement, a nearby programme of social and community services. He got to know Mary that year and later told her:

> I remember you as a cute English girl who came to all these meetings of the Puerto Rican group, and sat in the back of the room, looking very, very smart, and saying very, very little. ... But years afterwards in England, how different you seemed: not this quiet little person at the back of the room; quite the opposite, you had spunk! So much for first impressions![8]

At the same time, Danny observed that Mary loved partying and drinking, which he called her 'appetite for life!' He later asked her: 'Mary, how did you survive [being] surrounded with three hundred social workers in MFY? I didn't know it at the time, but you have certain thoughts about social workers!'[9] Mary did indeed have a

The War on Poverty

strong distrust of social workers. In Noisy-le-Grand, Mary regularly encountered social workers who terrified families. Daily crises left scant opportunity for parents to engage in calm dialogue with professionals. Given the harsh conditions in the camp, social services often removed children into state care. At MFY, Mary paid close attention to the social work approach. She wrote to the ATD team in France: 'We need to develop a scientific approach to our action to prevent social workers from leading us around by the nose.'[10] The MFY social workers had university degrees. This was different from France, where social work was vocational.[11] In the US too, however, a gulf separated social workers from people in poverty. Mary wrote on 24 October 1965:

> Dear Père Joseph,
> ...MFY social workers live nowhere near the neighbourhood they serve. They are very far from the people. A teenager commented sarcastically: 'Maybe they move to a different neighbourhood every day to help more of us!'
> The increasingly vocal resentment in this community is very much against social workers. People are developing strong awareness about the gap between social work and the population's true needs. Social workers are insulted as 'dictators' and 'enemies'...
> Mary[12]

Mary was interested in the work of Cándido de León, an educator originally from Puerto Rico. As director of MFY's higher education programme, he broadened his role from what was originally envisioned as an 'anti-juvenile-delinquency programme'. To show education 'as

Photos taken by Mary in 1966 New York City
© *ATD Fourth World / Joseph Wresinski Centre*

the door to a fulfilling life', he enlisted graduate students to tutor teenagers for 20 hours a week throughout the academic year. This external structure was meant to instil internal discipline. Looking back, de León later said:

> If they devoted one academic year to learning to study effectively and efficiently, they could continue on their own later. They bristled under these demands, and some never stopped complaining. But as they began to experience learning and even mastering some areas, complaints became part of their *shtick** and less authentic. I emphasised that programme staff had to stop 'discovering' that poor people can learn. Our obligation was to teach them *how* to learn; let them discover for themselves that they *could* learn. Two of the loudest complainers visited me later. One became a judge and the other became the District Supervisor for the New York State Division for Youth in NYC.[14]

For MFY to evaluate its programmes, de León advised they apply the scientific model used in industry: plan each step; execute it; and then measure how close you came to your target. Mary appreciated this systematic approach. However, she was frustrated by the distance between evaluation and people's everyday lives. She described De León's supervisor as: 'interested only in high-level

---

* 'Schtick' is a Yiddish expression meaning behaviour or comments that a person is well known for.

The War on Poverty

© ATD Fourth World / Joseph Wresinski Centre

change and not concerned with supporting people to improve their lives. He doesn't consider our work part of his research – even though our team is the only one using observational methods to thoroughly examine every one of MFY's programmes.'[15]

From MFY, Mary drew inspiration – such as when they influenced welfare support laws – but also frustration, such as the lack of jobs for newly trained young people, or the constant reassignment of social workers meaning a lack of continuity for family support. Mary particularly disliked MFY's over-reliance on psychiatric evaluation, not only for serious mental health issues:

> Whenever a person behaved in a way staff didn't understand, the staff felt they always had to take action. Whenever they didn't know what to do, instead of taking

© ATD Fourth World / Joseph Wresinski Centre

time to think the situation over together, the person would be shuttled off to a psychiatric ward just because no place was made for them. They simply needed individual support, something the social worker had no time to give. And the person sent away was no longer seen as a person trying to cope with poverty but as a case of individual inadequacy or breakdown.

MFY was soon to lose its grants and shut down activities. Mary reflected: 'I think that MFY was somewhat naïve. Because the staff there had earned quite good salaries, none of them considered staying on as volunteers after the funding cuts. They simply found good jobs elsewhere.' Professor Miller, who worked at the Ford Foundation which had funded MFY, noted that MFY 'had the positive impact of pushing the issue of poverty before the public and politicians to mobilise the community'. That said, he understood Mary's criticism and added: 'Despite the range of good services provided by MFY, these services were not built from the outlooks of the particular youths and families to be helped.'[16]

Mary also looked outside MFY at other War on Poverty initiatives. With many middle-class young people crossing the country to pitch in, their motivation impressed Mary; however, she saw drawbacks. She said:

> Americans are impatient for results. Any project without quick results was shut down. Or a funding stream changed, leading everyone to switch jobs. The whole country had high hopes for the War on Poverty. They believed that in five years, they would end poverty for good. But every institution was challenged, sometimes with physical violence. In this spirit of uprising, community residents turned against anti-poverty projects. Community members learned to organise themselves, and then surprised organisers by choosing their own goals.

The War on Poverty was only part of the wide variety of community organising initiatives in the 1960s. Everything was political. Civil rights demonstrators risked beatings, jail, and murder. Wresinski urged Mary to look for the worst situations of poverty, expecting her

The War on Poverty

In Alabama, Mary is second from the right
© *ATD Fourth World / Joseph Wresinski Centre*

to find places similar to Noisy-le-Grand. Instead, Mary insisted that racial segregation made poverty even worse:

> People are talking about the riots in Watts, Los Angeles. When white police injured a pregnant Black woman, riots broke out for six days. A local commission analysed the situation but ignored the root cause, which is the frustration of Black people with their inferior role in society. Following the commission report, virtually nothing was done to improve living conditions. So no one is surprised that new riots broke out again this month. Instead of investing in programmes that would help, President Johnson is spending more and

© *ATD Fourth World / Joseph Wresinski Centre*

more for this ridiculous war in Vietnam, where people are killed for nothing but to save face for the Great America.[17]

Throughout Mary's time with MFY, she volunteered with the Medical Committee for Human Rights. Formed in 1964, the committee provided health volunteers for the Freedom Summer campaign registering Black voters in Mississippi. In 1966, the committee was investigating discrimination in hospitals. On Mary's vacation from MFY, the committee sent her to Selma, Alabama, for two weeks to surreptitiously spy on hospital conditions. Lacking local knowledge of the area, and with a British accent to boot, she was highly conspicuous – and was promptly arrested. The committee was prepared, so a few hours later Mary was rescued by Donald Jelinek of the American Civil Liberties Union. Although the state released Mary, it later arrested Jelinek for practising law without an Alabama licence.[18] Mary concluded:

> My arrest in Selma showed me that challenging issues require long-term commitments, not just handfuls of individuals popping in for two weeks – which is why ATD needs long-term commitment from volunteers. The worst poverty cannot be dealt with in one meeting or from a desk. For anything to change, we need far more commitment, by which I mean keeping at it year after year and being prepared to really give something of oneself and do whatever it takes.

As Mary's year with MFY drew to a close, she urged Wresinski to visit the United States to experience it first-hand. In Noisy-le-Grand, she felt that ATD was rooted in its own approach to poverty and that her French teammates would not understand the value of what she was learning in the US. Contrasting the countries, she wrote:

> The greater diversity here allows more open ideas. You don't have the same rigidity when thinking about a person's future. It's a place where people experiment in ways that you can't in Europe. France is quite conservative. Even in England, history and tradition weigh people down. You're meant to build cathedrals that last a thousand years. But in the US, people always make something new that they might knock down two years later when it is no longer suitable.

> People move from place to place: different flat, different city, different state. You try out new approaches. You take a chance, and if you fail, you simply start over. Americans are daring. They really thought that they could end poverty in five years.[19]

Wresinski accepted Mary's invitation and they spent six weeks crisscrossing the country to meet people in poverty and to find ideas for shaping ATD. Wherever they went, Wresinski asked: 'What about people who are left behind?' He knew that many projects benefited only the most dynamic people. Mary said:

> Many leaders didn't make time to listen to the poorest people. Leaders said: 'They're too lazy to come to our meetings', as though no other reason might prevent someone from attending. That attitude influenced dynamic people in poverty. Those speaking publicly would insist, 'Not all of us are unemployed', or 'Many of us are not on welfare'. They knew society wanted to help only people seen as sober and serious.

Mary and Wresinski's journey began in Washington, DC, at the Office of Economic Opportunity which was evaluating the Community Action Program (CAP). This represented a significant change from previous generations of social reformers who considered poverty a sentimental issue. The old approach called on people to 'help the poor' to save their own souls, ignoring the rights and opinions of people in poverty, viewing them as unusual failures in a system considered functional. However, CAP was designed for systemic economic reform: welfare rights, access to jobs, and consumer boycotts. At the same time, there were tensions between national organisers and those working at the community level. At MFY, Mary heard these arguments:

> Washington would tell MFY, 'Your officials aren't truly representing people in poverty, so we won't send you one penny until you show us how people are participating and have power in their neighbourhood development programme.' I was struck by the ease with which policy makers spoke about poverty. I suspected that very few really knew what it meant to be poor.[20]

In Washington, Mary and Wresinski were struck to meet one policymaker who did experience poverty first-hand. Dick Boone, who founded the Citizens' Crusade Against Poverty, grew up in a struggling community of Appalachia. Working with incarcerated juveniles convinced him that people in poverty should be true partners in designing solutions. Mary called Boone 'one of the most impressive people we met'. He was opposed to an ever-growing welfare state because it would deem certain people unneeded to contribute to society and always dependent on assistance. Mary agreed:

> Welfare organisations don't attack the fundamental problem: to create a real place in society for people in poverty. They must be needed as contributors and creators, rather than just people whom one feels obliged to support. The risk is that, as welfare rights grow, they are seen not as rights but as a favour bestowed. The price to pay for welfare is an increase in control by society over the personal lives of families, dictating a way of life and cancelling out freedom of choice. Welfare benefits turn people into second-class citizens. Boone's vision was for paid employment to embrace different forms than in the past. He stressed work as essential to every person's dignity and value in society.[21]

Mary's fear about generous welfare benefits bringing an increase in control over personal lives was later borne out in western Europe, and very particularly in the UK where I now live – something we will return to in a later chapter.

Wresinski agreed about the importance of people contributing to society. Beyond public policy, he constantly asked people about the bigger picture, including culture and spirituality. He asked whether community development projects aimed to broaden people's perspectives on life. Beyond each person's need to earn a living, he wanted everyone to have a sense of beauty, grandeur, and being part of something larger than their own struggle.[22]

Mary chose their itinerary carefully. Avoiding the largest and best-funded programmes, she sought out small initiatives, which she considered 'more dynamic and less stuffed with stereotypes and concerns for the social workers' material well-being'. Mary saw a contradiction in community organising:

> Organisers genuinely want people in poverty to propose and lead projects. But the poor aren't used to being asked; they're used to a straitjacket, with others speaking in their place, supposedly interpreting their desires. So now those others (pastors, charity workers, etc.) have to be pushed out of the way for the poor to be heard. At the same time, many community organisers feel it's dangerous for people in poverty to become too political because that could jeopardise their funding.

On their visit to Jackson, Mississippi, they learned that when organisers realised that participants were questioning politics, the organisers took back control of planning. They continued the same children's activities with the same toys; but the project had changed, because the organisers reasserted control over decisions. Mary was frustrated to see how dependent on funding every project was. (It was to avoid being controlled by funders that Wresinski recruited a Volunteer Corps for ATD, initially providing only the barest bones of room and board, and later with a horizontal living wage for all.) In Mississippi, a Head Start children's development project was considered 'successfully completed' – and therefore its national funding was cut off. Mary wrote:

> Every single book, toy, and music record had been taken away by Washington. Many staff were determined to carry on somehow on a voluntary basis; but they had lost their offices. It was terrible. How naïve of the government to imagine that Head Start consists simply of kids playing quietly with toys, watched by parents who see no further implications for their families' lives! I wish the lost funds had caused a real revolution among people who tasted the cookie and were not prepared to let it go. One of the biggest dangers in fighting poverty is that people are quieted down by repeated crumbs and become too easily satisfied. After the Watts riots, summer programmes were funded to prevent other riots; but those are only crumbs. Come autumn, nothing more is done.

Her head buzzing with new ideas for the direction ATD ought to explore, Mary pushed on through the South.

Chapter 7

Racism, César Chávez, and Dolores Huerta

In Nashville, Tennessee, Mary and Wresinski met with the Southern Student Organizing Committee. Among white civil rights activists, Mary observed differences. Those from the North had their communities' full support and were celebrated for defending a just cause. But white students from the South who made common cause with Blacks were seen as betraying 'their own'. This was why southern students, whether Black or white, considered changing minds more important than changing laws. White southerners needed to learn that segregation was unjust.

Mary's next stop was New Orleans, where she and Wresinski visited the Desire Housing Projects reputed as 'unsafe for human habitation'.[1] Some 19,000 Black people lived entirely cut off from the rest of the city by a river, a canal, a railroad, and a major road. Mary said, 'The nasty conditions gave the feeling of a concentration camp: a strong atmosphere of a forsaken place.' Wresinski was invited to address the National Conference of Catholic Charities. Mary recalled:

> Most conference-goers were a motley crowd of the better-fed and more bourgeois clergy caught up in the rat race of making anti-poverty programmes conform to Washington politics, rather than using their own heads. Wresinski was invited to address them; but since he didn't speak English, I read a translation of his speech (despite the fact that I'm not

Catholic). I was quaking at the knees because that was the first time I ever spoke in public. We were quite disappointed because the only questions asked by the bishops and priests were about our funding and salaries.

Turning west, Mary then drove through Texas, New Mexico, and Arizona. She wrote:

We saw miles and miles of fantastic, unearthly country with an intensity that no outsider can penetrate, and a wonderful silence. It's not empty silence, but one that can be filled by the imagination about the billions of years before humanity was present. People there are still pioneers in close contact with the land. The enormous trees make one feel very small and unimportant. On a dirt road in New Mexico, we had the impression that outsiders do not understand the Indian way of life; Indians seemed neglected from every point of view, including by the civil rights movement.

In California, they travelled to Delano to visit the National Farm Workers, founded by César Chávez and Dolores Huerta, and using the slogan: 'Sí, se puede' (Yes we can). During Mary's visit, they were organising a massive strike by Mexican and Filipino grape field labourers. For fourteen-hour shifts without breaks, workers were

Mary, right, in Delano, California, talks to grape field labourers about the National Farm Workers' strike.

© *ATD Fourth World / Joseph Wresinski Centre*

often paid nothing. The employers' justification was: 'These people are degenerates, they're winos, and so we do the public a favour by giving these people work.'² Mary wrote:

> Chávez is genuinely extraordinary. The camps for workers are inhuman. Nothing is provided, except for a couple of beds and a stove. The camps for single men are the worst. One contractor pays in alcohol instead of money. I joined their picket line, while Père Joseph leapt about in the grape vines taking photographs and making everyone frightened that he would be arrested.

© ATD Fourth World / Joseph Wresinski Centre

'Viva la huelga' was the strike's rallying cry.
© ATD Fourth World / Joseph Wresinski Centre

Racism, César Chávez, and Dolores Huerta

© ATD Fourth World / Joseph Wresinski Centre

We saw an employee deliberately use a truck to run down a man picketing a grape-packing centre to frighten away the picket line. But instead, his action sparked a larger demonstration. It felt like a miniature revolution. The union was determined to improve working conditions; while employers were equally determined to prevent change.

Continuing for four more years, Delano strikers eventually won collective bargaining rights for all grape workers in California.

'Delano grape growers unfair to UFW AFL-CIO'

© ATD Fourth World / Joseph Wresinski Centre

© ATD Fourth World / Joseph Wresinski Centre

Next, Mary drove north to Berkeley to attend a Black Power Conference run by the Students for a Democratic Society who opposed the Vietnam War. The Black Power Movement used education and identity-building to empower Black people. Mary noted:

> The audience was mostly white and seemed to forget that they were part of the dominating white majority. I think the Student Non-violent Coordinating Committee are right to push their white members to organise white people in poverty. Many people, Black and white, told us how difficult it is in poor white communities to talk about civil rights of Black people. But nothing will change unless this is done. All people should be part of movements of interracial solidarity like the SNCC.

Turning back east, Mary drove through magnificent vistas in Nevada, Colorado, and Utah. Then in St Louis, Missouri, they were shocked. During the Great Migrations of African-Americans from the south to the north between 1916 and 1970, Missouri's location as well as its history as a slave state had combined to make this city one of the most racially segregated in the country. Mary wrote:

> We stumbled on the most awful, miserable area that I've ever seen. Just a few blocks from a spacious central city avenue was a sprawling Black neighbourhood where the residents' main occupation seemed to be rag-picking. I

Mary took these photos in St. Louis, Missouri.

© *ATD Fourth World / Joseph Wresinski Centre*

didn't see a single shop. The atmosphere was complete destitution: dilapidated housing collapsing, immense piles of scrap iron and rubbish, nowhere for children to play. There was a distinct feeling that no one cared a damn about this neighbourhood. If anyone cared, they wouldn't tolerate such conditions. In a nicer part of the city, well-dressed white people went about their business with confidence. We saw two young Black men there, their clothes untidy and the wrong size. They looked bewildered as if from another land.

From Missouri, they pressed on to Eastern Kentucky. Professor Miller had described to them the 'barrenness' of rural Appalachia. To address rising unemployment, War on Poverty projects focused on job experiments, such as training people to care for cemeteries. Despite the great natural beauty of Appalachia's streams and mountains, which Mary called 'vast and fantastic', deep poverty was also palpable: poorly built wooden houses in disrepair, coated with decades of 'dismal' coal-dust grime. Roads were poor; clean water scarce; malnutrition widespread. Mary wrote:

> Appalachia is a chunk of country quite remote from and left behind by the great America that presents itself to the world. It's not like the Deep South or a deprived urban neighbourhood where people live next-door to affluence and suffer from direct segregation. Despite the need for a general uplift – which is evident – anti-poverty programmes have difficulty making a mark because the roots of a particular way of life go very deep for people in the heart of the mountains.

In this isolated place where reaching a home might require 'half an hour of persuading the car to climb round and round a mountain road to the top', Mary felt there was more freedom than in the Lower East Side. She also noted that Vietnam seemed particularly far away. That said, she discovered that many young people enlisted 'both from patriotism and because there is nothing else for them to do'. She appreciated a visit to the Council of the Southern Mountains where 'unlike other groups, they didn't announce that they already know the solutions to poverty. They are humbly searching to always deepen their understanding.'

Their next stop was Chicago, where they visited JOIN (Jobs Or Income Now) and met 'a white woman from Alabama who admits she was a racist but [later] … realized that she was an accomplice to much injustice. She then devoted herself to struggle for the cause of black people; when the black movement asked white people to leave, she went to work with poor whites.'[3] It is likely that this woman was Peggy Terry, born into poverty and who became a leader in the civil rights movement eventually sharing the presidential ticket as running mate to Black Panther Eldridge Cleaver.[4] Mary and Wresinski also learned that the Commission on Youth Welfare was trying to improve relationships between the police and young gang members. Mary noted:

> One day, we found ourselves between two rival gangs, guns blazing. I hope some good is done by the youth commission; but a cop is always a cop, and they seem to walk on sensitive ground wearing hob-nailed boots. The police see no reason for youths to be together, so they put their heads down and try to break up everything they can lay their hands on – not very successfully as far as we could see.

That reminded me of the 'Sasquatch' technique used by DC police when I volunteered at Martha's Table. The teens they scattered were accused of nothing; but their very presence as a group struck the police as a provocation. Mary continued, 'We also visited Cook County Jail where the electric chair was explained to us in minute detail. Why hasn't humanity found a less inhuman way of dealing with crime and punishment?'

Their journey ended back in New York where another member of ATD Fourth World, Huguette, had moved from Noisy-le-Grand to develop a branch of ATD, with support from Danny Kronenfeld, Professor Miller, and others. Mary then returned to France with Wresinski. On their return, however, their teammate Gabrielle recalls seeing Wresinski sink into depression for months:

> He was devastated by racial segregation. He wished he could live in the skin of a Black man to experience first-hand the treatment he saw of labourers hauling away rubbish. He even referred to Noisy-le-Grand as a 'deluxe' shanty town because none of its residents were Black. That kind of racism was not part of their experience. Long after Père Joseph recovered his health, he continued to speak about that trip through the United States as a descent into hell.[5]

Mary too was deeply troubled. Having seen the segregation of vast neighbourhoods – some Puerto Rican, some Polish, some Italian – she said, 'No matter where we went, the very worst places were always Black neighbourhoods.' At the same time, while Mary called segregation 'a travesty of justice', she also noted: 'We saw that, for many, belonging to an ethnic community was a source of vitality. It created a more optimistic and dynamic sense of community than in poor communities in France, where policies deliberately scatter immigrants to avoid creating ghettoes.' But Mary's main conclusion was deep concern. The elderly woman who hosted her during her civil rights volunteering in Marion, Alabama, told her:

> We Blacks are in a constant state of worry. We might rejoice and feel hopeful one day, but by the next day it's quiet despair again. We're afraid to change anything, because every time things go wrong, it's always our blood that gets spilled. But in the end, maybe our blood is the price we have to pay for change?

Mary added, 'Her despair was palpable; but so was her belief that change must be possible, someday.'

In Noisy-le-Grand, as challenging as the situation was, ATD was starting to have an impact. Mary's insistence that Wresinski join her in the US profoundly shook things up, requiring ATD to take a wider view of very different situations of deep poverty, and also to draw lessons from the War on Poverty. Mary turned her notes into a chapter titled 'Organizations of Welfare Clients', published by Professor Harold Weissman in his book, *Community Development in the Mobilization for Youth Experience.* Her conclusion in that chapter, evaluating[6] six welfare rights organisations, was mixed:

> In less than a year, these groups have recovered well over $100,000 in entitlements for their members – a mirror of the extent to which the welfare system is not operating according to law. ... Protest and disruption have been needed. ... A nationwide organization of welfare clients now exists which hopes to put such pressure on the total welfare system that it will ultimately have to change.

> ... Such a strategy tends to overlook the possibility that repressive measures will be taken against individual clients. ... The success of welfare groups in changing the system will depend on their ability to act politically [and] to convince the broad electorate that change is required.

That concern for excluded individuals and for convincing the general public of the value of their cause helped inform Mary's shaping of ATD.

Chapter 8

'Immense but Hidden Potential' in Apartheid South Africa

Five years later, Mary observed racism on another continent. Back in the UK, Mary was studying at the London School of Economics, where a fellow student belonged to the Christian Fellowship Trust (CFT). This Quaker charity promoted mutual understanding between South African churches and UK community groups. When the CFT brought two South Africans to discover ATD Fourth World through Mary, this led them to award Mary a six-week study trip to Johannesburg, Durban, and Cape Town. The racial segregation known as apartheid – meaning 'separateness' – was established in South Africa in 1948 to benefit the white population. Throughout the 1970s, the apartheid government carried out the mass removal of 3.5 million South Africans of colour from their homes to territories designated 'Bantustan homelands'. Mary's study trip fell in the midst of this upheaval in May–June of 1973. Her goal was to see how people tried to resist.

Because the apartheid government refused all CFT requests, Mary had to use personal contacts to plan her itinerary. After a flurry of letters seeking people concerned about 'education, community relations, and social affairs', Mary flew to Johannesburg, where she was hosted by Ilse and Beyers Naudé.[1] Ilse was a senior lecturer in sociology at the University of Natal, a prominent speaker against the erosion of human rights, and part of the Black Sash, a white women's non-violent resistance movement.[2] Beyers had been a pastor of the Dutch Reformed Church. However his leadership of anti-apartheid activism led him to lose this title in the early 1960s. He was forbidden to preach to whites. Although still allowed to preach to Black people, he was constantly harassed by police. Since 1967, he was under a government ban severely restricting his freedom of travel, association, and speech. Mary noted: 'The Naudés are often physically attacked by fellow white South Africans who support apartheid. But the majority of white South Africans simply close their eyes to apartheid.'

The Naudés arranged for Mary to visit Alexandra, a Black township near Johannesburg. Her guide was an Indian man whose family had just been evicted from Johannesburg. However, he refused to live where the government wanted him, instead paying four times the market rate to rent a run-down flat. Mary wrote, 'He feels torn between devoting his life to resisting apartheid or fleeing the country to give his children the chance of a better life.' In Alexandra, Black South Africans previously lived as families. The mass removal programme meant the demolition of their homes. Children and grandparents were sent to the Bantustans. Only working-age adults could remain. They were assigned to live in dormitories built to house 60,000 people. The one Mary visited was bleak. Designed for 2,000 women, there were then only 700, sleeping four to a room. The single entrance was guarded, and electric gates throughout the building could isolate any corridor. For every fourteen women, there was a single toilet, sink, and cooking burner. No men were allowed in except to one public visitors' room. Mary wrote:

> During my visit, I was careful what I said so as not to create difficulties for my hosts. But after noticing the expression on my face, the guard accompanying me said, 'I can tell you're against this.' She tried to change my mind by insisting, 'These dormitories are a very good system. The women prefer it to living in the city, and most of them have been abandoned by their husbands anyway.'

The guard's sales pitch included telling Mary about evening literacy classes and showing her a 'social centre', but it did not impress Mary:

> I soon discovered that it is used mainly to distribute food to the numerous victims of tuberculosis. There was a lot of rat poison set out, but very little food. One of the few services

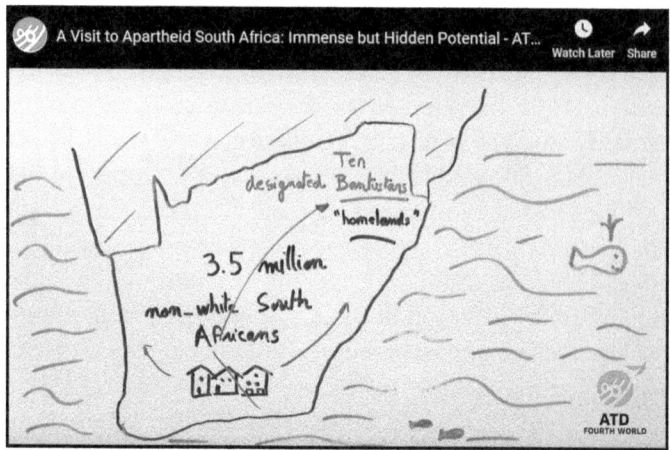

The apartheid government carried out the mass removal of 3.5 million South Africans of colour from their homes to territories designated 'Bantustan homelands'.

© Paul Maréchal

The Black Sash was a white women's non-violent movement to resist apartheid.

© Paul Maréchal

available to the women is contraception, because raising children is seen as a hindrance to the availability of the female workforce. One woman told me, 'Forced relocations destroy our families and our roots.'

Apartheid South Africa

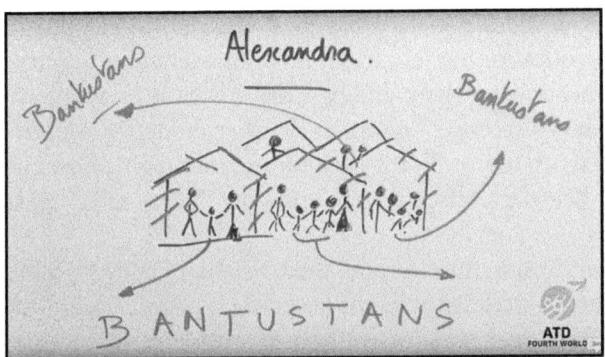

Alexandra is a township on the outskirts
of Johannesburg.
© *Paul Maréchal*

Mary knew that the men's dormitories were larger and also full; however her request to visit one was refused because these places were considered 'too dangerous for women to enter'. Most of the Black South Africans Mary met hated these dormitories, referring to them as prisons. She wrote: 'They also point out that the area surrounding these dormitories is plagued with violence, including sexual assault. Even the guard showing me around finally conceded that it was a mistake to build such large dormitories. She regretted that the planning committee did not include a single woman.'

Unlike the US with its widespread protests, South Africa lacked any freedom of speech. Resisters were imprisoned without explanation; the press tightly controlled; suspicion everywhere. She met with Black anti-apartheid activists living in constant danger of arrest. On the day they met, the police had raided their office, confiscated their publications, and closed it down. Mary wrote:

> Anyone could be an informant ready to denounce you so you always have to be very careful of what you say. This creates the most oppressive sense of isolation and distrust that I have ever felt anywhere. … The most important thing I've seen here is that Black people clearly have an immense potential; but it is mostly hidden because they work such long hours that they have very little energy left.

Mary also met with people in favour of apartheid: 'A white Baptist pastor explained that he considers it logical to separate people by skin colour. He could tell that I strongly disagreed, so he grew suspicious and began questioning me closely on political issues. Because he knew that my hosts were the Naudés, I did my best to avoid answering.' One of Mary's strongest qualities was her complete frankness about speaking truth to power. It's hard for me to imagine how challenging it was for her to exercise caution, knowing the potential consequences for others.

On Mary's return to Europe, the Christian Fellowship Trust asked for a report of 'no less than four typed folio pages'.[3] Hers was 33 pages long. In English, it was in addition to a 90-page report she wrote in French for Wresinski. In a follow-up letter, she advised the trust that future visits ought to 'serve the country in a more direct and immediate way'. For example, she proposed, future visitors should:

> have some knowledge and experience in community organisation or development ... [with] the object of documenting existing efforts of which there are no doubt many, but they are certainly not known to each other. ... Perhaps it would also be possible to have some long-term contact with some of these projects because it can be very lonely without the possibility of exchange with those outside. ... I think it very important that whoever is sent should be politically aware,

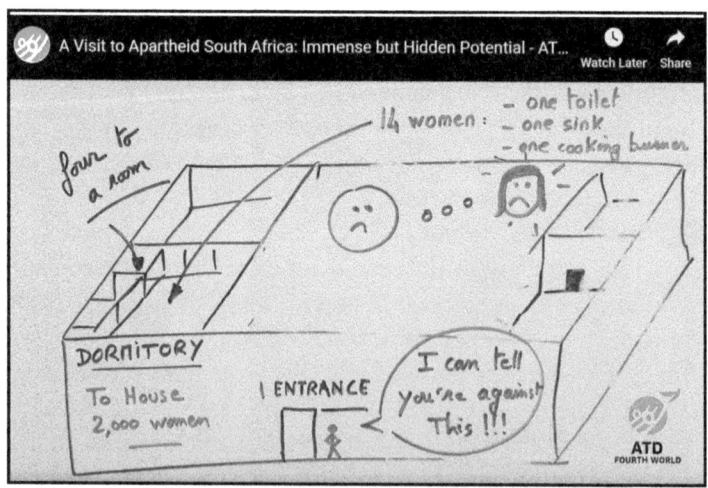

The guard showing Mary the dormitories said,
'I can tell you're against this.'
© Paul Maréchal

but should not wave any flag around as the risks taken by those seeking change are very great, and the choices [should be] made by these people only, i.e. those who are destined to remain in the country and take the consequences of their actions.[4]

As after her American travels, Mary was examining the big picture of movement-building. At this point, the trust invited Mary to become the first 'grantee' to join its UK Overseas Reception Committee.[5] In this role, she spent the next decade helping select other British candidates to travel to South Africa. Wanting grantees to do more to support non-white South Africans, Mary recommended grantees of Indian origin who spoke Indian or Pakistani languages, including an expert on religious minorities in the UK. Mary also helped welcome South Africans on study visits in the UK, where she made a point of ensuring that visitors would meet not only church leaders but 'ordinary people with their problems of poverty and oppression'. One of the South Africans welcomed by Mary, Nombeko Mlambo, felt 'big disappointment to find so much misery in a free country'.[6] Another, Mogobe Ramose, was not allowed to return home, having been exiled by the apartheid government while in Europe.

Corresponding faithfully with South African friends, Mary chose her words carefully to protect them, knowing that, in London too, the Special Branch of South Africa's secret police monitored

Mary, third from right, in South Africa in 1973
© *ATD Fourth World / Joseph Wresinski Centre*

activities, opening – and sometimes confiscating – letters. One of her correspondents was the Revd Theo Kotze, a close friend of Beyers Naudé. Under particularly close surveillance, Kotze was later banned for his anti-apartheid activities. He wrote to Mary: 'One of our main tasks is to help whites understand and accept a future that is already with us, a future that is *black with hope*!'[7]

In 1983, ten years after her study trip, Mary returned to South Africa. This trip, with teammate Brigitte Seinnave, was on behalf of ATD, which was just beginning to develop its work in Kenya and Burkina Faso (then Upper Volta). Apartheid remained firmly in place. In Mary's report, she compared the situation to that in 1973:

> In Soweto, people have been able to improve their homes. The houses look pretty, with curtains or decorations. Some have managed to add a room, and there are trees, bushes and gardens. I don't have the impression of bare ugliness as before. … But Alexandra looks dishevelled and abandoned, much like a shanty-town now. Some residents seem very poor. Children, dogs and goats all play in rubbish that is strewn everywhere.

In Alexandra, Mary reconnected with Bobbie who she met previously. She had brought her a book (published in the UK) about Bobbie's anti-apartheid organisation which was banned in 1977. Bobbie said that most of the others who worked there were gone now: 'Some left the country; others were arrested, banned, or imprisoned. Absolutely nothing has changed.' Mary wrote:

> At the nursery, Bobbie is delighted that they're fixing ceilings and windows – but it's in worse condition: the playground dusty, the kitchen needing repairs; and threadbare aprons. Children are open and smiling, their faces and bodies seem more marked by poverty. And in fact these are the luckier children because a hundred more are on the nursery waiting list.[8]

Mary was particularly struck that Bobbie's new Women's Legal Committee was impacting government policies. For example, every month divorced women had to miss a day's work to visit a social worker to collect alimony payments. To lose less pay, women preferred to wait a few months to collect several payments at once – but many social workers said this showed they could manage without the payments and should receive only one month's payment at a time. Bobbie convinced the ministry to change this.

Mary and Brigitte's also visited Jean-Pierre Lescour, a French priest who had volunteered with ATD in the UK and was now supporting mine workers to unionise. He spoke about men being tortured in the Johannesburg prison. Mary wrote:

> One was held for three months in isolation and interrogated every day. Because he did not see daylight for months, he lost his sense of time. Released now, he is still disoriented about time. Any man subjected to that kind of coercion can end up confessing to any crime. … Jean-Pierre's friends phone him daily so that if he disappears, they will know as soon as possible. … Labour unions are the only political organising allowed, since Black people are not allowed to join political parties. They are closely surveilled by the Special Police.

Next, Brigitte and Mary travelled to Lesotho, a kingdom of goatherds and shepherds landlocked in a mountainous enclave surrounded by South Africa and dependent on outside grants for food and development projects. In 1983, Lesotho's diamond mines were closed for poor production. There was no other industry, leading many men to move to South Africa for mining work – or to dance at weekly shows put on by mines for tourists. Mary wrote:

> Families without a man, or where the man lacks work, try to scrape by with a garden or selling craftwork, but life is hard. Winters are harsh because of the weight and cost of fuel. Many people live lost in the mountains, in places they can reach only by footpath. They walk, women and children carrying burdens atop their heads, or some go by horse.

Mary reflected on the nation's relationship to South Africa: 'Many South Africans who fled after the Soweto uprising came here for military training – and three months ago the South African army made a surprise incursion here. They targeted South African refugees they consider dangerous, but they also killed Lesotho citizens.'[9]

One of Mary's hosts was Phyllis Naidoo, a political refugee. When in Durban, South Africa, days after she gave birth to her third child, her husband was arrested, tortured, and jailed on Robben Island alongside Nelson Mandela. Because of their anti-apartheid activism, Phyllis was forbidden to work and placed under house arrest for ten years. The Special Police frequently raided her home. A year after her banning order was lifted, she fled to Lesotho – where the Special Police severely wounded her with a parcel bomb in 1979.[10] Mary's report describes Phyllis' home as a hotbed of activism supporting political refugees.

Phyllis' contacts helped Mary to discover Lesothan poverty. Mary wrote:

> In the mountains, elderly people, particularly widows, have no family and thus no way to survive. Despite the winter snows, there is terrible drought here, which brings hunger. The soil erosion is bad and the land is mostly boulders. When rains come, everything is washed away. Everywhere you see gullies several metres deep. ... Here, the poorest people may be men who spend months in the capital without getting chosen to work in a South African mine.

After spiking in 1982, the price of gold crashed just before Mary's visit. Gold mines with lower quality ore closed and fewer labourers were needed.

> Every day, men wait at tented mining recruitment centres. But some men are never picked: their health is bad; or they committed a fault at work; or they are known to have been in a labour union. The very poorest among these men never return home because they are so pained at not being able to earn anything. Of 300 to 400 men we saw waiting, a quarter of them sleep in the street. Last winter, three died of exposure and hunger.[11]

Mary and Brigitte visited a Maronite church project serving a hot meal to these men every evening, but it had taken ten months to be allowed to set up a tent for this. Most other churches – and the government – refused to rent land for the purpose, saying that these were 'undesirable' men who threaten the environment, and might even break into their church. Finally the Anglican Church found a temporary spot for the food tent.[12]

Another group of people whose struggles were particularly hard was young refugees from Angola, Mozambique, Uganda, Zimbabwe, and South Africa. Some 6,500 arrived after the 1976 Soweto uprising, when children led a protest joined by 20,000 young people and brutally repressed by the police. Most refugees had no profession and very little schooling, leaving them with 'no chance' of earning a living because of the unemployment rate. Mary noted: 'Some are as young as 13 or 14 and have no family or friends in Lesotho'. Mrs Malefane of the Christian Council of Lesotho told Mary:

> Sometimes these young refugees are aggressive with everyone, turning their anger on the world. Others would not accept that teenagers behave this way towards an adult; but I understand. They are lost. They have suffered. I wait for their anger to dissipate before asking questions. Then they start to calm down and explain to me their troubles. They must learn to live on their own, taking financial responsibility. The church gives them 40 rand that must last all month, so if they spend it on sweets, they can't pay their rent and have nothing left. ... Some teenage girls fall pregnant right away and have no family here to help them raise the baby as the custom would be.

Just as in France and the US, Mary was again seeing that, even where poverty was widespread, some faced more challenges than others – and once again teenage girls had specific struggles.

Discovering the profusion of international development projects in Lesotho, Mary wrote about 'expat mercenaries': white foreigners driving around the country 'without bothering to learn more than "hello" and "good-bye" in the Lesotho language'. This top-down approach to community development was the subject of Mary's conversation with Mpho Ndebele, a young activist for migrant rights, who had recently returned from the US where she trained as a social worker. Mary wrote:

> Mrs Ndebele said the most interesting part of her training was the notion that people meant to benefit from a project should participate in shaping it. In Lesotho, she explained,

before British colonisation, village chiefs listened to the people before making decisions. Respect for their authority depended on those reflections together. A proverb reflects this: 'A leader is a leader by the people'. But colonisers, who ruled through village chiefs, distorted this system by requiring that chiefs show loyalty to them instead of to the people. Colonial rulers paid the chiefs salaries and told them to give orders instead of consulting people. Mrs Ndebele said that people learned to obey as leaders learned to give orders.

Back in South Africa, Mary and Brigitte visited Beyers Naudé. Asked about the worst situations of poverty, Naudé spoke of those in the Bantustans dying of hunger, sex workers, people in cities cut off from family, people sleeping in the street. About migrant workers, he said: 'They are not allowed in cities and keep getting arrested, … shut into a cell with 39 others, crammed together like sardines. Boys only 12 and 13 may be held for weeks for stealing food. These people are forgotten by everyone.'

They discussed the worldwide spread of anti-apartheid protests. Mary was concerned that the boycotts had prevented any South Africans from attending the UN World Conferences on Women in 1975 and 1980. Naudé responded:

> I agree with some boycotts, but not all, and not all the time. Boycotts won't change our government's policy. But the existence of these has a powerful psychological effect on people here who are fighting for justice. We are totally powerless; but when others cry out for justice on our behalf, we know we are not forgotten or alone, and that is very important. …
>
> But the great weakness of Black activists here – and it's understandable because their struggle is to survive today, and because they lack the means to get information about the world – but their great lack is a clear vision of what society they would put in place tomorrow.

Although it was meaningful for Mary to reconnect with Naudé and other dissidents, her visit ended on a wrenching note. At the Johannesburg airport, she and Brigitte were detained by police for hours while all their papers were photographed. Although Mary made no notes during the trip, Brigitte's notes were copied. They immediately telephoned Bobbie, Naudé, and others to warn them. As Mary wrote disheartedly to Lescour: 'We also made a visit to the French Embassy in Libreville, Gabon, and saw a rather inebriated consul. I don't know whether that helped or not, but I do hope that there are no repercussions. Let me know when you can how things are going for you.'[13]

It wasn't until a decade later that apartheid was gradually dismantled, between 1990 and 1994. In 2015, I had the opportunity to follow in Mary's footsteps and visit South Africa myself. I travelled with an ATD teammate, Martin Kalisa, from Rwanda. Like Mary, I was fortunate to meet those trying to make a difference on the ground. For instance, in Orange Farm Township, on the outer edge of Johannesburg, we were given a tour by a group of mothers of children with disabilities who support one another as part of the Sidinga Uthando Self-Help Group. The mothers told us that traditional beliefs blame them for disabilities, considered punishment for immoral behaviour during pregnancy. These beliefs led fathers to abandon every one of these mothers. To dispel fears and start conversations with their neighbours about disability, many of these mothers agreed to paint their corrugated iron homes purple, showing bright murals of their children with speech bubbles like: 'Autism: Do you know what's going on in my mind? It's high time you learn about disabilities.' In this district of 70,000 people, the widely scattered homes decorated by this 'paint-it-purple'[14] campaign stand out like beacons to raise awareness, including of other families with disabilities who may not know about their group.

Martin and I gave several presentations about ATD, including at the lofty University of Cape Town, with its magnificent vista over the sea, and in Pietermaritzburg, the gritty capital of KwaZulu-Natal province. Everywhere we went, I was shocked to discover that one or the other of us was always firmly in the racial minority: some areas remain all Black; while more privileged places remain almost exclusively white and Asian. When we ate at a popular pizza joint, all the servers were Black, while Martin was the only Black customer. 'Why isn't the country more integrated by now?' I asked him. 'It's been more than twenty years since apartheid ended!'

'The Rwandan genocide was in 1994, the same year apartheid ended. But its impact is still with us. Twenty years is not very long for a country to move forward.'

One evening after twilight, in a garden scented with bougainvillea and jacaranda trees, Martin recounted to me and Lucille Luckhoff, our Quaker host in Cape Town, his experience of the grisly genocide, when he sometimes evaded ruthless killers only by clinging to rafters above their heads, helpless to prevent their butchery below. He says this left him 'with a deep appreciation for human dignity and what it means to be deprived of it'.[15] He points out that overcoming a legacy of such scorching evil requires a great length of time. This made sense to Lucille who, like Ilse Naudé, was active in the Black Sash resistance. She explained the deep entrenchment of segregation in housing, education, and every system in the country.

Overcoming painful legacies demands sustained dedication, as Martin and I saw at a day-long event for South African teachers run by Alley Lazarus of the Zakheni Arts Therapy Foundation. Dozens of teachers in attendance, almost all Black, not only teach in some of the most disadvantaged schools, but for the most had grown up studying at these same acutely underfunded schools. As teachers recounted stray bullets whistling into classrooms and their students' massive ongoing trauma, professional story-tellers improvised re-enactments of these challenges, honouring the teachers' experiences and offering an interlude for introspection.

Alley's motto is a quote from David Steindl-Rast: 'The antidote to exhaustion is wholeheartedness.' That unfaltering ardour, carried by the teachers and so many of the people Mary met on the front lines of the War on Poverty, is crucial to social change. But in Mary's view, wholeheartedness alone was not enough.

After her time in the United States, she and Wresinski spent weeks reflecting. One of their concerns was that most programmes they saw 'were directed at a mass of poor people but without any real understanding of the different levels of poverty'. Mary said:

> When many people in poverty do arrive at a better state, there will still be some whose situations have not improved, despite what was offered. This happened in Noisy-le-Grand where families in the camp are despised by those of a slightly higher level who say, 'Now that the welfare state is helping you, it's your own fault if you're still poor.'

They agreed that ATD's priority should be seeking out those most likely to be left behind to decide with them what kinds of projects could include everyone.

During their US visit, it was a struggle for Wresinski – who spoke no English and relied on Mary's translations – to grasp the loose nature of the movements there. One woman said to them, 'Oh, you're part of the civil rights movement just like us!' Wresinski agreed. Seeing how widespread this movement was, he expected that national coordinators were sending activists where they were most needed, or at least using a common publication to focus debate and build consensus. However, Mary explained, the many people and organisations working for civil rights all acted independently. The movement was so fragmented that it struggled to be effective. It lacked a systematic approach to prevent the most dynamic leaders in low-income communities from burning out or from moving to new jobs whenever funding ended.

ATD Fourth World considers itself a movement as well. But Mary and Wresinski wanted long-term institutions: a research institute, a Volunteer Corps, and a systematic approach to planning and evaluating every grass-roots project so that wholeheartedness would be bolstered by strategy.

Chapter 9

Solidarity in the Face of Racism

While racism was writ large in Mary's experiences in the US and in South Africa, over the years she saw that in each part of the world, racism is shaped by the histories and complexities rooted in that place. She also knew that racism exists everywhere, including in places where it is less acknowledged – and therefore hard to challenge.

In 1980, Mary wrote an editorial about racism and poverty for ATD Fourth World's UK newsletter. A sketch depicts a white woman clutching a Black child protectively. They are surrounded by four white children who are mocking them. This image represents a situation common among members of ATD in the UK: white women in poverty have children with Black men, some of whom are no longer present in their children's lives. These biracial children often face bullying that their mothers can't prevent. The mother in the sketch looks horrified. Mary's editorial connected racism to immigration, which in the UK is intertwined with colonialism. Using the term 'Fourth World' to mean people in poverty, Mary wrote:

> Racism is at the heart of misery. This is why the Fourth World must be the first to fight against it. … The Fourth World are forced to share the same living conditions as immigrants. … It is not true to say that all immigrants have better housing, better chances at school, better jobs than we do. Many of us suffer the same discrimination. If we want to get out of these conditions, if we want our children to be respected, we must all join together. It is our only hope. If

Solidarity in the Face of Racism

we don't respect each other and fight for each other, then nothing will ever change for any of us. Racism exists in the Fourth World, not because we don't like other people, but because we can't believe that others can be as unhappy and miserable as we are.[1]

Mary saw that conflict was rife in the run-down estates in Britain where families of many different origins lived in cramped quarters. As part of a European Union anti-poverty programme, Mary hosted monthly evening discussions with adults in poverty who chose to become activists with ATD.[2] In 1976-80, Mary focused many discussions on the origins of various British minority ethnic or religious communities. Regular participants in the discussions and guest speakers were invited to speak about their varied origins: Irish, Jewish, Muslim, Hindu, Sikh, Cambodian, Bengali, West African, and from the West Indies. Speaking about her father's Jamaican childhood, one speaker said:

Before independence, they were taught that England was their mother country. They didn't know their own history;

Mary's editorial for this newsletter said:
'We must all join together. It is our only hope.'

they learnt English history. He could tell you about every tree in England, and all the kings and queens, but he didn't know anything about his own history. So when they finally came here and were treated with prejudice, they thought, 'What the hell's going on – this is our country?'[3]

A participant from Manchester said:

Up to age 15, I didn't think of myself as Black – it was driven home to me. Going to a friend's house, I was waiting at the gate while they were inside the house. Black people are amazed that people call them 'Sambo'. My friends used to go out to clubs and I couldn't get in because I was Black, but they could get in. Slowly, things like that drove a wedge between us. They'd go their way and I'd go my way. ... I haven't committed any crime, but I've been arrested about twenty times in the last eight years. ... I was taken to the police station about 2 o'clock in the morning and questioned until 5 in the morning – at which time I was released. ...

Mary facilitates a monthly evening discussion
with adults in poverty.
© *ATD Fourth World / Joseph Wresinski Centre*

My mind used to get so depressed about it, I was absolutely shaken, I couldn't stand it. But I made up my mind not to let it get me down. ... That's just self-destruction.

In these discussions, immigrant parents spoke about child-rearing and the shock of discovering that, if their traditions were at odds with British expectations, social workers could remove their children into care. One speaker said that when her family arrived from Jamaica, in school the children were considered 'backward' because teachers could not understand their patois language.

The discussion about Bangladesh took place just nine years after the country gained independence. A guest speaker explained that the British Government had invited many South Asian men to serve as cheap labour, but that on arrival they faced frequent harassment and their families often felt isolated due to distance from extended family.[4] The group discussed the challenges for children of immigrants who adapt to British culture in school, but may feel a cultural gap with parents more rooted in their country of origin. One discussion participant said:

> Asians are not much liked. We're stamped out, not wanted, alienated, all the time. ... A friend recently visited Bangladesh and was overwhelmed by the welcome. Even with the poorest family he visited, he was never allowed to go without a meal. He wasn't asked, 'Are you going to have a meal with us'; he was told he was welcome. ... Here, things aren't very welcoming towards us. 'Please sit down and have a cup of tea'; no, that sort of welcome, we never receive.

Another discussion focused on Jewish immigrants. That evening's featured speaker was Grace Goodman, who in 1967 invited ATD to the UK to join her work, a project of specialised family support. Goodman explained to the group that her family of Sephardic Jews travelled from Persia to India, where she grew up. The family later moved to England where, she said: 'We were called dreadful names so often that we accept it. It's usually "bloody Jew". I have seldom heard a Jew referred to without the "b word" before or after the Jew. It used to hurt. Now I don't give a damn. We get used to it.'[5] Goodman's son-in-law described his mother's experience in Poland where Jews were banned from many professions and rights and targeted for violence in pogroms. His father immigrated to Britain from Russia: 'In the East End, my father and his friends had to go and do Hebrew classes til 9 o'clock at night. They always had to come out in gangs because there was a group of non-Jews around who used to do a bit of Jew-bashing. So they had to run home fast as a group.'

Goodman told the group how frightening it was to be Jewish in 1936 when Nazi sympathiser Oswald Mosley incited anti-Jewish riots in London's East End.[6] During the Second World War, Goodman lived in Manchester with her husband and daughter:

> To show how very recent and real the threat to the Jew is and was, during the war, a lot of us Jewish mothers got hold of some poison from the doctor. We saved our rations and said that if the Germans landed anywhere in England,

In Whitechapel, London, Bengali children play in uncollected rubbish during the 1978 'Winter of Discontent', a series of widespread strikes. This photo is in Fieldgate Mansions, a 19th century tenement block due to be demolished where the blocks were squatted by artists, local unemployed people and Bengali families for whom there was no official housing provision.

© *Dave Hoffman*

we were going to have one grand glorious party for our children, using up all our rations, and then we would give them poison and kill ourselves, because we were quite sure we were going to the concentration camps. That is absolute; it's as recent as that.

In these discussions, dialogue flowed freely, with Mary drawing out all participants. Whenever someone repeated an ethnic stereotype they had heard, it became a judgement-free opportunity to push the conversation to a deeper level to try to understand the experiences of different minority groups. Above all, Mary kept the focus on solidarity and keeping one's dignity in the face of different forms of racism and discrimination. She told the group:

One way of breaking down our isolation is to come together where we discover that we are all in the same boat, where we find people who listen and understand us, and where we can help each other.[7]

The most important question is how to help people in need, both here and in the countries people were born in. Each of us has the responsibility to look to ourselves and see how we can give help and courage and hope to people we know who are in need.[8]

Grace Goodman, an anti-poverty pioneer in the UK, invited ATD Fourth World to join her work in 1967.

© *ATD Fourth World / Joseph Wresinski Centre*

Together, we have learned that by starting to stand up for ourselves, we can get together with others to fight for those who have the greatest difficulties.[9]

Part III

'Women Always Seem to Get the Short End of the Stick'

Chapter 10

Violence against Women, and the Intersection of Poverty and Gender

The history of feminism in the United States is strong, including the 1848 women's rights convention in Seneca Falls, and Sojourner Truth's 1851 speech, 'Ain't I a woman?' In the 1970s, Gloria Steinem founded *Ms.*, a nationwide feminist magazine, and Helen Reddy topped the charts with 'I am woman, hear me roar!' But France is different. In 2018, when Catherine Deneuve said that the #MeToo movement was trying to ruin flirtation by condemning men for 'touching a knee, trying to steal a kiss',[1] many of her younger compatriots agreed.

On the continuum of feminism, I have the feeling that Mary stood somewhere between Gloria Steinem's radicalism at one extreme, and Deneuve's at the other. Mary believed staunchly in women's rights; but she was never strident about it. For her, a key principle was simply that women should be able to accomplish whatever they wanted. Perhaps this was why she didn't marry. She certainly enjoyed romance; but marriage and motherhood might have meant taking a back seat to a husband, which didn't appeal to her at all.

Even without marriage, there have always been men wanting to rein women in. My grandmother Frances was born to Czech immigrants living just outside of New York City. When she was 4, tragedy befell her teenage cousin. Mary Rucker was 'one of the most popular girls in Little Ferry', according to the *New York Times* report of the crime.[2] As the story was passed down to my father: 'There had been a dance at the community centre. Some man took a romantic interest in Mary and wanted to date her. She wanted nothing to do with him. Apparently he did not take rejection very well because he shot and killed Mary.' The newspaper quotes Mary's father insisting that this was 'no love matter', but adds about the murderer that this 'crazed man' was 'insanely jealous' having seen 'a young man accompany Mary' at the dance. He also threatened to kill her whole family – but she was the only one shot. The killer was 38 years old. Mary Rucker was only 17.

Early on Frances learned from her cousin's murder the searing lesson of consequences for women who cross the wrong man. She also once whispered to me that, before her marriage, she was raped. Maybe both of these crimes spurred her marriage to Floyd, which we all knew was an unhappy one. When cousin Bill looks back at their relationship, he notes that his own no-nonsense mother 'never would have put up with Floyd's boozing'. As for Frances:

> She was a traditional flapper. It was never clear why she married him, but she was about to become an old maid so I think she must have felt backed into it. Later she wanted out, and that's the main reason that Floyd wanted them to have a child: to keep her in the house. He also used to make snide remarks. Like saying, 'When I asked her to marry me, she double-crossed me and said yes.' Or when she turned 40, he used to say he was going to trade her in for two 20s.

That kind of scorn as well as violence against women both have a long history. In conversations with countless people over the years, I've heard again and again: 'girls should be seen and not heard' – 'women should know their place' – 'no one likes a pushy bitch'. One friend talks about reliving past trauma every time she's 'facing into' an encounter with any man who happens to behave in ways that trigger memories of her brutal sexual assault. This leads her to quickly back down into placating behaviour – although occasionally, she says, 'I manage to dig deep to find forceful energy that matches their natural ego state. I want to get heard and taken seriously, but it's hard to do without frazzling myself out.' As bleak as it is to know just how indelibly trauma continues to shape the world, I take hope from people like adrienne maree brown who founded a movement for 'pleasure

'Violence, poverty and gender'

activism' based on the idea that 'what we need is a culture where the common experience of trauma leads to a normalisation of healing'.[3]

And yet. Poverty can make girls and women particularly vulnerable to violence. One of the most fundamental elements of ATD Fourth World's approach is creating conditions for people in poverty to speak out about their own experiences and their own reflections. But some situations are so traumatic and deemed so shameful that they are even more challenging to voice aloud. In hushed tones, women have confided to me: 'Even after he raped me, I kept cleaning his house because I needed the job so desperately.' 'Because I was only 15, I didn't understand until much later that the men in the accommodation where social services had placed me were grooming me to be trafficked.' 'I don't want to be a hooker, but how else can I keep a roof over my kids' head?' Speaking publicly is often unimaginable. When the #MeToo movement emerged, I hoped it might create an opportunity for ATD to address the intersection of poverty and violence against women. But still, even as in Mary Rabagliati's lifetime, we continue to struggle with silence.

Society tends to blame poor men for violence against women in poverty. In fact, however, women are more often victimised by men who have power over them, including economic power. But while wealthy and abusive men often benefit from impunity, if a man in poverty shows even the faintest trace of anger, society is quicker to assume the worst. Awareness of this is deeply ingrained in ATD because of Wresinski's experiences and reflections on male anger. During the First World War, he was born in a French internment camp for enemies because of his father's origins in German-occupied Poland. In that camp, one of Wresinski's sisters died of malnutrition. After the war, his father eventually disappeared, leaving his mother alone to raise four surviving children. Wresinski wrote:

Joseph Wresinski as a child, at left, with his parents, brothers and sister
©ATD Fourth World / Joseph Wresinski Centre

My father shouted all the time, … cursing my mother and we lived continually in fear. Only much later, when I was a man, sharing the life ... of other families like our own, did I understand that my father was a humiliated man. ... He felt he had failed in life. He was ashamed of not being able to give his family security and happiness. ... A person cannot live such a humiliated life without reacting. The poor react in the same violent way.[4]

Reflecting on a man in poverty in Noisy-le-Grand who destroyed his own home, Wresinski said:

Behind his drinking, behind the violence in him, this man is not trying to *escape* but to *find* something that will allow him to look his children in the face, and that will lead his wife to put her arms around him and say: 'I love you. We've been through a lot, but tomorrow will be wonderful, you'll start working again.'[5]

I thought about this in 2009-12, when ATD Fourth World carried out participatory research on the violence of poverty. Activists with lived experience of poverty made it clear how painful it is to be stigmatised as the source of violence with no recognition of violence done *to* them. We concluded that when speaking about the violence of poverty, it's important to speak also about peace and the many ways that people in deep poverty create it. At the same time, we ended up focusing our work on institutional violence; we shied away from

The Noisy-le-Grand women's centre in the 1960s.
The poster on the wall reads: 'A good man'.
© ATD Fourth World / Joseph Wresinski Centre

evoking physical and sexual violence, in part because of the weight of shame and finger-pointing involved.

This is why I am struck by ways Mary's work pushed against the grain. In the 1960s, her journals recorded many instances of suffering of girls and women in the Noisy-le-Grand 'igloos':[6]

> *22 November 1962:* Mrs Perret[7] has been in the hospital for more than a week. She is in pain from her husband's beatings but no one explains her injuries to her. She tried to leave her husband. She slept in another family's igloo; but when a relative of theirs returned, they asked her to leave. Returning home, she discovered her husband living with a girlfriend. He threw her out. She said, 'Then he showed up drunk and threw stones at my friend's igloo. It's good to be in the hospital since I have nowhere to go.' Now Mrs Perret

In Noisy-le-Grand, fetching water was often a chore for girls or women.
© *ATD Fourth World / Joseph Wresinski Centre*

> heard from a neighbour that her igloo has been broken into and everything stolen: her clothes, the bed, even the stove.
>
> *23 November:* I'm investigating the Perret break-in. The home was trashed: several looters left nothing left but one rotted mattress. Most people won't talk, but finally old Mr Carlier told me he knows who took what. I asked him to get Mrs Perret's dresses back.

Mary did what she could to support women like Mrs Perret, and to reinforce their support of one another. She participated in global conferences on feminism where she convinced middle-class women to listen to women in poverty. Although she pushed ATD to start new projects for teenage girls, her premature death prevented that. Today, ATD still struggles to speak publicly about violence against women. Each person must decide whether and when to speak for themselves; and yet on this issue, many women prefer to remain anonymous, or to keep silent. We also still grapple with our worry about compounding stigmatisations about men in poverty. This is gradually changing, but at a glacial pace. A few people from ATD's founding generations are horrified at the idea of publishing Mary's writings about violence against women. That shocks me – but it's not representative of ATD's work today, so I want to write about the importance of Mary's stance, which included convincing Wresinki, a Catholic priest, to sanction birth control.

Chapter 11

Bedbugs in Birmingham and a Prison Visit in Pontoise

In 1963, Mary needed an appendectomy. It was the dead of winter, when the rudimentary conditions in the camp were too harsh for post-operative convalescence. She returned to England for the operation – which Wresinski deemed an opportunity to assign other tasks to her. Several former volunteers were scattered around England. Mary was to recruit as many as possible to return to Noisy-le-Grand. Mary's second assignment was spending six weeks in Birmingham helping a non-profit group while learning from its approach.[1]

In Birmingham, Mary discovered a community of 'back-to-back' houses, cramped early Victorian buildings without hot water. Several households shared one outdoor laundry basin and one outhouse. Each home had just one bedroom, a small living room with a coal fire, a coal cellar, an attic, and a tiny kitchen with a small gas stove. These houses were notorious for bedbugs, attracted by flour in the wallpaper paste.[2] Mary wrote on 7 March 1963:

> Dear Père Joseph,
> There's so much to do in the kindergarten. Once, the teacher left me alone with the children. I can barely keep order, and they know it, so they were perfect little devils. On top of that, I've caught bedbugs.
> But don't worry, I'm being spoiled too. My godfather lives nearby. On Saturday night, his son took me to a fancy dress

party. He dressed as a toreador and I as a flamenco dancer. Everyone watched us dance the 'pasodoble'. I loved it!

It's really crazy to work in the depths of poverty when we could be happy doing something else. Is that mean? Although I love the families in Noisy-le-Grand, sometimes I just want to travel the globe. Yet of course I'm as poor as the other volunteers. So to afford it, maybe I'll marry an explorer – just for two or three years, to see the world. It would be impossible to bring a husband to the camp. Anyway I'm happy tonight, and tomorrow is a new adventure.

To study anti-poverty work here, I had great success last week. While visiting the housing officer, I 'borrowed' one of his reports about halfway houses. It's quite interesting. I had copied out most of it when he telephoned to ask if I knew where the report was. I pretended to look and said, 'Bother, I must have taken it by mistake'. I returned it, and began translating what I copied.

I'm visiting several low-income families. One mother is pregnant with her eighth child. One of her sons has been diagnosed with tuberculosis. I'm trying to help her with housework and home organisation – quite a challenge.

The community centre here has family planning. Now that contraceptive pills are legal and free in England, most mothers are thrilled. Husbands dislike condoms, but blame pregnancies on wives. Some men refuse to recognise an unwanted child. All couples should have the chance to plan their families. You told me that the only morally acceptable method is 'natural rhythm'.[3] But the chaos of poverty makes that hard to follow. Besides, if the rhythm method and the pill have the same goal, isn't it hypocritical of Catholics to allow only one? How can any woman organise her life with exhausting pregnancies year after year? It's too easy for priests to preach. For one thing, they're all men, and for another, babies don't wake them at 3 o'clock in the morning.

I'll leave it for now, as you're probably working too hard, as always.

Thinking of you all, Mary

In a letter jam-packed with anecdotes and ideas – like her fantasy about a temporary husband just to finance her travels! – Mary did her

In the camp, babies were born at home.
© *ATD Fourth World / Joseph Wresinski Centre*

best to convince Wresinski that overcoming poverty means letting women choose their family size. Although Britain legalised the birth control pill in 1961, it was so new that the Catholic Church had not yet taken a position. In France, where the pill was not yet legal, middle-class society often discussed imposing limits on families in poverty. Outsiders would say of the Noisy-le-Grand camp: 'They should all be sterilised'.[4] Wresinski pointed out that in wealthy families servants provided significant childcare support, while in Noisy-le-Grand, mothers with difficulties managing often lost their children into foster care. This societal control over families in poverty spurred Wresinski to defend their freedom to have large families.

However, Wresinski was also well aware that repeated pregnancies compounded struggles. He noted: 'Whenever a mother in the camp loses her temper with a neighbour, she shouts, 'I hope you get pregnant again!' They consider additional children a burden. They are weighed down by problems. It's not normal to wedge an entire family into a 9- by 15-foot space with nowhere to relax or work on a project.'[5]

On Mary's return from Birmingham, she continued visiting women. Babies were born at home, and Mary once acted as a midwife. She recalled: 'Doctors refused to set foot in the camp because of poor light and the lack of water, to say nothing of dogs everywhere.'[6] Following each birth, Mary brought parents birth registration forms, although couples with irregular immigration status preferred not to fill out the forms.

The daily journal Mary wrote is something asked of all of us in ATD Fourth World's Volunteer Corps: to record our interactions with people. In the moment, they serve as a place to put all that we have witnessed and to help us reflect. Later they can become tools for supporting individuals understanding their history or for thinking about policy, or for research.

I experience the rawness in this extract from Mary's journal. In amid accounts of a drunken driver crashing in the middle of the camp, seeing a father scavenge for cigarette butts to make new cigarettes, and a circus horse getting loose and galloping crazily through the camp, she also wrote:

> *16 June:* Everyone is talking about the Delauney girl's suicide attempt:
> 'She slit her wrists so it must have been for love.'
> 'If everyone with a bad love story killed themselves, there'd be no one left!'
> 'It's not her fault. Just see how filthy her mother is.'

In 1964, Mary helped sociologist Jean Labbens do research with 50 families in the camp. In his book, about a correlation between insecure housing and weak self-image, he devoted several pages to single mothers:

> Although never married, they usually lived for several years with the father of their children before he died or left. These women may have several passing relationships, and are sometimes accused ... [of] having loose morals ...

The Noisy-le-Grand camp
© *Gérald Bloncourt, ATD Fourth World / Joseph Wresinski Centre*

in the camp, where lone women are looked down on and considered threatening by other women.[7]

Partnered or not, Mary's research showed that a third of these mothers lost their children into state care.[8]

> *25 March:* Social services are placing four of the Barre children in foster care. The whole family brought the girls to the convent. Their little brother cried, and Mrs Barre was holding back tears. Mr Barre came too, although the couple is separated. At the convent, Mrs Barre handed me the paperwork, saying, 'You're faster'. When the nuns told us to leave, the daughters grew very upset. The youngest clung to her mother's skirt and the oldest cried.
> Heading back to camp, both parents agreed, 'At least they'll have lots of food there. And it's so clean!' But Mrs Barre couldn't hold back tears any longer.

Noting in her journal, 'Women always seem to get the short end of the stick', Mary recorded many agonising situations for women and girls, which included domestic violence, miscarriage, medical malpractice, and seeing their children permanently fostered away from them. A 20-year-old mother of children aged 8 months and 1½ tried to have her third pregnancy aborted illegally, but she died during the procedure.

Activities at the women's centre continued, with Mary noting: 'For once, the summer party we organised was lovely. In the past, women were anxious the food would run out and ate as quickly as possible. But this time, everyone was relaxed and at their most dignified and friendly.'

One young woman in the camp, Mariette Acevedo, was a machine worker whose employer required staff to work in silence, race to the toilet, and do unpaid overtime. Suddenly she was laid off, along with 20 other female machine workers, typists, and stenographers. Although a union helped them try to sue the employer for severance pay, the case dragged on because the company made secretive legal changes to its name. Mariette's sister called her crazy for testifying in court regularly and being seen as an 'unemployable troublemaker'. Mariette said, 'No, the other girls are crazy for protecting that stupid boss. Not me. I won't shut up now!'

Mary tried to help Mrs Legrand when her husband fled the police along with their 13-year-old son, Joël. Mrs Legrand wanted to report this as a kidnapping – but police in two neighbouring towns refused, with one saying: 'Not my jurisdiction'. In Neuilly-Plaisance, the chief said, 'Just wait, he'll probably come home on his own. In the meantime, request a foster family for Joël so we don't evict your whole family because of him. As for your husband, you should throw him out yourself. Unless you do, my hands are tied.' Feeling unable to protect Joël from his father's influence, Mrs Legrand told Mary: 'When the fair came to town, Joël got so drunk he vomited all night. Later, he said proudly, "I got plastered, just like Dad". What will become of him?' Mrs Legrand also recounted her own background to Mary:

> My mother had tuberculosis, so we children were always sent to foster care during holidays. My sisters weren't sent the same place as I was, so I don't know them well. To this day, I'd never ask them for help, even when I need it. When I got married, we lived with my mother-in-law. But the landlord didn't want us and it was really overcrowded. So when we heard Abbé Pierre's broadcast about helping the homeless, we came to Paris. At first, they put us near the Porte de Vanves flea market – terrible, thirty strangers per tent. Here, there's more privacy. But now my husband drinks more because he works clearing out junk. Landladies offer him drink as payment for emptying their cellars. Then he drinks all afternoon. My dream is a two-room flat where my daughters could have their own bedroom, and I'd sleep in the kitchenette.

Such a modest dream – and yet so far removed from her life.

A few weeks later, Mary discovered another shocking situation. She wrote:

> *30 June:* Mrs Delauney has been beaten up. Last night, Jocelyne Vincent invited Mrs Delauney into her igloo with Mr Vincent and three other men. Jocelyne and Mr Vincent both tried to kiss Mrs Delauney. She started kicking and punching. Mr Vincent stole her watch and tried to rape her while the other men watched. Mrs Delauney is proud of having fought him off. Père Joseph is furious with Mr

Vincent because it's clear he's been pimping out his wife. But when the policeman accused Mrs Delauney of having loose morals, to my surprise, Mr Vincent jumped in to defend her honour. Jocelyne was silent – although whenever the officer addressed her, she gave him her sultriest look until he blushed and stammered. When Jocelyne had to respond, she agreed with everything her husband said.

The following winter, Mary invested a lot of time to support a woman whose teenage son, Gilbert, was arrested with a friend for stealing a radio and cash from their former boss. The friend, Antoine, wrote to Wresinski saying that Gilbert had no visits from his parents. Mary brought this message to Gilbert's mother and step-father. She noted:

> Mr Masson was in a bad mood. Mrs Masson was upset too, saying: 'It's shameful having him in jail! Antoine's parents told everyone, and now you know too!' When she calmed down, she explained that she did try to visit Gilbert twice but in two different prisons, she was told she was in the wrong place. Her letters to Gilbert were returned stamped 'addressee unknown'. When I asked if Gilbert needs a lawyer, she said: 'The court-appointed lawyer is enough. He messed up and has to pay consequences.' But the next morning she came to say she *does* want a good lawyer. She disagreed last night only because her husband was listening. She said:
> 'He thinks Gilbert belongs in juvenile detention and doesn't want me visiting him. It's because he isn't Gilbert's father. He wants to throw Gilbert into the street. But Gilbert's problems are my husband's fault. He always shouts at the kids. On Gilbert's days off work, my husband yells at him for lounging around. So Gilbert always has to go out, and then he hangs with the wrong crowd. I agree Gilbert needs to learn a lesson, but not in jail.'

Mary drove Mrs Masson to Pontoise to request permission to visit Gilbert. During the drive, Mrs Masson grew increasingly anxious. By the time they reached the Hall of Justice, Mary noted that 'her whole body was trembling'. After receiving the visitor's permit, they queued at the prison gate with many other women. Over two hours, the women spoke about prison conditions. Gradually feeling less shy,

Mrs Masson told the others that this was her first visit and she needed information. She felt better meeting others in her situation. After Mrs Masson visited Gilbert, she and Mary went to a coffee shop where Mrs Masson said:

> Gilbert messed up because he's fed up with the camp. He hates it so much that he wants to take off. That's terrible for a mother to hear. But there's no reasoning with my husband, especially when he's drunk. If I'd known, I wouldn't have married him. But once it's done, you have to stay put. My husband is nice to me; but it's the children who are important. I should leave him. Gilbert can't come home; and I can't leave him in the street. When he's released, I'll pack my bags and leave with the kids.

Mary asked who they could stay with. Mrs Masson's father walked out when she was young. Her mother remarried and had six other children; however, all were removed into state care with Mrs Masson sent to a group home. She told Mary:

> They offered me nursing training. But I was afraid of failing. I regret it. If I were a nurse, I'd have another life. Later, an aunt and uncle took me in. But they made me feel like a foster kid. They lived in the sugar beet region where I worked on a farm. I was proud to earn money, but I never saw a penny; my aunt kept everything. She kept me under lock and key too. I wanted to date, but was never allowed. Finally I ran away and got married. When Gilbert was little, he was sick and got bad medical care. That's when I moved to Paris. He spent a few months in the hospital and I found work as a chambermaid. My husband stayed away and wanted me back home, but I couldn't leave Gilbert. Then I got sick. While I was hospitalised my husband divorced me. He kept our oldest son who I never saw again.

Gilbert left school at age 14 because his mother hadn't known children were allowed to stay at school longer. Now her hope was for her younger children to earn the school-leaving certificate at 15. Mrs Masson was happy to hear Mary suggest that ATD's evening tutoring classes could help. Mary concluded her journal entry: 'Unbeknownst to her husband, she's saving up to move out of the camp. But whenever a family member gets sick, she uses the money for health care. Just recently, her daughter needed a hernia operation and Mrs Masson had appendicitis.'[9] Another dream – and a plan – were sadly quite out of reach.

Mary was 21 that year, an age at which many women in the camp already had several children. Accompanying them in their struggles with physical hardships, exploitative employers, and abusive relationships must have felt overwhelming to her. I see her dogged commitment to writing as a way for Mary to begin understanding these women's harsh realities. Mary felt they deserved the world's attention.

Chapter 12

Losing Custody of Children in Family Court

During the month of Gilbert's arrest, another mother in the camp told Mary that a social worker threatened to remove her children. Mrs Hervé protested:

> I'm keeping them! My husband has work now, and look how warm their beds are, with sheets for all of them. Social services are only poking around because someone wrote them a bunch of lies, saying I go out drinking at night, abandoning the children alone. But you know I don't drink.

Mary drove Mr and Mrs Hervé to family court in Pontoise. Because of a mix-up, the barrister scheduled to defend them was unavailable. By telephone, the barrister advised Mary to ask the court to reschedule. In her journal, she wrote:

> Court was in session already. I barged right in with the Hervés, to the surprise of everyone present who didn't understand what business I had there as I'm neither a barrister nor a social worker. It was clear that no one in the room felt sympathetic to the Hervés. The social worker said, 'All the lawyers in the world would make no difference. The children must be removed from that worthless milieu.' Then I was sent out. When the Hervés came out of the courtroom,

> Mrs Hervé was crying. Every time she tried to speak, she was told, 'Shut your mouth or you'll be put in jail.'

Fifteen minutes later, the Hervés and Mary were called back to hear the judgement read. The decision was that the four oldest would remain in foster care. For the three youngest, a court-appointed doctor was asked to make a recommendation. Mary was shocked that the judge spoke only to her, instructing her to make sure the children would be present for the doctor's visit; to prevent the parents from making a scene; and to explain everything properly to them. Mary wrote: 'He spoke as though the parents were complete imbeciles. The next court date is in a month and I will make sure the lawyer can be present.'

The medical visit went well. The doctor said, 'These children are perfectly healthy. Why was the judge concerned?' However when Mrs Hervé received a letter with the new court date, she neglected to tell Mary until the last minute. It was too late for the barrister to be available, so once again Mary alone accompanied the Hervés to court. She wrote:

> Mrs Hervé cried during the whole drive. Their youngest turns two today and she fears losing him. At court, we waited two hours in the hallway. When Mr Hervé stepped away at one point, his wife confided:
> 'If we lose the children, he'll leave me. I don't care if he leaves, but I want to be with my children. I've been very unhappy with him. … If I'd known what marriage was like, I'd never have married anyone.'

© ATD Fourth World / Joseph Wresinski Centre

In the courtroom, the prosecutor built a case against the Hervés, his every word mocking or insulting. He blamed them for not being legally married. He cited court records from the removal of their older children that called Mr Hervé 'lacking in intelligence, lazy, incapable, brutish, and an occasional drunkard'. A similar record about Mrs Hervé added that she was 'incapable of raising children'. Mary's journal continued:

> The doctor's report was positive about the children's health; but he noted that their home lacks the material necessary for hygiene. The prosecutor summarised the social worker's report stating: 'It is obvious that the children are in an impossible situation in terms of medical, physical, and moral health. They must be taken into care immediately.'
> I asked for an explanation of 'moral health'.
> He said, 'According to one child, Mrs. Hervé is sleeping with another man'.
> The judge asked my opinion. I said I had always seen the children happy and healthy. I spoke of the parents' sorrow at losing custody of the older ones and pointed out that if all children were removed, the parents would be devastated. I described improvements in their home. 'But these improvements are so small', the judge said. He tried to be kind, explaining legal terms so the Hervés would understand. He talked about acting for the children's good. But the prosecutor and social worker kept interrupting to insist that not one child remain in the home.
> The judgement was that all children be removed, with a hearing to reconsider in one or two years. On leaving the courtroom, the prosecutor called us into another room with the social worker to discuss the children's removal. With one phone call, he could have the police pick them up before we got home. But this controversial procedure would spark protest from neighbours. So he offered us a few weeks to prepare the children's departure if we pledged our word of honour that on the fixed date I would drive the children to the social service office in Versailles. I asked if the children could live near Noisy-le-Grand, to facilitate contact visits; but they wouldn't promise because it depends where

placements are available. Our drive home was quiet. Mrs Hervé was upset, but kept tears back.

At this point, Mrs Hervé spoke to Mary about her own childhood in foster care and her struggles at school where she was considered 'the worst student in her grade'. She had work in a factory, a laundry, and as a live-in maid. In a previous marriage, she also had a child who was removed into care. Mary asked why she had never mentioned this before. Mrs Hervé said, 'It's too painful'.

When the appointed day for the children's removal came, Mrs Hervé grew confused about the dates, thinking on the eve that they had two more days together. But the next morning, she had the children beautifully dressed and ready at 10 a.m. Mary took a family photo. When Mrs Hervé told the oldest child, age 7, that he would make lots of friends in the group home, he said, 'I don't want friends!' Mary wrote:

> At the end of the journey, the oldest said, 'I don't want to stay here!' He started cursing, but his 5-year-old sister said, nicely, 'Please, be polite'. We were shown around the group home. Mrs Hervé was very pleased when a teacher said, 'He's so cute!' about her youngest. The director spoke nicely to us and Mrs Hervé was relieved to see a happy atmosphere. When we had to leave, her two youngest clung to her skirts screaming. But Mrs Hervé just gave them each a quick kiss and let the director carry them away. She held back her tears until we were in the car and then said, 'I'm glad I've seen the place and I know they'll be taken care of'. But she continues to blame her husband. She said:
>
> Everyone in our street is on my side. They know that any father who really cared would have managed to keep the children. Anyway, all he talks about is moving out. I'll get the children back myself and he'll never see them again. How soon can I ask when they're coming home?

That summer, Mrs Hervé left her husband and moved in with a neighbour. However, every night he came by to harass her. She wished she could move closer to the foster home. Mrs Hervé looked for work, but the nearest factory was hiring only young workers, and other employers distrusted anyone living in the emergency housing camp. Her husband had torn up the identity papers that would have allowed her to register with the town hall as a job-seeker.[1]

Mary compiled a document defining common characteristics of families in the camp. It noted:

> The families in Noisy-le-Grand are perhaps not the poorest of all when they continue to live as families. However, what makes them very poor is living in constant fear that the slightest problem might cause them to lose this richness, as did Mrs Hervé when her children were removed.

Although I never met Mrs Hervé, poring over Mary's reports, I feel I can hear her voice. Here in the UK, social services often discriminate by confusing poverty with neglect. A mother who lost several children into forced closed adoptions told me: 'Once you've had your children taken off you, people vilify you. That's why having your children removed by the state is even worse than being raped, something that I've also experienced.' As jarring as that comparison is, this mother's words express how violently she experienced the forcible removal of her children.

All around Mary, women and girls were feeling crushed. In her report she listed material poverty – poor housing, food, work, clothing – and physical poverty – ill health and inaccessible health care. She identified 'spiritual poverty', noting: 'People lack a reason for belief or hope. At the same time, they have a strong spirit of hope'. And Mary also described what she called 'mental poverty': 'They lack possibilities for education and achieving their potential. They are considered unintelligent. (A visiting reporter was surprised by Mrs Klein, saying, "But she's so smart!") Many also have mental illness and no possibility of treatment.'

Faced with such daunting challenges, how might solutions even be imagined? Mary said that living in Noisy-le-Grand 'often felt unbearable':

> The young people in particular are harsh, impatient, and lacking the perspective of their elders. But what else can young people do with their sense of revolt if not take it out on us, who insist that everything can be changed? When they look around them at the present, they must panic, imagining that the future may be no better.[2]

Mary constantly discussed this with Wresinski – but in the squalor and chaos of Noisy-le-Grand, they were frequently interrupted by camp residents. After one interruption, Wresinski told Mary, 'Lock the door! We need calm to think; this can't work.' (To my delight, I know this because many of their meetings were recorded, painstakingly transcribed, and archived, so that decades later it's almost like I was in the room with them!)

In 1966, with ATD Fourth World growing, Wresinski felt they needed a protected setting for research and training of new volunteers. As plans were made to replace the igloos with a housing project, Wresinski proposed that a few volunteers remain to run cultural projects, while others move to Pierrelaye, on the other side of Paris. François Mauriac, a Nobel laureate in literature, was convinced of the importance of ATD's work. He published an appeal in the *Figaro* newspaper, raising enough donations to purchase the Pierrelaye building that became ATD's international centre.[3]

Mary was one of the first to disagree about moving to Pierrelaye. She worried that 'what we were trying to achieve would fall apart. We had always shared our lives with the families. How would the camp manage without us?'[4] Gradually, however, Mary came around. She wrote to Gabrielle:

> Père Joseph is making us terribly insecure by moving the offices, and jumping from one idea to another. I'll keep complaining! But there's something meaningful about this perpetual insecurity. It's hard to put into

Ongoing construction in Pierrelaye would later transform the building on the right into a conference centre.

© *ATD Fourth World / Joseph Wresinski Centre*

words. Perhaps it prevents us from succumbing to self-satisfaction with our projects? It keeps us from thinking that our main goal is to just continue one specific project.[5]

Looking back later, Mary felt that moving to Pierrelaye had opened doors for building a wider anti-poverty movement:

> Unless you're creating something new, you stagnate, treading water. Many volunteers left because of this. ... As long as we remained in the chaos of the camp, we were holding ourselves back. By creating an international centre, we became freer to broaden our vision. In Noisy-le-Grand, there was one mother who was never able to stand up for herself. She later became someone to reckon with, and I'm convinced that would not have happened if we had not broadened our approach.[6]

Mary drew a parallel between the life of one woman in poverty and the path of ATD:

> One mother used to move frequently from one igloo to another. Her family was terribly poor and their home was an awful mess where you couldn't find anything. But each move was a fresh start. They were still poor, but they could find their belongings. When things got difficult a

For the International Year of the Child, ATD Fourth World mounted a billboard in front of its Pierrelaye centre stating: 'The world owes me the future.'

© *ATD Fourth World / Joseph Wresinski Centre*

few months later, they could move again. That mother was teaching us that she could start over as long as she could have a change. Sometimes you just need a change, or you're tired of seeing the same faces. ATD has to look for fresh starts to be optimistic and to progress. ... Being dynamic gives hope.[7]

The frustrations in Noisy-le-Grand led many volunteers to leave after only brief stints. Mary and Wresinski were convinced that making a meaningful difference would take decades; so by 1967, Mary's new role in Pierrelaye was training new volunteers before sending them to the camp, hoping that would help them make a long-term commitment to anti-poverty work. She said: 'I don't have any time to do anything, as organising thirty to forty people takes all day – and at night I dream about them! But it's quite fun, really, and very active. In the evenings, we sometimes listen to Mozart by candlelight.'[8]

Most young people agreed that Mary's approach was fun. Her teammate Ursula Jomini recalls: 'I'm not sure what her secret was for connecting with young people, but many of them appreciated her enormously.'[9] Ghislaine Adriaensens was trained by Mary and recalls: 'As soon as one of us arrived, Mary would immediately give us a responsibility. She looked for ways to make common cause. This was in an atmosphere of shared responsibility with no suspicion. She wanted to convey to us the importance of building ATD together.'[10]

That togetherness was essential. Just as the work in Pierrelaye helped the Noisy-le-Grand projects, Mary said: 'For some volunteers to be in an office is meaningless unless others continue alongside people in the

ATD Fourth World's new Pierrelaye training centre in 1967
© ATD Fourth World / Joseph Wresinski Centre

From left, Ursula Jomini, Mary, and Stuart Williams
© ATD Fourth World / Joseph Wresinski Centre

Ghislaine Adriaensens, centre, with some of ATD Fourth World's members in the Philippines
© ATD Fourth World / Joseph Wresinski Centre

worst situations: in the middle of shit, illness, hunger, ignorance, and the sense of revolt that makes people insult us just for being present.' In Pierrelaye, with more time for in-depth work, Mary reopened her dialogue with Wresinski about birth control. This was only one tool for improving women's lives, but it had finally become legal in France during Mary's year in the United States. In 1967, France also lifted a ban on spreading information about birth control. At the time, the Pope had still not taken a position on contraception and some Catholic theologians were recommending it be approved in certain conditions.[11] This time, Mary prevailed on Wresinski, who agreed:

> In extreme poverty, motherhood weighs heavily. ... Many women tell me they plan to get their Fallopian tubes tied. Under no circumstances do we have any right to force people in poverty to have seven or eight children. We could even say that they have no right to give birth to so many children if they won't be able to offer them a modicum of love. ...
>
> Think of the woman who has six children and hates her youngest. Or who has seven children and hates her husband. The destruction of the last scraps of love in a home weigh on the children ... Only when we have measured all of this can we help a mother choose a solution that will not lead to years of remorse. We must never forget the child who knows he was unwanted and who grows up where everything shows that the likes of him never will be wanted; this child is lost. ... The sacred nature of the family ... shows that birth control, even against the husband's wishes, can be justified because the very nature of human love requires it.[12]

In another speech, Wresinski went further:

> There are situations where a woman is in danger and is the only one who knows it. I believe that she may be raped by her own husband, who drinks and has created a situation where it is practically impossible to raise children. For her, I consider [birth control] a case of legitimate self-defence. It is this woman's obligation to protect herself and prevent another child from being born into such conditions ... even if the husband does not know and would not agree.[13]

By speaking about marital rape in 1967, Wresinski was 25 years ahead of his country, which only in 1992 outlawed it (and which continued to presume consent to all sexual relations within marriage until 2010).[14] Mary had persuaded him of the urgency of finding ways to support women in poverty. Her commitment to bearing witness to so many of the things endured by both girls and women around her underlies most of her journal writing, which would prove useful in later years when Mary prepared to represent ATD at United Nations conferences on women.

Part IV

Founding a UK team: 'The Best and Worst of Humanity and of Myself'

Chapter 13

Frimhurst Family Centre: 'The Threat of Violence Is Always in the Air'

In 1968, shortly after Mary moved to Pierrelaye, Wresinski proposed that she move again, this time returning to Britain. He asked her to join the staff of Frimhurst Family Centre where she would live in a single household with dozens of people in poverty. Huguette had refused to move to Frimhurst because she didn't feel ready for the heavy responsibilities involved. Living directly with families sounds overwhelming to me, so I understand why Mary said, 'I wasn't very keen to go.'[172] I was quite comfortable in France with something meaningful to do. I had friends and felt secure.'[173]

However, Mary agreed to give it a shot. Impressed, Huguette said: 'Mary was very brave to go.'[174] Mary later called Frimhurst the harshest experience of her life, even compared to the stark material deprivations in Noisy-le-Grand. She recalled:

> Frimhurst was a tremendous shock: the state of the house; the smell; the noise; the feeling that anything could happen. I wanted to run back out. A friend had the same first impression, saying 'It was the first time I found myself with people I did not know or understand and who were in the majority. Alone and terrified, I didn't know what to do'. I experienced a physical upset in the first weeks. The whole system has to get adjusted to shocks, strangeness, and fear of the unknown. Violence erupts constantly but

unpredictably. Will threats be carried out? Will I be able to cope? Will I ever bridge the gap separating me and them? Will they ever trust me? Can I trust them?

Despite this, Mary became so passionate about Frimhurst that she dedicated sixteen years to it, founding a branch of ATD Fourth World in the UK. The families referred to Frimhurst by social workers were almost all at high risk of having their children removed into care and had already had 'unimaginably harrowing experiences'.[175] Because Frimhurst represented the last chance to keep families together, Mary described enormous pressure:

Frimhurst Family Centre
© *Mary Rabagliati, ATD Fourth World / Joseph Wresinski Centre*

> There was nowhere to hide, and my entire identity was challenged. I discovered the weight that volunteers represent for people in poverty. There's the weight of our presence, even if we say nothing. There's the weight of our position in life, which can feel like an accusation for anyone with a feeling of inferiority.

Although Mary had not imagined what moving to Frimhurst would be like, it had a decisive influence in shaping ATD's action in the UK to this day.

Frimhurst opened ten years earlier as one of seven residential centres for those considered 'problem families' – the term for anyone stuck in poverty despite the post-war economic boom. The wartime destruction of housing led to a housing shortage and to unauthorised squatting by homeless families, often in former military camps.[176] When authorities cleared out the camps, they needed somewhere to send these and other families in need, which led to creating 'recuperative centres to assist and rehabilitate' them.[177] Most centres were managed by 'wardens' or 'matrons' who instructed mothers in cooking, cleaning, sewing, and parenting. Mothers and children were sent to the centres for several weeks. Husbands, considered bread-winners with no role inside the home, were not invited.[178] Each warden's authority was absolute; thus, whenever a new warden was hired, house rules might change.[179]

Grace Goodman, founder of Frimhurst Family Centre

© *Mary Rabagliati, ATD Fourth World / Joseph Wresinski Centre*

Frimhurst, however, functioned very differently. Founded by Grace Goodman and Margaret Gainsford, specialised family social workers, the approach was based on a participative ethos. Fathers were included, and admission was longer, for months rather than weeks. Instead of domestic instruction, the stress was on valuing children and parents so as to reinforce positive relationships. At weekly meetings of residents and staff, parents were allowed to complain about the staff and the rules, something unthinkable elsewhere. Frimhurst's fierce independence valued families rather than trying to domesticate them on behalf of the authorities.[180] Historian

Dr Michael Lambert notes: 'Frimhurst was very much in the vanguard, even if the other homes disapproved of the more liberal atmosphere it engendered. Frimhurst had trained social workers, and emphasised parenting over female domestic skills. This was by degree, but it signalled a wider shift in social work during the 1960s.'[181]

Wresinski first visited Frimhurst in 1961 on a tour of all seven British recuperative centres. Eager to learn from others in solidarity with people in poverty, he appreciated Goodman's personality, approach, and belief in the hidden potential of people considered 'hopeless' by others. They developed an enduring friendship.[182]

Frimhurst is a large Victorian mansion in the heart of the Surrey countryside and just ten miles from Farnham, where Mary's family was living in the 1960s. In the early 1900s, Frimhurst was the country estate of Dame Ethel Smythe, a suffragist and composer. Later, it became a country club where Rita Hayworth was among the guests who played snooker. After the Second World War (when it was requisitioned), Grace Goodman and Margaret Gainsford scraped together savings and loans from friends, family, and a bank in order to purchase Frimhurst. As social workers in London, they met many families 'so defeated and vulnerable that they couldn't resolve the difficulties they were facing'.[183] Goodman said she based Frimhurst on her own experiences as a mother feeling she 'knew nothing' and needed to learn from others: 'At Frimhurst, nobody knew all the answers. Nobody was going to tell you what to do. But by living with each other, learning from each other, making our mistakes together, we'd learn and help each other.'[184]

In 1966, Goodman, by then running Frimhurst alone, was attacked by a male resident. Hospitalised for a year, she realised that if she had been killed, the project would have died with her. She invited many organisations to join her – but none agreed with supporting the aspirations of the most disadvantaged. Finally, she turned to Wresinski who convinced Mary to move to Frimhurst along with a new French volunteer, Marie-France Aurières. Mary recalled:

Grace Goodman, centre

© ATD Fourth World / Joseph Wresinski Centre

Mrs Goodman opened doors for families. But her staff was disgusted because she deliberately hosted the most violent families, who were impossible to work with. Several staff had nervous breakdowns. None continued long. For me, however, things were different. Two of us arrived together, already connected to a movement behind us, with a broader perspective. Without that meaningful link, I wouldn't have lasted at Frimhurst. I could express discouragement, anger, and sorrow to others who could relate. When things went badly, instead of accusing us of failure, Père Joseph would encourage us, saying, 'Get outside! You'll suffocate in that house; it's time for an outing'.[185]

Mary described Goodman as a woman 'who felt extraordinary freedom to speak her own mind and wanted to offer that freedom to families in poverty'. After generations dependent on the good will of others, families deserved to make their own choices. Mary appreciated the idea of Frimhurst as a place where everyone could learn together:

Marie-France Aurières (at right) with Mary during a visit to Mary's parents in Farnham, just 12 miles from Frimhurst

Provided courtesy of Paul de St Croix

Usually social workers are made out to be super-humans who never make mistakes. But living together at Frimhurst, it's clear that families make mistakes; and we volunteers also make mistakes. We all spoil things. Volunteers can forge a real relationship with the families because we are human, and we do make fools of ourselves at times.

Although Mary considered Goodman's relationships 'brilliant', she also found her approach scattered:

Mrs Goodman had not structured Frimhurst, and she never explained. You had to follow her around with pencil and paper, observing. Nobody had ever questioned her. Our questions enabled her to begin putting her approach into words. She said

Children playing at Frimhurst
© *ATD Fourth World / Joseph Wresinski Centre*

she had no pedagogy; her approach was respecting and accepting people as they were, without judgement. She told us her hopes for them. She was curious about people, which gave her a way of understanding suffering. Everyone trusted her, people from any background. She took time to get to know everyone. She spoke of Frimhurst's residents as 'families who have lost heart and feel they have been got at by society'. Our approach was to have faith in these families to start with; then they began to have faith in themselves.

Frimhurst housed seven or eight families at a time, each staying six to nine months. This meant at least 20 children there, and sometimes over 30. It was a single community sharing one kitchen and large living room. Although a small living room was reserved for staff, Mary said, 'Our flat is inevitably open to all who need something or someone – which is constantly.' During weekdays, when older children were at school and fathers either working or job-hunting, the staff ran a nursery for toddlers. This allowed mothers to organise running the house. Mary said:

> Each group works out its own rules – not without difficulty for those who are used to being told what to do. Food is cooked together, the mothers helping Ruby who does the shopping and organises the kitchen. The kitchen is the source of food and warmth, and also where feelings are expressed first. Food is the focus for complaint, jokes, anger, threats – and

© ATD Fourth World / Joseph Wresinski Centre

in the last resort it's a weapon. How many times have plates of food been thrown across the room!

Ruby was a local staff member who did not live at Frimhurst. An administrator, Mrs Gadd, ran the office and encouraged job-seekers. Families described both women as grandparents to them and particularly enjoyed Ruby's nurturing personality. During nights and weekends, however, only Mary or Marie-France were available, which felt draining, as Mary wrote:

> Often at night after a long day, we volunteers are needed again. Someone is sick, afraid, or worried; they had too much to drink and are creating a disturbance; or there's a row. One family rowed for months on end, invariably starting after everyone was in bed. Sometimes it ended in an injury requiring the police and an ambulance. The threat of violence is always in the air, along with the deep unhappiness of those who feel they are failures and nobody cares.

When Mary had time for a step back, she explained the purpose of this insularity:

> Frimhurst is for families to find not just their feet but themselves: to understand why their lives are a mess, and to untangle where they want to go in life and how to get there. Living together, each person sees himself more clearly as

Mary, centre, notes: 'How many times have plates of food been thrown across the room!'

© *Miroslav Marik, ATD Fourth World / Joseph Wresinski Centre*

their action or words boomerang back to them. There is no escaping the effects on others of forgetting to clean the bath or playing the record player too loud. At the same time, people are supportive. Individual strengths are brought out and valued, for there is always something that each one can do well.

One example of this was a woman who 'never felt she knew how to do anything'. Even in the simplest daily chore, she would 'only push dust around but never manage to get rid of it'. But gradually, Mary discovered this woman's talent for story-telling. With encouragement, she became the one that all the children wanted to hear a story from. Mary explained:

> Once she felt valued by others, sweeping felt like less of a chore and life became easier. Each time a person was able, for the first time, to feel they had done something helpful for others, something they hadn't imagined themselves capable of, it was such a special moment. That freedom leads them to become ones who will reach out when they see someone else suffering to offer encouragement.[186]

It was new for Mary to be in such close quarters with young children. Writing to Hélène von Burg and Jeanpierre Beyeler, who were founding an ATD team in their native Switzerland, Mary said: 'I'm learning to appreciate children for the first time in my life. Some are so beautiful. And some have a great need for love and affection. You can actually see just how much love matters for their development, and how they suffer when love is in short supply.'[187] Mary was particularly struck by a 2-year-old girl who arrived at Frimhurst unable to speak or walk, showing almost no facial expressions and hiding her head when people looked at her. Mary wrote:

> We concentrated from the start on encouraging her parents, and helping them to communicate [with her]. Within two weeks of arriving, she had started to walk. Soon she was smiling and became very sociable. ... Children need love to survive; but this is just as true of adults. All people need someone to encourage progress. We have proved that there

is no such thing as a 'hopeless' family without value who does not merit time and money being spent to help.[188]

In a 1974 television interview, Mary presented this project to the general public:

> [Frimhurst is] an exemplary model of what one can do with people who are considered useless and have virtually been discarded by society because they don't conform in a way they're expected to ... We have faith in them to start with. They get to have faith in themselves, and to see that they have something of value to other people. What is a shame in the social welfare services – although it gives people a lot, it helps people a lot – it doesn't provide people with an opportunity to *contribute* something, which is essential. This is what we do here, and what can be done in any community virtually, if people believe in it.[189]

A visiting journalist described the centre this way:

> Frimhurst is not a clinically swept and scrubbed white-walled institution in which people creep around like frightened mice. It is clean, but not sterilised. The kitchen is a warm centre of talk and tea. The nursery is tumbling over with toys and children's art. The library, in a converted stable, is quiet, dominated with travel posters and the gleam of polished wood. The garden is stocked with vegetables. A new clubroom is being built. ... Among the 367 families who have lived here over past years are couples who married too young, who had no stable home, or indeed any home at all. ... During their stay, they learn that with their insights and fortitude, they have something real to offer society.[190]

A visiting MP described Frimhurst as: 'Rather chaotic! If you feel a bit messy yourself and walk into a pristine room, you stand out like a sore thumb. But Frimhurst was all rather warmly shambolic. So, if you felt a mess yourself, well then you were quite at home.'[191]

Although Frimhurst was not 'sterilised', Mary's natural energy and elbow grease were sorely needed to scrub, sweep, and regularly redecorate the gigantic house. She was also an avid gardener who filled vases with fresh flowers. Mary called herself and Marie-France 'a good pair of domestic workers'[192] who were almost 'too busy to think'.

At the same time, worried that it was 'too easy for us to bury ourselves here',[193] Mary also worked on fundraising, recruiting local volunteers, and establishing ATD Fourth World as a legal British charity. While her year in the US laid the foundation for others to start an ATD team, now she was in the lead to set up a new branch of this movement. Looking back in later years, Mary confessed:

> Frimhurst challenged who I was and helped me understand what it means to truly listen to another person without trying to give a quick answer. I discovered the weight of our conversations and questions. This taught me to listen more intently. You shouldn't say, 'I'm listening' unless you're truly open to understanding what a person has to say and putting yourself in their shoes. For anyone who is naturally active and wants to be helpful, that way of listening does not come naturally. We had to admit that none of us had immediate advice to offer. Instead, we really took time to think together about how to respond to what each person wanted. …
>
> Being at Frimhurst gave me the unique chance to experience the best and worst of humanity; to perceive and make my own choice for the best and for the worst in myself; and to learn that there are no limits to which we can go in overcoming human misery, and thereby liberating all of humanity.[194]

Chapter 14

'Kicking Myself for My Temper'

As people in poverty continue to tell me today, the UK roots of ATD Fourth World are deep in the soil of Frimhurst where Mary gradually came to see living together as an essential learning process. Grace Goodman – who never lived there herself – knew she could count on ATD, so she shifted her attention to a new project in London. Although Mary felt committed to Frimhurst, life there was immensely challenging:

> Frimhurst is where I often wept with frustration, exhaustion, and anger. Misery and poverty can make people behave harshly. We all lived under one roof night and day with

© *ATD Fourth World / Joseph Wresinski Centre*

all of our day-to-day bitchiness. In their troubles, families in poverty judge you and blame you for everything that's gone wrong in their lives. They often lashed out at volunteers, saying exactly what they thought of us: 'You're an idiot. You've got your nose in the air. You insult people all the time. You don't know how to listen.' It's hard to hear, especially when you've come to help. But it was important that the families feel free to say anything. This doesn't mean they were allowed to walk all over us. But there was a constant possibility for confrontation where families in poverty could try to free themselves from whatever life had done to them, using us as punching bags.

That treatment inspired a request to a donor: for the kind of punching bag used to train boxers. Mary drew a face on the bag, placed in Frimhurst's children's club:

> so that whenever children want to beat someone up they can just go at it for hours on end. Mrs Goodman says a punching bag is wonderful therapy – plus just think of all the money we'll save by having fewer broken windows. Hopefully, we volunteers will get fewer bruises too![195]

One mother described another aspect of the boxing metaphor, telling Mary: 'You volunteers are like seconds in a boxing match. After each round, you sponge the boxers down, put back the gum shields, and send us back in the ring.'[196] Frimhurst was a place of last

Grace Goodman
© *ATD Fourth World / Joseph Wresinski Centre*

© Mary Rabagliati, ATD Fourth World / Joseph Wresinski Centre

resort, accepting social service referrals for families that other centres refused. Quite often, living as a family was a challenge passed down to them over generations. In an editorial of the *Frimhurst Journal*, Mary gave examples of this: One resident was a father who never met his own father and lived on the streets from the age of 14. Another was a recently divorced 23-year-old with five children, the oldest born when she was 15. Having grown up in hostels for the homeless and children's homes, she had 'very little, if any, self-respect left'.[197] Describing Frimhurst residents, Mary said:

> Parents and children suffer badly from separation into hostels and institutions. We have seen them, years later, wake from nightmares, terrified. Not only does this separation cause terrible anxiety for the children; it also sets up a barrier between parent and child. ... They have spent their whole lives with a feeling of failure and living in intolerable conditions that are impossible to believe until you witness them. They have a sense of isolation and loneliness that can be greater than any other difficulty. ... Whole families arrive with insatiable appetites, their children going so far as to steal other children's dinners.[198]

As in Noisy-le-Grand, many families felt trapped by social services. Prior to Frimhurst, for example, a divorced mother of two lived in a

© *Mary Rabagliati, ATD Fourth World / Joseph Wresinski Centre*

second-floor flat when one of her children slipped going downstairs in icy weather. Seeing the bruise, a social worker accused the mother of pushing her daughter downstairs. To avoid another fall, the family began sleeping at a friend's ground-floor flat. However, the social worker then sanctioned her for not sleeping in her own flat. Mary said:

> Poverty is often a choke-hold. They haven't much money, and on top of that, they are boxed in by being suspected of child abuse even before children are born. They need to live in a certain way to protect themselves: learning how others expect them to run their household budget; raising children so as not to lose custody of them; learning to collaborate with barristers if they go to court. Frimhurst is where you fight for your life, for the chance to remain as a family, and to get back into the world again. At Frimhurst, parents who often did not grow up with their own families can learn from one another how to bring up their children.

This made for a context of desperation. Given the constant proximity of everyone in Frimhurst, Mary said:

> Our role as volunteers is very delicate, involving us almost totally in the lives of very unhappy families. Living together, we share some of the effects of isolation from society. We

have to take responsibility; yet not take responsibility away from parents. We have to allow choices to be made freely; yet ensure the safety and welfare of everyone. We try to share the best that we have, but also to be frank about our weaknesses, our fears, our lack of faith and courage. We receive from them lessons in living; but we also feel the bitterness, anger, violence and hatred of rejected people.

As in Noisy-le-Grand, Mary's concern focused on women and girls, whom she described as 'deprived of affection [and] needing a friend to talk to'.[199] Discovering the intelligence and aspirations of one teenage girl, Mary took her to visit Pierrelaye by way of encouragement. A year later, however, Mary despaired: 'She left home because of her mother's constant criticism. She's dropped her ambitions and stays with various girlfriends, all of whom live with their boyfriends. She could have made something of herself – but now she's pregnant, which will make it hard for her to get training. Poverty is a cruel trap for girls.'[200]

At the bottom of the drive leading to
Frimhurst, some children look towards a canal.
© *ATD Fourth World / Joseph Wresinski Centre*

In another family, Mary said that the father, 'W.', admitted to 'punishing his wife for his mother's rejection of him'. Gradually, however, as the Frimhurst team gave caring attention to both husband and wife, 'they came to feel that they were valued in their own right'. The improved relationship of the couple helped their parenting as well:

W. began for the first time to show interest in his children, particularly when his efforts to praise them were appreciated. For example, encouraged to help his 6-year-old son lose his stammer, he succeeded. When volunteers put the first painting of W.'s 3-year-old son on the living room wall, W. was so proud that he brought all the other fathers to see it.[201]

Even with occasional steps forward, Mary always found Frimhurst challenging:

> We must find ways to make whatever happens into a useful learning experience; encourage confidence when self-esteem is lowest; and somehow keep hope going when despair is the greatest. ... The families must endure us – our incompetence, blindness, deafness, and the limits of our commitment or caring. It it up to us to help families to face responsibility for themselves, their partners, children, and other families.

In considering her own faults, Mary longed for somewhere to hide her temper. Systemic injustice enraged her; but equally she had – and regretted – outbursts over petty annoyances. She recalled:

> You had nowhere else to go at the end of the day. Even when you had a day off, you'd keep thinking of the families; and in

© ATD Fourth World / Joseph Wresinski Centre

> the evening, you'd have to make up with those you'd argued with. Once, in a terrible mood, on my way out, I shouted at a mother, 'I hope the house burns down with you in it!' Of course, the minute the words were out, I wanted to sink into the ground with shame. I spent the day kicking myself for my temper. It was terribly hard to talk to her again that evening. But in the end, it does people good to see your true self; and my true self has a temper – especially when I've slept badly and I see children deliberately bashing a bird's nest or trampling the flower garden. And when I know I've behaved badly, perhaps it keeps me from becoming pretentious and helps me learn forgiveness.

Families did indeed forgive her. One mother later recalled, 'After arguments, Mary always came back.' This mother explained:

> Even when I was small, no one wanted me. They said I was no good. I kept running away from the places where they put me. The teacher used to call me names. Living at Frimhurst, I was trying to commit suicide. I could have got in trouble with the court, but Mary never gave up. We used to have disagreements. She could have said, 'I'm washing my hands of you!' Instead, she would come back after an hour, saying, 'Go get your kids, let's go out somewhere nice together.' The most important thing is knowing you've got people who care about you, trust you and say you're worth helping. Now I tell my kids they're worth it. I pass it on by

© ATD Fourth World / Joseph Wresinski Centre

going to other people who have got no one. I tell them that everyone is worthwhile.[202]

Despite her temper, Mary's presence was making a difference.

Chapter 15

Dreamers and Lunatics? Changing Minds

'The parents who live at Frimhurst – and who ordinarily are the first to criticise it – were ready to take to the streets to defend the house, insisting that it *must* stay open because it is the only place where anyone has tried to understand and help them.'[1] Mary was very struck by this about-face, which occurred after two fruitless years seeking permission to replace the drainage system. They were stuck in an administrative quagmire. Suddenly – on the eve of the scheduled opening of a new children's play centre at Frimhurst – the district health committee decided to close down the house because of the dilapidated sewage drains. In addition to parent protests:

> The local newspaper published a magnificent article protesting the decision and calling Frimhurst 'a centre of worldwide renown'! Everyone took sides, which was excellent publicity. Finally, it was agreed that we will not be closed, and we received permits to begin building a new sewage system. The director of the Surrey Public Health Department himself cut the ribbon to the children's play centre in front of a big crowd of social workers, friends, and local officials.[2]

Although Frimhurst prevailed, Mary worried that ATD Fourth World had no voice of authority. From the beginning, Mary said:

> Wresinski told everyone, 'We shouldn't shut ourselves away to become poor with the poor'. Constantly thinking of our

© ATD Fourth World / Joseph Wresinski Centre

education, he worried about us becoming small and stupid. He repeated that families in deep poverty deserve to be joined, not by specialists in poverty, but by esteemed people who know and love the world, able to share something universal through literature or art or history.[3]

Goodman spoke to Mary about the importance of connecting Frimhurst to the wider world in another way:

> Mrs Goodman told us that our daily life in Frimhurst was like a microscope to show us what was missing in society. In that small context, we could see a reflection of the whole: how relationships go wrong, creating all sorts of other problems; and how much potential there is for society to benefit when people have support to regain their self-respect.[4]

During her year in New York, Wresinski advised Mary: 'It's very important that you study at a university. A diploma will give recognition to everything we are trying to do.'[5] Mary agreed, noting that in Noisy-le-Grand: 'Often, I tried to help a camp resident communicate with administrative offices but was insulted by officials for being only a "volunteer".[6] Mary wrote to Hélène and Jeanpierre, 'It seems I shall have to get some kind of diploma. I don't know yet where or what subject I should study, but everyone says that only academia can help us develop authority.'[7]

In 1970, Mary decided to study social administration. To enrol in the London School of Economics, Mary began staying with a friend in London during the week, returning to Frimhurst on weekends and holidays. She studied under Richard Titmuss, who – despite never having secured any formal credentials – pioneered the academic field of social policy. Mary was also taught by Kit Russell, OBE, who was 'more interested in people than in research'[8] and who remembered Mary as frequenting music parties, and as 'a very rare and wonderful person, an inspiration to everyone who knew her'.[9]

Even while studying, Mary remained connected to ATD's international work. Wanting Marie-France to 'widen her horizons', she sent her for a visit to Hélène and Jeanpierre Beyeler to discover ATD's approach in Switzerland.[10] Mary considered such links crucial to staying the course in the face of challenges:

> We are constantly shaken up. The poorer people are, they more they upend our plans and disturb things we thought we could count on. This leads to constant confrontations and self-doubt, which we find umpteen ways to avoid. For all of us, these are hard issues to discuss with teammates. … [But we need] co-volunteers to remind us of our fundamental beliefs.[11]

Twice a year, Mary made the long ferry crossing to France for meetings of senior Volunteer Corps members. Having attended similar meetings myself, sometimes corresponding to triy to include others who had to miss them, I'm struck by Mary's efforts to fill in Gabrielle when she was unable to attend a session. She wrote: 'Père Joseph worries that the Volunteer Corps agrees too much. He said we need to move ideas forward so we don't become like certain social workers who have only a small project that will never get people out of the shit of poverty. Instead, he thinks volunteers should have big political ideas that mobilise society.'[12]

In 1970s Britain, many young adults were involved in power struggles: as labour unionists, feminists, or on behalf of the elderly. At

Dreamers and Lunatics? Changing Minds

Frimhurst, however, Mary wrote to Gabrielle, 'We remain somewhat isolated, I think because we make a point of choosing to work with families in the greatest difficulties. Time and again, we're called dreamers and lunatics.'[13] One young person discovering Frimhurst, Fran Bennett, recalls, 'My parents warned me to be careful, saying: "Communist organisations hide under other labels."'[14] Determined to change minds, Mary invited many young people to come see Frimhurst for themselves, helping with the upkeep of the building and grounds. Evening campfire sing-alongs were part of these voluntary work-camps. Fifty years later, one participant wrote, 'I was in awe of the fire of Mary's dedication.'[15]

Every year, these work-camps hosted more than 100 participants of a dozen nationalities. Some arrived on their own, while others were sent by schools or organisations like the Scouts, the Friends Service Council, the United Nations Association, or the Christian Movement for Peace.[16] Stephen Baker, 19 at the time, recalls:

> Mary was quite different. Nobody spoke like that. You couldn't help but respect her. She was authentic, passionate and fiercely loyal. Mary was challenging to all the world and unafraid of argument. Most of us don't like being challenged for the way we live. It's bloody cheeky! But she was quite at ease with it, and quite clear on right and wrong. She wasn't controlling; but she kept an eye on me when no one else really did. You can easily go off the tracks. She kept tabs on where I was, what I learnt, how I developed.[17]

Stephen Baker, left, with Richard Barnet

© *ATD Fourth World / Joseph Wresinski Centre*

Mary challenged Stephen to get a job on a building site. This was partly to donate his earnings to Frimhurst

Stephen, with Barbara Schumann
© ATD Fourth World / Joseph Wresinski Centre

as part of his room and board and also to set an example for job-seekers in Frimhurst. He says:

> The world of building sites was quite a shock to my system because I had a public school education; but Mary also wanted to look at my welfare. She was, to some extent, my 'employer' but I never felt what she expected of us was a burden. And then she'd invite us all to go out and have fun with her, in a pub or seeing a film together. It was liberating. Then she sent me to Switzerland with a rucksack and a bike to spend nine months working with Jeanpierre Beyeler. I trusted her and it was fine. She was a tough cookie – she could take you to the cleaners! – but also extraordinarily compassionate and gracious. Once I left a car window open and her favourite jacket was stolen. 99.99% of people would have gone ape. I would have! But Mary just explained to me, 'It's London, you need to close the windows'. The whole of our lives was important and needed to be taken care of. Unlike most people, she wasn't out to make a name for herself or get one over on you. You sensed quickly that she was genuinely interested in your future, not trying to get something out of you. Her concern for my education and well-being were remarkable. She encouraged me to go to university.[18]

Colin Barham was 20 when he joined ATD's team in Frimhurst. He recalls:

> I had recently lost my grandmother, my girlfriend, my job and my car. Looking to rebuild my life, I trawled through the literature of the day and discovered Frimhurst. I began there as a driver and handyman: painting, repairing windows, gardening. It was also necessary to help with meals and washing up. I don't remember seeing a TV or radio; but I did discover a record player and an LP with Wagner's Tannhauser. On weekends, Marie-France and I drove the children to a local woodland setting where they could have fun and experience nature directly. So I earned my keep while waiting my chance to go to Pierrelaye.[19]

Pierrelaye had become the place to train young people interested in ATD's International Volunteer Corps. About his work in Frimhurst, Colin continues:

> Mary was mostly living in London, but I understood that she was an important figure within ATD and had the ear of Père Joseph. Her energetic and determined personality shone through. She had a reputation as a hard worker that was more than justified. There was a feeling of togetherness. She inspired and encouraged people to work hard and was very kind and respectful. Smartly but modestly dressed, she gave the impression of an intelligent person who enjoyed the finer things such as good wine and food.
>
> Communal staff meals were the highlight of the day. When Mary was present, her active say made them even more fun and interesting. Meals were discussion forums about anything and everything, always intellectual and never banal or trivial; but also full of humour and sometimes sharp debate. Mary was well spoken and always prepared both to listen and argue her point forcefully. After supper, discussions continued into the late evening with community spirit.

Colin enjoyed six months at Frimhurst. However, he struggled in Pierrelaye where he was assigned to do manual work with men who had been homeless and lived very difficult lives. Their work was supervised by Bernard Jahrling, recently qualified as a mason and now overseeing the construction of ATD's international centre. Colin writes:

Bernard was good-natured. But his companion, Jean-Pierre, was of quite a different character. His quick-fire temper could be triggered if things seemed to go wrong. I was always concerned that Jean-Pierre would one day attack me. I eventually found life in Pierrelaye too arduous and scary and did not complete my full term in France. It occurs to me that Mary must have worked amongst similar unpredictable people as Jean-Pierre. This shows how brave she was.

Although Mary was stressed by violence in Frimhurst, ultimately she focussed more on changing her own mindset. In a *Frimhurst Journal* editorial, Mary wrote:

> To begin to understand the families here, I had to empty out my own preconceived ideas. This took real discipline. More than anything, they need people who can lead them to explore and understand their environment and enlarge their narrowly limited horizons. We invite them to use us volunteers for whatever they dream of accomplishing. They can invent their own projects and change their own destinies. This begins with each person discovering what they want out of life; then developing the self-confidence to make choices and trust others. Once a family manages to live as a family, they can handle everything else.[20]

In 1974, Pathway Films made a documentary about Frimhurst. Mary noted: 'Families are referred here by social services … for six to nine months, longer, it depends on the family. We don't like to be rigid.'[21]

After Mary's death, social service referrals changed because of pressure to create more assessment centres where families would be put under surveillance, often on camera 24/7, as a way to gather evidence for removing their children. For this reason, ATD stopped taking these referrals and it was no longer viable to continue a permanent residential project in Frimhurst. Since then, we've used Frimhurst for much shorter term projects, where families or individuals in poverty come for a week of well-being activities or a working session to develop our Giving Poverty a Voice programme. This is why I've never lived for more than a week or two at a time under the same roof as families in deep poverty. But during even those short periods, sometimes it feels like the raging injustice and sheer chaos of poverty are seeping into my every pore, which leaves me all the more in awe of Mary's role in Frimhurst.

Dreamers and Lunatics? Changing Minds

Mary in 1974, being interviewed by Pathway Films
© *Pathway Films Camberley by A.J.Dalley and D.J. White*

© *ATD Fourth World / Joseph Wresinski Centre*

In the 1974 documentary, Mary went on to describe how relationships with families evolved after their departure:

> When they go, we keep up with them. We go see them or they come see us. But then we're no longer responsible for them and we have an altogether different relationship. ... Giving people services doesn't provide them an opportunity to contribute and gain a sense of achievement. Conversely, what can be done in any community ... is to allow each person to realise that they are in fact completely capable of doing something useful to other people.[22]

This aim would soon lead Mary to take a new step in developing ATD in Britain.

Chapter 16

'Providing a Megaphone' while 'Everybody Else Had Their Clipboards'

After completing her LSE degree, Mary returned to life in Frimhurst. However, she was convinced ATD Fourth World needed to focus more energy on changing systems. In 1977, ten years after her arrival at Frimhurst, two other ATD volunteers, Stuart and Isabelle Williams, took over that responsibility, freeing Mary to develop a national centre in London. Since joining Goodman, Mary had collected names and addresses of people across the UK who were interested in ATD and wanted to support it. Her voluminous correspondence and newsletters prepared the work-camps, raised awareness, and requested donations. During that first decade, an ally of ATD in London: 'had been keeping our correspondence in her sitting room cupboard, bulging with newsletters, greeting cards, and carbon copies of letters. ... Each scrap of paper represented our hope that others would join our work.'[1]

To replace that cupboard with a proper setting for strategic communications work to flourish, Mary set off with two other volunteers, Fran Bennett and Brigitte Seinnave. During their first year in London, they sometimes worked in separate places and usually couch-surfed at night. Fran remembers a temporary office, first in Marylebone and then Euston. She adds, 'Once, I just slept on the floor of the office.'[2]

Mary recalled:

Providing a Megaphone

Between the trees stands the Victorian property of 48 Addington Square occupied by ATD Fourth World.
© Peter Marshall

Eventually, through a friend of a friend of a friend, we found a house that would become the ATD centre in London. Although we didn't have any money, we borrowed from all sorts of places. Later, we scraped together donations to pay it back bit by bit. Now that we have this house, we volunteers live here; but it isn't our house and it isn't the house of people in poverty either. We are using the house together for a common purpose. It is a place where all the hopes and aspirations of the poorest people will be engaged.[3]

The sprawling building she purchased stands at 48 Addington Square near Waterloo Station in South London, where I now live. Purchased from another charity, Cambridge House and Talbot, the house had been used as accommodation for local groups doing social and community work. In the 1960s, Addington Square had been home to the notorious Richardson Gang. Just opposite number 48, those reputed as London's most sadistic gangsters carried out torture sessions. Fortunately, the Richardsons were imprisoned before ATD moved in.

But number 48 was run down with a leaking roof, dangerously faulty wiring, and no heat. Because the square was then open to through traffic, Stuart recalls, the ruckus was constant, with 'taxis racing by and newspaper delivery vans hurtling through the square and up into central London at 5 o'clock, five or six mornings a week with copies

In front of 48 Addington Square, from left: Stuart Williams, Fabienne Klein, me, Stephen Baker, Françoise Vedrenne, and Isabelle Williams
© ATD Fourth World / Joseph Wresinski Centre

of the Evening Standard.' Even so, the house was a haven for Mary. She reflected:

> In Frimhurst, just seven or eight families consumed all our energy. To survive, it was almost impossible to see beyond those few individual crises. Our minds were hemmed in from all sides. We needed another physical place in order to learn and develop a more far-reaching approach where together we could begin influencing policy. We wanted to meet new people and form alliances with others also trying to convince society that a new approach was needed to overcome poverty.[4]

Although Mary had passed on the daily running of Frimhurst, she continued investing energy for the team there to get a fresh perspective without feeling 'hemmed in on all sides' as she had. Isabelle Williams says:

> We could get bogged down because Frimhurst was non-stop. With sleepless nights, you were not always straight in your thinking, and could easily lose the sense of the big picture. ... Mary was enormously important because she laid the ground for us to have time and space to reflect.

Providing a Megaphone

Back row: Stuart, Stephen, Barbara, Helen; middle row: Jessica Ballin, Miriam Fernando, Mary; front: Isabelle and Ursula
© *ATD Fourth World / Joseph Wresinski Centre*

She ensured that we could have time off, but also time to think about our understanding of poverty. When we came to Frimhurst, she had already struggled to establish that basis that made it possible for us to last. That was huge. She started in Frimhurst in conditions that – it's hard to imagine how she managed. She was a mover and a shaker. She played a very important part in the support and inspiration we got from the London team.[5]

Living in London gave Mary the opportunity to attend many public events. Fran considered her particularly talented at building relationships with policymakers: 'She could hold her own in any company. As much as she was at home with families in poverty, she was just as confident meeting MPs or ministers. She was always vibrant and able to persuade others.'[6] One Parliamentary staffer recalls Mary at a conference on family policy and poverty at University College London:

> There were a lot of 'experts' at the conference, and it was all rather boring – until the afternoon when Mary, clearly frustrated, stood up and asked how many of us had bothered to consult the families we were supposed to be trying to help. She invited any of us to visit Frimhurst. Since meeting

Mary in the spiral stairwell of Addington Square
© *ATD Fourth World / Joseph Wresinski Centre*

Mary, I emphasise the need to talk to people affected by social policy instead of laying down the law from on high.[7]

Margaret Thatcher's 1979 election made it important for ATD to work with the Conservative Party. In fact, ATD's principle is always to reach out to all governments and parties because all can benefit from thinking together with people in poverty. Mary's charisma helped her connect with two Conservative politicians: Sir Peter Bottomley, then MP for Woolwich West (in south-east London), and his wife the Right Honourable Baroness Virginia Bottomley of Nettlestone, then a social worker and later named Thatcher's Minister of State for Health. I interviewed them about their memories of Mary over coffee across the street from the Palace of Westminster, in the bustling lobby of Portcullis House.

VIRGINIA: My particular interest was the underclass, the people left behind, the downtrodden. The worst thing that can happen to a family is to have your child taken into care. That's such a humiliation: you're not even able to look after your own child. I remember that ATD uniquely embraced all those who society had stripped of any sort of dignity and pride – the ones that everyone had given up on – and made them feel valued as human beings, as spirits, as citizens. Mary had a Velcro approach: she picked people up. That's my lasting impression and belief.

And ATD wasn't over-professionalising. Many social welfare agencies inevitably had files and notes and reports, and it was very much a professional relationship. Whereas ATD's relationship is essentially one of forgiveness, solidarity, and warmth in a non-judgemental way. That was particularly unique at a time when everybody else had their clipboards and reports and their psychometric profiling and their Freudian theories.

Asked about Mary's approach to advocacy, they finished one another's sentences:

PETER: She was clearly direct, clearly persistent –
VIRGINIA: Quite an emotional woman, speaking for the inarticulate. … Mary was not manipulative, not devious, she was *totally* authentic. … Some voluntary organisations and welfare organisations are very professionalised. But my sense is that with ATD, it's more an all-embracing commitment to volunteering. There are other organisations that use volunteers, but –
PETER: But they're daytime or by the hour, and ATD is by the life!
VIRGINIA: Exactly, yes, a whole life commitment as opposed to 'I'll give you Thursday mornings'.
PETER: When we had some sort of 'do', Mary and I made sure that you always heard the voice of people who were experiencing whatever we were trying to share or to change. So it wasn't speaking *for* people, it was –
VIRGINIA: – providing a megaphone –
PETER: – and others there had to learn.

At Frimhurst, from left, the Right Honourable Baroness Virginia Bottomley of Nettlestone, Dave Burningham, and Eileen Donovan
© ATD Fourth World / Joseph Wresinski Centre

> VIRGINIA: We both take the view that impossible people change the world. If you really care, you *are* impossible. So that wouldn't have put either of us off!
> PETER: Putting it in a slightly different way, Virginia often says if someone asks you to do something four times, you probably ought to do it.

That does sound like Mary's persistence! Asked about feminism, Lady Virginia said:

> I had some colleagues always going on about 'feckless women' and 'bad women' – when it's so evident that the problem is overwhelmingly with feckless, irresponsible *men*. But that didn't need explaining to people like Mary. I think we both took it for granted that it was the women who had the stamina, tenacity and a sort of resilience to cope in appalling situations. I think in ATD there was affirmation and solidarity with the responsibilities of women. ...
>
> In poverty research, you talk about 'the bottom decile'. The group Mary was serving were defined in a dismissive way in almost every encounter. They were most often referred to as 'benefit scroungers'. In the Housing Department, they would call them 'problem families'; every government agency defined the people she served in some demeaning,

Providing a Megaphone

'To understand and be understood': Addington Square became a place to host discussion forums called "Fourth World Evenings"
© *ATD Fourth World / Joseph Wresinski Centre*

condescending way. So Mary wanted to give these people dignity and affirmation.

That's why ATD stands for All Together in Dignity: to change this view of people struggling the most. Sir Peter added about Mary's approach:

> Mary worked with the ones who had already given up. … ATD was dealing with people who had slipped through the whole thing and hadn't been picked up. There wasn't a quick solution to half their problems, life hasn't been resolved. … I don't wish to judge and say it's people who don't move forward. They have become part of the [ATD] community.[8]

For Mary, interacting with MPs gave food for thought about why Britain's long history of fighting poverty had not accomplished more:

> Ours is a country that was very far ahead of others in the 16th century with the first introduction of the 'Poor Laws', which taxed Londoners to pay for charitable hospitals. Today, both the state and many charitable societies are still concerned with the poor. There are whole libraries of studies on poverty. But it is all done without coherence. The approaches of different social workers are not linked up

with research on the way poverty is passed down intergenerationally, or with research on basic income. Many people choose one area to work in without looking beyond it. So you have a lot of data on poverty, but a lack of comprehensive thinking to inform policy. The societal expectation is that people in poverty should manage to pay their rent on time and their children must succeed in school. But when your life has been a series of obstacles, those achievements can take a generation or more.[9]

Making long-term change was a daunting challenge, but being established in London gave a strong foundation for Mary's next steps.

Chapter 17

A Westminster Abbey Exhibition and Being a Rottweiler

The International Year of the Child (IYC) in 1979 was a breakthrough for Mary's awareness-raising work. The director of the UK Association for IYC, Judith Stone (who was at school with Mary), recalls:

> Mary took the lead in ensuring that voices of the poorest children and families were heard during the year and that we listened to them speaking of their experiences of poverty, homelessness, the threats to their families' health and unity, and their aspirations for a better life. Mary moved with ease between the families whose lives she shared, and the very sea of the establishment with its wealth, privilege, and power. There, she became an eloquent and effective advocate without alienating the powerful allies she needed, but also without ever compromising her integrity or principles.[1]

Cover of *UK children OK?*, a pamphlet created for the International Year of the Child

As part of the UK association, Mary co-led with the Child Poverty Action Group and Family Service Units to create a pamphlet called *UK Children OK?* which focused on extreme poverty and included a section challenging the removal into foster care of children 'from geographical areas of social deprivation'.² Jo Tunnard, who produced this pamphlet with Mary, says:

> *UK Children OK?* was no dry, dense report but, rather, a punchy collection of evidence – facts, photos, family quotes – with ten action points for government. Typically, when politicians talked of setting targets for halving child poverty, Mary would ask: 'But what about the other half?' I knew Mary well in the late 1970s through my work at the Child Poverty Action Group and then the Family Rights Group. She stood out as a committed ally of families in poverty, their formidable champion for social justice. Her vision was crystal clear and she worked tirelessly for the change that was needed. She was innovation and compassion rolled into one.³

ATD Fourth World's collaboration with the United Nations led to a UNESCO conference attended by Ruth Lister, then director of the UK's Child Poverty Action Group. (Lister, who remains a steadfast ally of ATD, later became a professor at Loughborough University, and in 2011 was appointed Baroness Lister of Burtersett, a life peer of the House of Lords.)

For the international year, ATD also created 'Children of Our Time', a travelling exhibition of 189 photographs, showing how children in

Mary at the 'Children of Our Time' exhibition
© *ATD Fourth World / Joseph Wresinski Centre*

poverty look at their families, the world, and their rights. For instance, one caption read:

> Nicole: Often I look out the window and see the houses full of people who have all sorts of problems, like us. Noise from traffic going past goes round and round in my head. The cars never stop, day or night. On the other side of town are some really nice houses where it's quiet and peaceful. Those families haven't got people upstairs who shout at their kids all the time, or neighbours who fight, or water you can hear running, and doors banging about all night, or televisions and transistors turned up loud so they can't hear the noise the neighbours are making. They're alright and good luck to them, but do they know how lucky they are? Sometimes at the window, I start dreaming. I say to myself, those nice houses aren't for me.... The way things are, my life will always be like this: slums, noise, shouting. I can see myself living the same way, I already shout at my little brother. It's the same with school work: I'd like to pass exams and work with children. But look at my dad, he can't get any work. No, I'm telling you, at 16 I'll get any old job, just like my brother did.[4]

In this 1979 photo from the 'Children of Our Time' exhibition, Bengali children play with an abandoned car in Whitechapel, London, in the courtyard of Fieldgate Mansions, a 19th century tenement block due to be demolished.

© Dave Hoffman

© ATD Fourth World / Joseph Wresinski Centre

After being displayed by UNESCO at the Centre Pompidou in Paris and at the European Parliament in Brussels, the exhibition came to the UK. For six months, it toured the country before being installed at Westminster Abbey where its launch involved Baroness Faithfull of Wolvercote, a leading campaigner on behalf of children, as well as the Right Honourable Lady Soames, who was Winston Churchill's daughter – one of those who had vetted Mary's mother Sandra during her application to become a custodian at Chequers.

Some 18,000 people came to see the exhibition in the UK. Many agreed to get involved with ATD. Some were journalists, including from Thames Television and the News Agency of Nigeria.[5] Having collaborated on smaller exhibitions for ATD, I'm hugely impressed by that number of visitors. I can also well imagine how much work went into it. There was the aesthetics of the final product; the partnership with a national institution to host it; and above all maintaining ATD's ethos so that the families of the children portrayed and quoted felt the pride of co-creation. It was eventually published as a book in French, which Mary translated into English.

Mary also helped plan the exhibition's tour in the United States, which included: United Nations Headquarters in New York; San Francisco City Hall; a Los Angeles arts centre; and the University of Dayton, Ohio. In New Orleans, it was displayed at the International Trade Mart near Canal Street Ferry. This was promoted on a radio broadcast, whose moderator stressed that the tour was sponsored by donations from working-class people: 'We would especially like to thank all the trade unionists, the seafarers, the operating engineers for realising that poverty is a place that we, as labouring people have once come from, and it's a place we must try to bring others out of.'[6]

The featured guest speaker, Reggie Chapman, was an electrician who met Mary when she was preparing the exhibition. She convinced him to donate a month of his time to promote it, even though their first meeting at a Mardi Gras event was not easy. Chapman remembers:

> We got in an argument. She was basically coming from the perspective of disadvantaged, hopeless people who just cannot seem to ever take care of themselves. Let's say they rely on welfare programmes. I was coming from the viewpoint of a man who's learning a good trade, working off-shore in the oil field. So she's speaking of hopelessness; and I'm speaking of a land of opportunity. So here we have a tremendous dichotomy, a very contradictory situation, people who are here for opportunities; and another group who see no opportunity. Somehow we need to get those together so that people who take advantage of opportunities are able to share that information with their fellow men.

However, after spending time with Mary, he was able to explain the importance of ATD's work:

> The main goal is to open people's eyes. ... Without changing the perception of the poor by the people who are not poor it will be virtually impossible to gain a lot of ground. ... For many of us, poverty is just next door – we try to look the other way and pretend it doesn't exist. ...
>
> [ATD] moves into an area and lives at the same level of income as the people they are trying to help. They're not talking down to anybody or coming in as big-time earners with fancy cars or anything – they live in the same housing, and gradually are able to relate to people who are often very suspicious. Part of it is: they will not start an action unless they hope that they can continue. Too many do-good programmes come along, last a little while, and fold. And this tends to make people not want to participate in anything. The lady I met spent five years of her time before she was able to see signs of hope in people's hearts.[7]

Standing, from left: Mary, Stuart Williams, and Anneke van Elderen
© *ATD Fourth World / Joseph Wresinski Centre*

That was Mary all over! Never one to shy away from heated discussion, she deployed her insights and charm so successfully that Chapman was now promoting the very cause he had argued against.

Stuart Williams, who worked closely with Mary for 10 years, recalls:

> She was combative and bold. She would directly question others, including Father Joseph, about whether what ATD was proposing was practicable and effective. And she had a bite! In the associative and political world in the UK, some considered her a Rottweiler! She represented a constant and tenacious reminder that demands being made by organisations to benefit those in need, or legislative proposals being weighed for their impact, were (invariably) inadequate, inappropriate or incomplete. And like a Rottweiler who has hold of your leg, Mary wouldn't let go![8]

Stuart hit the nail on the head! Mary did indeed have a bite. Many people in poverty appreciated that she never minced words. But it could be hard for some teammates to get along with Mary, particularly if they were soft-spoken and retiring. Her brother Paul remembers that Mary disliked some people's 'saintly' approach to social justice work. Fran Bennett, who lived with Mary in London, recalls:

Mary was quite irritated by a teammate who acted as though individual acts of love and generosity were enough to end poverty. She and Mary always rubbed each other up the wrong way; they were almost allergic to each other. It would not surprise me if this was in part due to a different way of thinking about how to solve problems: one is about individual acts of love and generosity, but the other – whilst also about relationships – is about collective voice, organisation, influencing, agitating, policy and practice change, etc. In Mary's view, we needed to raise our collective voice to agitate for broad social change.[9]

Anneke, another teammate of Mary's, once told me:

> Some were afraid of Mary; but she wasn't really aware of it. She raised her voice at times, but I don't think that was what scared people. It was more the strength of her passion for life and justice. I think it came from the crucible of her years in Noisy-le-Grand. Society inflicted such violence on the families in poverty. Mary and the first ATD volunteers lived in equally harsh conditions with no protection at all. Because they chose to go there, no one understood. They were called stupid to throw their lives away. And they were asked to build a relationship with families that was not based on judgement or fear. Learning to forget your biases and meet people empty-handed; listening instead of lecturing – you don't learn that on your own. It's through confrontation; and it changes you as a person. So Mary had to prove herself. I think she created a real armour for herself.[10]

A year later, we spoke again and Anneke put it this way:

> It enraged Mary to have to be patient with someone not taking initiative and being too wishy-washy. I'm that way too. That's part of why she got on so well with Père Joseph. She made him laugh, but he also loved fighting with her and didn't like getting adoration from others. He had a kind of freedom next to her; when they were together there was a

Ursula Jomini
© ATD Fourth World / Joseph Wresinski Centre

kind of equality. And the sweet gentle people were afraid of them both.[11]

Ursula Jomini, from Switzerland, admits:

> Mary scared me at first as I did not understand and speak English well when I joined the London team. She reproached me for having no common sense. Sometimes she had fits of anger and we didn't always know why. But I also discovered how lonely she was, always surrounded by foreign teammates. Building a movement in a non-French-speaking context, I think she must not always have felt understood.[12]

Huguette too was struck by the challenges Mary faced as the only native speaker of English among ATD's founding members: 'Our work was very francophone at the time. Mary was culturally isolated among us. It was exceptional of her to manage it.'[13] Fran cited this as one of her reasons for leaving ATD's Volunteer Corps, instead going into public policy work: 'ATD was so French in the 1970s! I wanted a wider perspective.'[14]

Ursula continues:

> Mary's strength was that, after an angry outburst, she would come back, apologise, offer a small gift, strike up a conversation. One thing Mary said touched me: during those

> years when she was the only ATD volunteer at Frimhurst, she experienced intense moments with families, sometimes joyful; but she felt hatred at times. People pushed her to the limit of becoming violent or wanting to flee. That's how much people needed recognition, listening, tenderness. Even if she tried to give all she could, it was never enough to fill what they lacked since childhood.
>
> Mary was a hard worker. She demanded a lot of herself, she dealt with everything, at every level. Sometimes, after a long day's work, she suggested outings to forget everything, have fun, take your mind off things. She'd invite us to the pub, or a concert, or an exhibition. Mary made an effort with each of us to ensure that we were not alone in difficult times, for example, when there was a death in the family, or at Christmas, when she knew someone couldn't make the journey home.[15]

So yes, Mary definitely had a Rottweiler side that could be frightening (as I discovered when she first sent me to iron my clothes!) but even with people whose personality was less combative, she always made amends for her temper; and her sense of joy was contagious. Anneke also remembers Mary taking the whole team to the Isle of Wight 'and she had us hanging overboard just for the thrill of it.'[16]

To follow up on the exhibition, Mary began a new project:

> We go to speak in Hyde Park at Speakers' Corner to meet new people – even though we have to speak to hundreds before connecting with one who decides to turn up at our next meeting. We write letters to about 4,500 people each year. Having every single one of their addresses is the result of a conversation or a meeting because we don't believe in purchasing mailing lists. And every one of these people represents some hope for everything we are trying to accomplish.[17]

Going to Speakers' Corner was of a piece with the monthly evening discussions Mary continued to organise with parents in Frimhurst and former Frimhurst residents. The idea for these discussions grew from her year in New York when she reflected:

> In France, we're putting down roots and building a long-term commitment; while in America we saw that we could connect with others who aren't afraid of trying something new to make our work more political. Others in Europe still do not understand that our motivations are not sentimental or purely moral. We need to show that people in poverty should not be seen as passive recipients of aid. Our goal is not to show that the poor should be loved; rather, it is to show that people in poverty have been excluded from humanity. We were already certain that this was the crucial issue; however, visiting the United States gave us the idea to start community meetings. We began sharpening our understanding of poverty by making sure that people would identify their own needs.

Beginning in 1973, these 'Fourth World Evening' discussions took place in London with some participants travelling in from Frimhurst. Each discussion focussed on a theme, often with outside guests, as for the series about ethnic and cultural differences, or when an alderman was invited to explain how local councils spend their money. Written summaries were mailed to participants following each discussion. Themes ranged from disability to inflation to proposed laws about foster care, adoption, and abortion. A discussion called 'Family Situations' included speaking about suicide.[18] A series about human rights made connections with other campaigns, for instance with a nuclear disarmament activists speaking about the right to peace, or speaking to a trade union official about the 'right to work and to be considered as workers'.[19] Sometimes the discussion was replaced by a cultural outing, for instance to the House of Lords, or to Loseley Park, a manor house frequented by Queen Elizabeth I in the sixteenth century.

During the International Year of the Child preparations, the themes Mary organised included: the world of play; the world of drawing and painting; primary school education; the broader context of how children learn; 'the child as citizen', a discussion featuring Sir Peter Bottomley as the main guest; children in care; laws about the care and protection of children; the lives of children in immigrant families; the spiritual life of the child; and child abuse and neglect, with a guest from the National Society for the Prevention of Cruelty to Children.[20] Whatever the topic, Anneke insists:

> Mary wasn't afraid of anything. When she set the theme as sexual abuse, it was tricky of course, but she was good at helping people open up when she knew there was something they wanted to say. She was so straightforward, and never treated anything as pitiful. It was all about each person carrying their own dignity instead of just moaning about trouble.[21]

Having done my share facilitating similar discussions, I'm particularly impressed by that. Even when I know in advance what participants want to share about a thorny subject, there is no level of trigger warnings and 'trauma-informed' practice that guarantees things will work.

Stephen Baker describes Mary's facilitation style:

> Mary was extraordinarily capable of holding onto the expectations and demands of people from very different backgrounds, whether the political elite, trade unionists, or families in poverty. She knew each and every person in the room so she could call on people and be sure they could stand up and say what needed to be said.[22]

The goal was for all participants to speak freely, understand more about society, and develop reflections on their individual identity and history.[23] Mary recalled:

> We had already spoken about many issues [with] parents at Frimhurst. But they were not accustomed to being consulted and speaking out themselves. Gradually we realised they deserved the chance to meet and to speak out in a broader context. So we began these wider meetings. We always invited guests, not just as speakers, but as outsiders to whom people in poverty could speak about their own history. Around the same time, Wresinski began something similar in France, which meant that we could consult each other, with both groups able to learn from what the other was doing.[24]

In the early 1980s, these Fourth World Evenings connected with similar discussion forums that ATD was running across Europe and in the United States. Mary considered these international exchanges

Mary at a 'Fourth World People's University' in France,
which was developed on a similar model
to the 'Fourth World Evenings' in London

© ATD Fourth World / Joseph Wresinski Centre

important for broadening context: 'Families in other countries live in quite different material conditions; however, discovering that they experience the same situations as we do proves to us that our situations are not the exception, but the same as that of many others everywhere.'[25] Together, they all sharpened their focus on human rights. Mary led discussions about the history of poverty and workhouses in Britain. Given the massive spike in unemployment (which reached almost 12% in 1984[26]), they spoke about how being out of work impacted identity and what they needed 'to live in dignity as workers'. This was in preparation for an international event organised by ATD in Brussels: the 'Human Rights Festival' of 15 May 1982. To travel to

Mary in a team meeting preparing for the Human Rights Festival

© Luc Prisset, ATD Fourth World / Joseph Wresinski Centre

Ursula at the Human Rights Festival in Brussels
© *ATD Fourth World / Joseph Wresinski Centre*

While preparing for the the Human Rights Festival, Mary was concerned that the English media had not responded to ATD's press releases. Because the UK delegation was preparing to perform a play in Brussels about workhouses and the history of the poor, Mary decided the group should wear costumes representing work done by people in poverty throughout history while 'occupying' the offices of The Times and The Guardian, which is why Mary dressed as a maid. This stunt did result in interviews and short articles in both papers.

© *ATD Fourth World / Joseph Wresinski Centre*

Belgium, Mary explained, all the Fourth World Evening participants wanted to pitch in to raise money. 'Several knitted cardigans to raffle off. One mother stitched material into sheets to sell; with the profits she purchased better material to sew more sheets. After stitching many sets of sheets, she donated the profits to the trip.'[27]

The festival led to a new book. Drawing on fact sheets contributed by participants in poverty, Lucien Duquesne, a French member of ATD's International Volunteer Corps, stitched the facts into a narrative about a new International Centre of Human Rights where the chair is constantly interrupted by people in a large 'grass-roots' contingent who point out violations of rights he believes are already being respected. Mary oversaw the translation into English, as *An End to Injustice*. On its publication, in February 1984, the book was mentioned in the House of Commons during a debate about family policies. Mary saw this as a sign that ATD was 'becoming known more and more for its experience and its optimism'. However, despite the triumphs of the exhibition and the book, Mary remained down-to-earth, reflecting:

> In fact, we remain little known. On top of that, when budget cuts hurt people in poverty, there can be a sense of discouragement. However, we are seen as a movement which tries to see the possibilities, and which cannot sink into pessimism by accepting a public discourse that says, 'There will no longer be employment for everyone.' Instead, we try to find new possibilities. We keep saying: everybody can learn; it is always possible to do something positive, and to involve new people.[28]

Chapter 18

An Alliance with Social Workers to Denounce a Culture of Risk

About the Fourth World Evenings Mary ran, she once said:

> Right at the beginning, there was only one topic we kept off limits: social work. We actually banned the words 'social workers' for the first two years. Social workers play such a massive role in families' lives that we wanted to avoid speaking about them so as to make room to speak about everything else. There is so much else to talk about. We wanted people in poverty to see themselves in other dimensions of life, from culture to politics to everything else.[1]

Despite this, Mary, like everyone involved in ATD Fourth World, knew the massive role social workers play in the lives of families living in poverty.

In 1988, when I was living with Mary at ATD's international centre in France, she hosted a visit from Dina Wardi, a social worker who came for a month to learn from our approach. Mary knew that the isolation and exhaustion of poverty can drain people to the point where it is hard to even feel hope, let alone to participate in any project. Mary enlisted Dina's help with a project doing research based on people's 'lived experience' of poverty, an approach ATD was beginning to develop that is now widely accepted in academic circles. Mary also

From left, Geneviève Tardieu with her children, with Mary,
Dina Wardi, and Gabrielle Erpicum

© Bruno Tardieu, ATD Fourth World / Joseph Wresinski Centre

proposed that Dina live in Herblay, a residential community run by ATD and somewhat similar to Frimhurst. In Dina's report on this, she stressed the balance struck between considering needs and difficulties, while also inviting every family to engage with various projects:

> In Herblay, as well as in Frimhurst, I saw a wide range of activities that families were exposed to: children's Street Library activities;[2] a youth club; a women's club; Sunday nature walks together; an outing to watch the Concorde airplane take off; a policy campaign against unemployment; preparations for the World Day for Overcoming Poverty; and more. All were opportunities that people were left free to choose or not. There was no requirement. Despite everything that might have held them back, many families chose to participate frequently. ... The frame of reference here is very different from that of conventional social work agencies. In our work, people are seen in terms of psycho-social pathologies that require treatment, whether for 'disturbing behaviour', substance abuse, or mental well-being. However, in Frimhurst and Herblay, ATD teams are accepting, available, and understanding, these attitudes making up their mutual daily life (not a one-hour meeting in an agency, as is the case for social workers). The relationship is developed free of interpretations and conditioning.[3]

That different frame of reference helps to explain why dialogues with social workers remain extremely fraught for most people in poverty. Navigating this impasse remains our very biggest challenge, especially when children are in danger of being removed from their parents. According to *Prospect Magazine*:

> The UK has a forced adoption problem. The UK is unusual, compared to the rest of Europe, for the frequency of forced adoptions. … Data from 2014 suggests that almost half of the 5,050 children adopted in the previous year were given new homes without their parents' consent. In England alone, 80,000 children were removed from their parents in the year up to March 2021.[4]

Occasionally, children must be removed from parents who are acting with wilful cruelty. But the vast majority of the families we get to know in ATD are simply struggling to cope with poverty. The appropriate response would be compassionate early help to support loving families to succeed. Instead, we often see people who were themselves abused in the care system as children and then made homeless when they aged out of this system at 16. Their childhood trauma can then be compounded by the emotional harm of having their own children removed despite strong bonds of love – and despite the fact that these removals are inherently traumatic and also create additional risks of harm. In family court, the priority for the local authority sometimes becomes defending its own initial decisions rather than uncovering the truth of how best to protect children's well-being.

In many ways, the realities for families in poverty have worsened since Mary's time. The Adoption and Children Act of 2002 made it easier for local authorities to secure a placement order from a court resulting in a contested closed adoption. The basis for this includes 'the risk of emotional harm' in the future, as defined in the Children Act 1989.

Dr Simon Haworth has taught social work at the University of Birmingham and served on ATD's Board. Once a year, I travel with a group of parents living in poverty to teach a session of Simon's class. We are always touched by his passion for inculcating in his students the values that lead him to challenge many social work practices today. It is delightful that Simon is always game to join in the Theatre of the Oppressed exercises I propose, even at the cost of having his

An ATD Fourth World group of parents living in poverty deliver a
session of anti-poverty practice training to
social work students
© *Diana Skelton*

student berate him (as part of the role play, of course!). Simon calls future 'emotional harm' a 'rather hazy classification' sometimes used simply to avoid uncertainty:

> The inherent disconnect between risk of potential future harm and actual events of child harm occurring can be forgotten. If we expect risk to be there, it is easier to find and confirm [and] … even more difficult … to challenge. … In court, this can sometimes be reinforced through the opinions of experts such as psychologists, who tend towards an individualising narrative that excludes wider social forces. [… Separation is brutal and emotionally damaging for parents and siblings alike, thus constituting other forms of emotional harm. Certainly, siblings can

find it very hard to understand why their brother/sister has gone, and self-blame can ensue. Separation at any age is hard to understand and accept, but as a child it can be overwhelming and devastating.[5]

As social workers try to gauge the risk of future emotional harm, one factor they consider is whether either parent was removed from their own home in their childhood. Because this is assumed to weaken their capacity to become good parents, during a woman's first pregnancy, she will be assessed; the decision to impose a closed adoption may be finalised before the child is even born.

In 2019, Amanda Button, a senior ATD activist who grew up in poverty in Lincolnshire, explained to our board of directors what it feels like to have social services remove your children:

> As a young mother, I was convinced there was something fundamentally wrong with me. I am normal, but agencies I went to for help made me believe I wasn't. Poverty is about what life throws at you. There are so many places you go to ask for help; but you feel ashamed. You know people are judging you. You hit rock bottom, where you feel there's no point in getting up in the morning. You might as well be six feet under. The situation we were in was so abnormal that it stripped our humanity away. People have their soul destroyed.

Simon Haworth and Amanda Button, at the University of Birmingham
© *Diana Skelton*

In addition to the prevalence of adoptions being forced on families in poverty for fear of possible emotional harm in the future, a 2014 policy change impacted children in care. Some children's social care services were privatised, 'making children in care a highly profitable industry. One report revealed that the 10 largest social care providers made more than £300m in profits in 2021. "If mothers had even a fraction of that money, many times their kids would not be taken away."'[6] *The Guardian* adds: 'The majority of providers are privately owned, and the average cost of an unregulated place is £948 a week, with average operating profits of £330 a week.'[7] Lax regulations about the accommodation of 16-to-18 year olds in care have compounded the shift putting children in the hands of providers whose intentions orbit around profit.

This has led to heart-wrenching consequences. I recently interviewed an activist who grew up in Derbyshire. (To speak anonymously, she chose the pseudonym 'Rachel White'.) Her voice taut with trauma, she explained:

> Children's Services placed me in adult accommodation when I was 15. They housed me with seven men over the age of 18. I was abused by all of them. I was groomed and sexually trafficked in that accommodation. I ended up in the hands of a gang and was trafficked up and down from England to Scotland for sex. The social worker used to come out once a week to sign for my rent because I wasn't old enough to live there. She didn't check in, nothing. She used to take me to LiDL, buy my shopping and leave me. She didn't ask me what was going on there, or anything about my pregnancy at age 17. ... Social services might not have been the ones trafficking me up and down the country, but they were the ones responsible for that care. ... Today teenage girls are still being housed without supervision on barges and canal boats and on caravan estates. They're living with adults, and how do we expect exploitation to not go on?

Rachel, Amanda, and many other parents and young people have felt excruciating torment in their interactions with children's social care. At the same time, these members of ATD work alongside social work allies like Simon and others who are convinced that their profession's values require them to challenge poverty-ism and improve policies. Amanda explains that ATD's approach made a fundamental difference:

> Before, we would have gone under. But at ATD, I met others in the same situation and I got to know people who could help me. Here, I don't feel like people talk to me only because they're paid to. People are all treated as equals. It's not 'them' and 'us'. People are welcomed for themselves.

ATD core workers believe that we try our best. I was asked to help. That gave me a sense of purpose. And I meet people of so many different cultures and levels of education – that opens things up. When we come together with others, you feel honoured in your soul. Meeting ATD, I knew I could be involved here long term. If I screwed up along the way, I could come back and start again. The ATD centre is more than a building; it's where we feed our souls. It's our saving grace.

Thanks to Mary's Rabagliati's example, we are continuing today to recruit allies both within the social work field and outside it. In 2016-19, in a partnership with the University of Oxford, we carried out participatory research on 'Understanding Poverty in All Its Forms', with Amanda and other experts-by-experience as co-researchers.[8] When launching those research findings we began a partnership with Amnesty International UK, Just Fair, and the University of Essex Human Rights Centre. With support from these institutions, in 2023 ATD presented 25 pages of evidence to the United Nations Committee on Economic, Social and Cultural Rights. In reviewing the UK Government's compliance with its commitments to these rights, we drew their attention to:

- poverty-ism, i.e. discrimination due to socio-economic disadvantage, and the ways it skews children's social care interventions towards harsh investigations of families in poverty;
- the use of contested closed adoptions instead of kinship care, which could protect children's well-being without permanently severing ties with extended family and community;
- the impact of cuts to family support services (including youth services), community-based resources and housing support services, which disproportionately affect families in poverty;
- the inconsistencies in assessing possible future emotional harm to children and the need to consider emotional harm caused by removing children from their parents;
- the quality gap between for-profit care and those run by charities or local authorities;

- and the inappropriate accommodation of 16 to 18 year olds in care.

To bolster our evidence, we are running peer-led study groups and focus groups on poverty, social work, and the right to family life. My co-researchers include Amanda, Patricia Bailey, and six other activists with lived experience of poverty and social service interactions. Simon and other social workers advise us. We rejoiced in 2023 to see Amnesty feature our work on the cover of its members' magazine, proclaiming: 'The deepening conditions of poverty in the UK are a human rights violation.'[9] The article includes an interview with Patricia, who explained that support she received from ATD motivated her to support other parents in moments of crisis. She said:

> It is shameful that the poorer you are in this country, the more likely you are to have your children forcibly taken from you. … The forced adoptions are horrendous because they affect everyone – siblings, parents and grandparents are never going to have contact with that child again, forever. I absolutely want those things changed. … Families want to stay together!

Although we don't know yet what this work will lead to, having Amnesty give credibility to Patricia and our work with other experts-by-experience gives me hope that someday society may make the changes Mary was calling for from her arrival at Frimhurst.

Part V

Bringing the World on Board

Chapter 19

The United Nations: Women's Conferences in Mexico, Copenhagen, and Nairobi

Mary's commitment to feminism came not only from her Rabagliati and McLaren fore-mothers, but also her mother. Her brother Paul recalls:

> Mum was no activist but was quite outspoken in her feminist views. Distrusting the values and mores of a society 'run by men, for men', she longed for a world that legislated for equality of opportunity for women. She was quick to see through any attitude that reeked of paternalism. She was forthright when she encountered anyone with a male chauvinist attitude, and was happy to have it out with anyone brave enough to try and defend such views. I remember her delight at the publication of Germaine Greer's *The Female Eunuch* in 1970 with its searing examination of the oppression of women in contemporary society.[1]

At the same time, Mary's experience – as well as Wresinski's childhood in poverty – made her wary of middle-class movements that failed to invite women in deep poverty to contribute their own thinking. The typical approach of suffragists was described this way by Royal Holloway, University of London: 'Many campaigns achieved something primarily for middle-class women; but on the basis of saying they had to act for, or speak for, the others who could not.'² This was a method Mary would rail against whenever she got the chance.

© ATD Fourth World / Joseph Wresinski Centre

In 1975, when the United Nations organised the first ever world conference on women, set in Mexico City, the event had particular resonance for ATD Fourth World because it had only recently been recognised by the United Nations as a 'non-governmental organisation' allowed to participate in international conferences. Mary saw this as a unique opportunity to bring voices of women in deep poverty to the widest possible audience. She travelled to Mexico with Huguette, Wresinski, and also Alwine de Vos van Steenwijk, who had been an ambassador for the Netherlands before abandoning her career to join ATD's Volunteer Corps.

Conference preparations began in 1974 when ATD consulted women in poverty in different countries. During Mary's consultations in the UK, one woman told her:

> If you've got nothing, you go without. I had hopes and dreams, but I felt ignored. Some girls were laughed at, and others were pushed into a corner. At that age, you don't know how to get job training. And when you've lived in institutions all your life, nothing's ever been your own. I wanted a home of my own, to belong somewhere. So to get out of there, I got married at 17. I only knew him three weeks. And then with children, you're shut indoors and you feel cut off, just looking at the washtub with no money for a pub or an evening class. So all I live for is day to day. My only hope is that my daughters don't have to go through life like I've had to.³

Feminism initially appealed to this woman; but listening to the feminists featured on TV at the time, she was disappointed: 'There was only a certain class of women speaking out for women as a whole. When they say motherhood is menial, I don't agree.' Another woman in the same meeting felt less pessimistic, telling Mary that staying at Frimhurst had helped her to stop feeling 'tied to the kitchen sink' by motivating her to find a job. She said: 'Now life is better because I can have a laugh and joke at work. After that, I can face going home and the kids don't get on my nerves anymore.'[4]

Mary was also struck by how women spoke about their husbands. With long-term unemployment becoming entrenched, many men felt useless. Mary saw this as damaging individual self-esteem and also families as a whole. She said:

> Men in poverty are in an increasingly difficult position. We have to be sensitive and understand the consequences. If there's no place for men in the world of work, what kind of future can they have? It's a concrete question every day: for harmonious family life, each person has to have a place. But many men feel less and less like they have that place in their own families.[5]

Before the conference, ATD wrote a study and drafted a 'Fourth World Women's Charter', inspired by Sojourner Truth's speech, 'Ain't I a woman?' The charter was printed on a poster in English, French, and Spanish, later published by the UN Economic and Social Commission for Asia and the Pacific.[6]

Sending a delegation of four people to Mexico was a big investment but they raised money for airfare from a women's club in Geneva. To avoid hotel costs, they convinced a friend of a friend to host them – which to this day remains common practice when any of us travel for ATD.

At the conference, they met Betty Friedan (author of *The Feminine Mystique*) and visited families in a precarious mountain settlement. While Wresinski and Alwine observed the official meeting of government delegations, Mary and Huguette ran an exhibition stand at a more informal gathering of 6,000 women marked by 'passionate candour', as Alwine described it. Huguette recalls:

> The conference was really huge with a lot of bigwigs – but the women there were not poor at all. Some of them had good messages but our message raised a question beyond sexism. We asked that female solidarity refuse to exclude a single woman. We hoped that women could show a new way forward by making sure that progress for any of us could be progress for all women.[7]

Throughout the conference, the ATD delegates worked eighteen-hour days meeting every possible journalist or delegate and updating written contributions that they hoped might influence the conclusions of the governments. To distribute the charter, they slipped a copy into every mailbox of the main hotel rooms. As Mary put it, they needed to convince others to free women in poverty from 'the circle of misery where they are kept in roles of reproducers and feeders of their children – and then judged if they don't conform to what is expected'.[8]

Accustomed to diplomacy, Alwine had high hopes for the conference – which were dashed when her former colleagues proved loath to give ATD the respect they had given her as an ambassador. To others in ATD's international centre, she wrote:

> The conference opening was splendid [with] women from every corner of the earth. ... However, we were soon indignant at government platitudes. Many delegations were headed by men. Privileged women took sides in men's power struggles instead of paying attention to the underprivileged. And the acrimony about western imperialism took precedence over every other issue, which stifled efforts to evoke the realities of women in deep poverty. The official action plan adopted is useless.[9]

Mary too was frustrated. She later wrote: 'Mexico was a battle for the privileged. We spent all our time talking about those who were absent.'[10] Despite this, they found a way to be heard. Alwine noted:

This photo was taken by the ATD delegation during their trip to Mexico.
© *ATD Fourth World / Joseph Wresinski Centre*

© *ATD Fourth World / Joseph Wresinski Centre*

The delegates also took these photos in Mexico.
© *ATD Fourth World / Joseph Wresinski Centre*

When our right to address the conference was revoked, our anger drove us to find dozens of allies among the conference staff. Every secretary, waiter, and chambermaid we approached helped us distribute the charter on banquet tables and in bedrooms. A bellboy who read our charter called his friends over immediately, saying: 'Hey, you've got to hear this, it's really good'.[11] And every woman we spoke with, privileged or not, was moved by the question of poverty.[12]

Among the women they won over was the First Lady of France, Anémone Giscard d'Estaing, who later visited ATD's international centre with the French minister for women's issues. To follow up on the conference, Mary, Huguette, Alwine, and Wresinski organised a women's congress in Pierrelaye. Mary wrote hundreds of letters to women they had met. She was also invited to contribute an article to the Women's Forum newsletter of the British National Council of Social Service. Her article asked:

> What does equality with men signify when your husband is out of work, underemployed, underpaid, and unrepresented by unions? What does equality signify if your husband is constantly ignored by others – except when he is looked down on or mocked? What meaning can world development have when the cost and conditions of living undermine your mental and physical health and when, despite free education, you remain barely literate and are unable to convince your children that they have a chance to develop their own potential? There is no doubt that women can lead where men have failed – but how will women lead, and in whose name?[13]

More confidentially, Mary spoke with many women in poverty in Britain, sharing news from the conference and asking their opinions about a proposed change in the abortion law. The women's opinions about abortion differed; but several agreed that they felt coerced into sterilisation. Mary explained in an ATD discussion group:

> Some couples in poverty have sterilisation proposed when they are very young and not prepared to take such an irreversible step. Some women who were sterilised without warning felt that it had not been explained sufficiently, and that they consequently suffered physically and mentally. Many women (and men) think that doctors are inclined to decide *for* their patients, telling them what is in their best interests, rather than helping them choose. They said a woman should not be pushed into choosing an abortion because of bad housing or low income, or because other people thought she already had enough children. This kind of situation is most likely to occur in the poorest families.
>
> Women in poverty also noted that even if there are people willing to foster and adopt unwanted children, 'The likes

of us don't get a chance to take care of those unwanted children.'[14]

Times had changed. With birth control much more widely accessible than in the 1960s, Mary saw that family planning was being turned against women in poverty. Many social workers had long distrusted the parenting skills of people in poverty leading to removals of children into care. Now that same distrust was driving some health professionals to coerce mothers into birth control, sometimes without informed consent by carrying out a tubal ligation immediately following a delivery by caesarean section. The Fourth World Women's Charter stated: '[Women in poverty] demand the right to plan their families freely without threats and pressure from social and medical services or from public opinion. Their decision to limit the number of children they have must be their own choice, and not imposed on them because of their poverty and vulnerability.'[15]

In 1980, a second world conference on women was organised in Denmark. This time, Mary was the only one representing ATD. She wrote to Wresinski, comparing it to Mexico: 'Here, there's less "feminism" and more political activism. ... The situation of women in poverty risks being banished from the agenda.'[16] Although Mary was interested in the debates about colonialism, Zionism, and capitalism, she regretted that no connections were made between poverty in both the global North and the global South.

Her speech drove home points made in ATD's 1975 charter – adding the challenge of children's removals into care through this example:

© ATD Fourth World / Joseph Wresinski Centre

Phyllis is 38 and works as a full-time cleaner. She looks 50. She suffers from a chronic kidney ailment; however, she does not see her doctor often because, first, she is used to pain and discomfort and has a very low expectation of health. Second, she sees doctors as a threat to her family because they are sometimes the ones who involve social workers in removing children from their parents' custody. Although Phyllis lives with her youngest child, her five older children were taken away and brought up in children's homes. In those institutions, the notion of training and qualifications did not enter into her children's experience. The older girls were both married and had babies at 16 and 17 years. Phyllis' family has been dispersed. She has suffered particularly from her children's absence; even worse, they are inclined to blame her for depriving them of a chance at family life. Their situation is not exceptional. We calculate that between 4 and 5 percent of women in rich countries suffer this way.

Mary's speech went on to argue that women in poverty are excluded in three ways: She said:

1. They are excluded from the ideas flowing through society – ideas that give us our identity and strength, the conviction of our rightful place in the world, and of our contribution to equality, development, and peace.
2. These women are excluded from new living patterns. Development brings new standards of living and new standards to live up to. It is perfectly possible and lawful for a mother in West Germany to see her children taken away on the grounds that she is illiterate and cannot care adequately for them.
3. They are excluded from human rights. As we urge our governments to ratify the Convention on the Elimination of All Forms of Discrimination Against Women,[17] I plead that we take care; these rights must not become standards against which women will be judged. The woman who is not educated, not in good health, not able to make the contribution she would like, and still struggling against all odds to bring up her own children must not be condemned as useless and worthless. Solidarity to me means joining

> together to fight for the dignity of the poorest women, for their aspirations, for their liberation. In achieving theirs, we will achieve our own.[18]

Mary felt that a policy banning discrimination was not enough. She called for extending solidarity and respect to all women. Her speech convinced the conference to adopt a resolution put forward by ATD to ensure that all development projects take the needs of the poorest women into account; and also that government reports to the United Nations on women contain particular emphasis on progress made with regard to the poorest women.[19]

The third world conference on women was the climax of the UN Decade for Women. Held in 1985 in Nairobi, Kenya, with 12,000 participants from 157 countries, it was twice as big as the Mexico conference. Because others in ATD were more invested in events for the International Year of Youth, Mary was again ATD's sole representative.

Although most travel funding was reserved for women from the global South, Mary convinced UNESCO staff to fund her travel as someone 'concerned with the critical literacy issue'. Her housing was arranged at the University of Nairobi.[20] To prepare, Mary returned to interview many of the same women she had interviewed in 1975. This time, often their teenage daughters joined the conversations. She wrote a paper called 'Access of the Poorest Women to Education and Training'.

During the preparation, the British minister for foreign affairs invited Mary to collaborate with members of the Government delegation. Mary was shown an advance copy of the Government's response to the UN questionnaire on advances during the Women's Decade. Responding to the minister, Mary objected vehemently:

> I would like to express the extreme concern of ATD Fourth World:
> 1. that gains made have not benefited all women equally, and that women in the lowest socio-economic groups have benefited least of all;
> 2. that the real conditions of the most disadvantaged women and their future prospects are not made visible in the evaluations of women's progress, and that this means priority cannot be given to developing policies to improve their condition.

> In the attached note, I have drawn out priorities for the coming years, restricting my observations to the interrelated sectors of education, employment, and participation in public life, with a brief comment on health. In Nairobi, we will be asking delegations how their governments have progressed toward implementing the resolution put forward by ATD in Copenhagen. Can we count on you to support us in this question?[21]

The minister, Baroness Young of Farnworth, was won over and promised to support ATD's contribution in Nairobi. She also made copies of Mary's eight-page note for all the departments preparing the UK report for the UN.[22]

The gigantic Nairobi conference was later referred to as 'the birth of global feminism'. In Mary's report, she recounted:

> It was quite a logistical challenge to contribute to the government negotiations. Just being able to print, photocopy, and staple together documents meant racing clear across the city each time. To speak with diplomats, we had to catch them quite early or quite late in the day since formal negotiations filled their time. That said, every government read our proposals for the three amendments to the text on education. All the diplomats I spoke with agreed to support them, including those from Austria, Bulgaria, Egypt, Ghana, Ireland, Jamaica, the Philippines, Senegal, South Korea,

© ATD Fourth World / Joseph Wresinski Centre

Women's Conferences 213

© *ATD Fourth World / Joseph Wresinski Centre*

Tanzania, and the UK. (The French government could not support anyone, as their representative had a quarrel with the chair of the conference.[23])

In addition to lobbying, Mary convened a workshop on the question: 'What Future for Girls of the Most Impoverished Families?' Sixty workshop attendees, of eighteen nationalities, agreed to stay in touch with ATD.

On Mary's return to London, she began corresponding with those 60 women. Baroness Young asked Mary to help welcome delegations of women from Spain and Portugal visiting England. She was interviewed about the conference on the BBC and Radio 4. Following the Radio 4 broadcast, the vice president of Her Majesty's National Women's Commission told Mary: 'You answered questions brilliantly. Our membership has always been somewhat middle class. We would, however, very much like to represent a broader section of society in our membership and thus to extend membership to the "women of the Fourth World".' Mary agreed, but continued to address her Government with vehemence. To the Department of Health and Social Security, she wrote:

> We are quite concerned about risks for the most disadvantaged women and their families when policies intended for the health and well-being of all families are not very carefully monitored and difficulties evaluated. Every question relating to parental rights and responsibility is particularly delicate; so too is the question of free choice

in family planning. All of us have to face these questions based on the actual experience of very disadvantaged families, and in particular through two and sometimes three generations of the same families, whom I have followed personally.[24]

When asked to reflect on all three women's conferences, Mary wrote, in ATD's French national newsletter:

> Ten years ago, ATD brought together for the first time dozens of women in deep poverty from different countries. The voices in the room were shy and hesitant, and some women wept because they couldn't find the words to express themselves. At the same time, it was joyous, just because we knew that other women wanted to listen to us, even at the United Nations. So much has changed since then. So many women, men, and young people have learned to speak out, and have promised to overcome poverty together. We all set out to look for people who were still in the shadows to share with them our hopes and encourage one another to rise up together.
>
> The conference in Nairobi was also joyous, filled with song, dance, and growing friendships. Thousands of women looked back at a decade of fighting injustice and oppression and building solidarity. Their message was: 'We can no longer wait for development, equality, and peace to come to us. We must set out to make it all happen.'
>
> For us, as members of ATD, we will continue, as before, to be on the lookout for people who have been the most beaten down by life so that, all together, we can move forward. In the future, our granddaughters must each have a profession they are proud of, work that is worth their time, and a role in their communities and nations that enables them, and their brothers, husbands, and families to contribute to shaping a world of justice and peace. Despite the obstacles, we will go onward.[25]

Chapter 20

Travelling in Africa: 'She Missed the Memo!'

Between 1956 and 1975, 45 of Africa's 55 countries gained independence. This led to a huge influx of non-governmental organisations (NGOs) from the global North. Elisa and Philippe Hamel, a French couple based in Senegal for ATD Fourth World throughout the 1980s, recall:

> NGOs were all busy setting up new development projects. Very few emphasised the need to sit down with the people concerned, to think with them about the stages of the project and how to involve the weakest people, which would mean taking more time to get the project up and running. Overseas development agencies were focused solely on 'big projects'. At the time, it was all about concerts to benefit aid to Ethiopia. Everything had to go quickly. No one spoke about people living in desperate conditions every day because of long-term poverty. International aid was

Philippe and Elisa Hamel in Dakar in June 1984

© *ATD Fourth World / Joseph Wresinski Centre*

Mary, at left, joins the Hamels for the launch
of their project in Dakar.
Provided courtesy of Philippe Hamel

only focused on short-term catastrophes like famine and armed conflict.

In 1981, ATD Fourth World organised a seminar for participants from several French-speaking African countries. This led ATD to start a team in Senegal, not to run projects, but to connect the African seminar participants to one another, particularly in Burkina Faso, the Ivory Coast, and Mali. As relationships deepened, the focus was always on learning from those who were offering solidarity to people in the worst situations of poverty. The Hamels, who were responsible for this team, say: 'Père Joseph thought there should be a parallel but separate team for English-speaking Africa. He was very aware that there were big differences between French-speaking and English-speaking countries, partly because the ways they had been colonised were different.'[1] Their reflection is striking because today, if anything, the differences are even sharper. The *New York Times* reports: 'Support for [democracy] is declining in Africa, while approval of military rule is on the rise. ... That shift is happening much faster in former French colonies than in former British ones.'[2]

The Hamels' daughter Catherine tries to braid Mary's hair.

Provided courtesy of Susie Devins

Travelling in Africa: 'She Missed the Memo!'

It was Mary who set out to develop ATD's network in English-speaking Africa. To understand her rationale for this project, we first need to hear how she was reflecting on the direction of ATD at that time. Mary had been part of ATD for more than two decades, in France, the United States, and England. In 1983, in an open letter to other senior members of ATD's Volunteer Corps, she wrote about the material conditions of their work:

> When we began, nothing was easy, but our purpose was great; and the Volunteer Corps needed to demonstrate that

In London, members of ATD organised a large bon voyage party for the start of Mary's African responsibilities.
© *ATD Fourth World / Joseph Wresinski Centre*

Joseph Wresinski, at right, attended Mary's bon voyage party.
© *Isabelle Williams, ATD Fourth World / Joseph Wresinski Centre*

purpose. ... We had almost no means, but I was invited to work towards an ideal: to end injustice, cultivate hope, and appeal to others to make the same commitment. With no running water or electricity, we were awfully cold in the winter. We were never quite as hungry as the families; but the food in our mess hall reflected the emptiness of our donation box and the drunkenness of the cook. My stipend at the time was only five francs, and none of us could afford a car or a nice vacation.

We have always aimed to demonstrate our fundamental beliefs through the community of the Volunteer Corps. We argued everywhere: first among ourselves about how to live in a way that the families could be proud of; then with the families about refusing to accept that more dynamic families take advantage of the weakest ones. We argued with institutions that they should respect the families and support them with the means to live in dignity; and we fought with people from other backgrounds so they would change their mentality of hand-outs and instead treat the families like people with responsibilities. We did all this without the most basic means: of the language, of decent clothing, of knowledge, of political strategy, and even of diplomas. To defend the families' dignity and honour, little by little, we understood that we needed to train ourselves, to think, to read, to speak, to write, and to become true professionals to be able to represent and serve people in extreme poverty. Training has become part of our life.[3]

Her letter described the ways that the Volunteer Corps was gaining security. In 1962, conditions in Noisy-le-Grand were almost impossibly harsh. But twenty years later, the Volunteer Corps Association had become an independent charity with enough donations to ensure health care and pensions. Mary said:

This meant that even people from an insecure background or in fragile health would not face obstacles in joining the Volunteer Corps. This Corps has the responsibility of looking after our own. We have never abandoned a volunteer because they fell ill or were in an accident. Nor have any of

Me, at left, facilitating a computer workshop during
an ATD Street Library in Brooklyn
© ATD Fourth World / Joseph Wresinski Centre

us been obliged to deprive our children because of ATD. On the contrary, I've always felt a great understanding, and even indulgence, for each of us. This respect for all of us has allowed us to continue to choose freely whether to continue with ATD. I think this is what prevents us from becoming harsh fanatics. It ensures a sense of loving-kindness throughout ATD.[4]

When I joined ATD, in 1985, the team in New York City included Geneviève and Bruno Tardieu, a couple with a toddler and a newborn baby. They did live decently – earning only minimum wage but with support for health care costs, as well as community support of other Volunteer Corps members. At the same time, their family life reflected ATD's ethos. Their flat was in a deeply disadvantaged neighbourhood, not far from where ATD ran a Street Library project for children. To get a discount on rent, Geneviève spent a few hours each week assisting the building superintendent. Their toddler attended a daycare with sliding-scale discounts for low-income families. And their baby napped in the ATD office while her parents were engaged in deeply fulfilling work. Watching them combine parenting with working was part of what attracted me to the Volunteer Corps.

Later, I had three children of my own. After the first was born in Washington, we uprooted our little clan several times to join teams in France, New York, France again, Madagascar, and finally the UK when our youngest was 14. Despite this constant flux, and despite my passion for working long hours, they say they have not felt deprived by this upbringing. They grew up getting to know kids their age: some of whom were living in emergency housing shelters or in informal settlements alongside a massive rubbish tip; and others whose parents were embassy diplomats. When my oldest returned to the US for university, what shocked her was meeting young people who could *afford* travel – but chose to stay put because they enjoyed mixing only with people of similar backgrounds. Now she works as a clinical social worker serving vulnerable teenagers with serious mental illnesses.

Although the course is uncharted, I do think ATD has managed to find a balance: ensuring more security for us than Mary's first cohort had; while retaining an ethos of minimal salaries that do not change with our seniority or responsibilities. At the same time, when Mary says 'we argued ... among ourselves about how to live', that resonates for me because we constantly interrogate our way of living.

That question was on Mary's mind in 1982 when she asked other co-founders of ATD: 'Why do we feel so insecure? It seems to me that it's in the places where our teams have the most means of funding and opportunity that we have the hardest time achieving our goals. I think we're looking for something new.'[5] The following year, Mary connected this question to the global South:

> When our movement was small and young, and when our only resource was our determination, we defended the dignity of families in poverty by taking direct action: more or less punching and kicking to gain each little victory. Now we have matured into a movement that is articulate, that can write, that can organise extraordinary events. But I worry that having more means at our disposal might someday make us forget the kind of community we aimed to shape. What are our priorities in a world where people in poverty are being crushed, humiliated, and excluded more than ever before by technological progress? I'm glad that our Volunteer Corps is now starting from scratch in Africa, Asia, and Latin America. It is an opportunity to leave behind our security and credibility. Wherever we go,

Provided courtesy of Paul de St Croix

we can learn from others while continuing to bear witness to
the hope, honour, and dignity of the most excluded people.[6]

Unlike the majority of NGOs in the global North, Mary did not imagine that ATD had solutions to preach; she saw how much there was to learn from the global South. She also felt it was crucial to shake things up without letting newfound security lull us into a rut of renewing prior grants and continuing projects even after situations on the ground had changed. Jeanpierre Beyeler remembers that this was also Wresinski's concern: Originally, he made a point of developing our work in Europe, but in the 1980s, he decided to reach out, first to Guatemala and Haiti. Our work in France had gotten so big and rigid that he felt it was out of his control. We needed a fresh start. And we needed to go very slowly to avoid the mistake of 'exporting' a European approach. Hundreds of organisations were swooping in with their 4-wheel drive jeep development projects to fork out assistance – just like what had been happening in Noisy-le-Grand before Père Joseph arrived. Some members of ATD wanted to start big development projects too, engineering a new approach to agriculture or setting up craft workshops for sustainable jobs; but Père Joseph said: 'No, we must join the pace of people in each country'. This was Mary's strength: building relationships with people on the ground without imposing anything, and knowing how to hear and listen to their own ideas about how to create change.[7]

Mary had seen the shortcomings of big development projects during her year in New York when she reflected: 'The methods of action of Mobilization For Youth are very interesting; but most could never work in a shanty town. In Noisy-le-Grand, residents are too cut off from normal neighbourhoods that have schools, churches, cafes, and so on. Also, no one feels rooted in a shanty town.'[8]

By the 1980s, ATD's European and American projects were run in more organised neighbourhoods, similar to those where MFY had worked. But when Mary travelled to Africa – in 1983 to South Africa, Lesotho, Senegal, Ghana, and Togo, and in 1984 to Kenya, Uganda, and Burkina Faso – some people she met reminded her of Noisy-le-Grand because they too were often cut off. While Africa has communities with strong traditions of mutual support, some people slip through gaps in these networks and struggle alone with homelessness. This was often the legacy of colonialism which ripped apart established social supports for its own ends. Mary's

Salome Muigai
Provided courtesy of Salome Muigai

drive to let everyone know what inspired her during these visits led her to launch a newsletter in 1983 called the 'Letter to Friends in Africa'. Today, it has broadened into a worldwide network, with a newsletter called 'Letter to Friends Around the World' and a website: OvercomingPoverty.org.[9]

In 1992, thinking about how ATD might harmonise its approach internationally, she said: 'The idea is not to flatten out our vision of the world. Rather it will be an opportunity to return to the source of our inspiration: empty-handed, ineffective, and therefore humiliated and silent, dependent on others.'[10]

In reading about Mary's African travels, I wondered how she was perceived there. Salome Muigai enlightened me. I first encountered Salome in 1987. Then a teacher in a school for girls considered 'delinquent',[11] she travelled from Nairobi to Paris to take part in a

The 1987 UNESCO seminar organised by Mary
© *ATD Fourth World / Joseph Wresinski Centre*

seminar organised by Mary at UNESCO. My role was logistics, such as meeting participants at train stations to help them navigate the Metro to reach the homes of ATD friends hosting them. I wrote to a friend at the time:

> The most interesting parts of the seminar were outside the conference room when people got to know each other and talked about the strength that gets them through rough spots and pushes them further. Mary and Jeanpierre's exhibit of all the participants' messages looked damned professional in the UNESCO lobby. It's really something to see such sharp presentations – and then to take a closer look and realise that the words are those of people the world isn't used to listening to.

Although Salome worked closely with ATD in the 1980s, when I travelled to Kenya in 2015, she had fallen out of touch. Some internet sleuthing helped me discover her on LinkedIn. Her reply to my message was immediate and gracious: 'The tenets of ATD remain close to my heart and I welcome the chance to renew contact.' A few weeks later, in her beautiful home, she warmly hosted a wonderful evening for my group of five: three members of ATD Tanzania, a Rwandan from ATD's African regional team, and me. With some of Salome's family and friends, we were a group of ten. Before the meal, Salome invited us to join hands and circle the table while she led us in a traditional prayer – to which she added acknowledgements to LinkedIn for our reconnection, a juxtaposition spanning centuries that delighted me.

During and since that visit, Salome and I spoke several times about Mary. When I asked her what she thought of Mary as a white European travelling in Kenya, she said:

> I first met Mary at the World Conference in Nairobi. She was talking about poverty in Europe and North America and I was attracted to her because in Kenya we didn't know there was poverty over there. Most white people only talk about poverty in Africa. Her awareness of poverty was a big contrast to all the other white people I had met. They were always surprised to discover poverty. Travelling to Kenya was the first time they had the experience of seeing poverty. Mary was also the first white person I met whose

whiteness meant nothing to her. Other white people in Africa found privilege as white people. But Mary missed the memo! When Mary was in Kenya, she would act like an African too. If she was invited somewhere, she wanted to bring others along. I really think she was colour-blind. She just had a total unawareness of colour. I haven't had that experience with anyone else before or since. Mary prepared us for humanity.

Mary was actually well aware of the more typical disdain of white people towards Africa. On one visit to Kenya, she wrote about three white European women living there:

It's clear they've stayed in their own circle and don't appreciate Kenyans. They don't read the local press, and some of their remarks about the country verged on being offensive. I asked them to start reading the local press to send us clippings about important issues here. That will help them educate themselves about how people here make efforts to overcome poverty. I had a heavy heart to see the opulence they live in and their lack of curiosity about how people around them live.[12]

While Mary was not interested in using whiteness to gain privilege, her childhood gave her particular awareness of the realities of white Europeans in Africa. Her father was born in South Africa – but before coming to that, let's take a brief detour through their engrossing family history, because Mary's upbringing was steeped in these stories.

The Rabagliatis descend from Mary's great-great-grandfather, Giacomo Gaetano Francesco Rabagliati, who was born in Genoa, Italy, in 1797, the son of a tailor. At the end of the Napoleonic Wars, he took part in a failed 1821 liberal insurrection – which led to his exile. Next, he joined the liberal constitutionalists in Spain until his capture in 1823 by the French who imprisoned him in Montpellier.[13] Upon release, he moved to Scotland as a political refugee. Advertising his services in the *Kelso Mail* and *New Scotsman* newspapers,[14] he then is said to have gone to Abbotsford, the home of the novelist Sir Walter Scott, in order to teach him Italian.[15]

Giacomo's eldest son, Andrea Carlo Francisco, qualified as a medical practitioner and left Scotland to become house surgeon at Bradford

Mary's grandparents, Julia and Andretto,
on Isipingo Beach, South Africa

Provided courtesy of Duncan Rabagliati

Mary's grandfather,
Andretto Rabagliati

*Provided courtesy
of Duncan Rabagliati*

Royal Infirmary. His son, Andrea Francis Honeyman Rabagliati, known as Andretto, followed his father into medicine, becoming an expert on tropical diseases. In 1908 he married Julia Bright. Because of Andretto's tropical expertise and because 'his Italian last name was a deterrent marketing-wise', the couple set sail for Australia,[16] where Andretto purchased a far-flung rural practice with horseback the only mode of transport. But with Andretto often away on house calls, it fell to Julia to rub down the horses and muck out the stable. After their daughter Helen was born, Julia told Andretto she refused to care for both the livestock and the family. This led them to Durban, South Africa, where Mary's father Alexander (called Sandy) was born in 1914.[17] When the First World War broke out, Andretto was posted to France and East Africa.[18] After the war, Andretto returned to Durban but also travelled regularly to Nairobi. In both places, he set up nursing-home clinics. The family's youngest child, Francis, was born in 1920.

In 1929, when Sandy was 15, his father's health deteriorated rapidly, and his parents travelled to Yorkshire for medical attention. Andretto was admitted to a Leeds nursing home where he died shortly

Travelling in Africa: 'She Missed the Memo!'

Julia with her children, Helen, Francis and Sandy (at right)
Provided courtesy of Duncan Rabagliati

afterwards at age 51. Not wanting to return to Africa without him, Julia and the children remained in Great Britain. A few years later, Helen married Charles Gaitskell and they moved to Kenya, where they raised their four children on a farm.

Mary's Uncle Francis also ended up in Kenya. In the Second World War, he served in the RAF Coastal Command and lost one eye when his plane was shot down. With his vision damaged, he was no longer assigned to combat but to flights ferrying personnel or equipment, travelling to Canada, the United States, Egypt, Sicily, India, and Kenya. On one occasion, he flew Emperor Haile Selassie from Kenya to Ethiopia. After the war, he obtained a degree in agriculture, settled in Kenya, and worked for the agriculture department advising farmers. In 1954 he married Anne Marshall, a farm manager in Kenya, and they had four children.[19]

Although Mary did not travel to Africa until she was 31, her childhood included regular visits from her cousins who were growing up in Kenya. One of Helen's daughters, Julia Moss, recalls, 'Mary was a little older than me and I looked up to her. Mary really impressed me with her piano playing. We had a lot of fun together.' Julia also explains how her immediate family experienced the upheavals in Kenya. During the 1950s, the Kenya Land and Freedom Army waged war against the British army and European colonists. Julia calls these events – often referred to as the 'Mau Mau Uprising' – the Kenyan War of Independence. She explains:

> Our father avoided [being targeted in] attacks on whites, partly because he was well-liked, but also because a lifelong Kenyan friend working as his servant warned him that the Mau Mau might compel this friend to lead them into our home. Our father helped his friend to leave the area and to set up a butchery in another part of the country so that he would not have to deal with this pressure.[20]

With Mary's family so thoroughly entwined with Kenya and South Africa, I imagine that before travelling there she must have thought quite deeply about the post-colonial legacy, including the cruel ways that Western governments and individuals plundered the continent for wealth and power. As Salome remembers, Mary wanted people in Africa to know about poverty in the global North. During my visit to Salome's home, one of her friends, responding to what I said about poverty in the UK declared: 'Here in Kenya, we finally threw off the iron fist of the British Empire – but it is still crushing the poor in Britain!'

In 1983, Mary wrote about what she wanted ATD to learn from Africa:

> We have much to learn from volunteers who have gone before us: from the Africans who have chosen to stay with their families, their villages, and their people. [On our journey] we met dedicated teachers who, without books, paper or pencils, often without benches for their pupils, continue to instil learning into the minds of children who laugh at them because the children can earn more money than their teachers in the streets and markets. We found nurses and doctors, imprisoned within the institutions of the sick, the 'mad' and the 'bad', with neither equipment nor medicine nor sufficient food, accused by fellow citizens of exploiting or profiting from those in their care. We saw social workers turning their backs on jobs with higher social and financial rewards in order to care for those who count for no one.
>
> We encountered 'volunteering' by ordinary people: schoolchildren who work enthusiastically to help build their school, to cultivate the fields, to help prepare their own food, to sweep out their classrooms; mothers who – to pay for food and their children's school fees – leave their families

at dawn to join long queues for public transport to go work, returning only after dark; and men who teach their trade of shoemaking, metalwork or crop tending to young people in order to ensure their dignity and independence. ... [They are] living and working in conditions which can only make us profoundly respectful. Each one spoke of their hopes. For, faced with the most disastrous or difficult economic, political and agricultural conditions, we never met an African who did not say to us: 'I believe in my country and in my people.'[21]

Salome Muigai was one of the volunteers Mary learned from. A childhood bout with polio left Salome with lifelong disability and a deep understanding of exclusion. As a member of the Constitution of Kenya Review Commission in 2001-05, she took the lead to ensure that all forms of diversity would be protected in the new bill of rights. In our 2023 conversation, she spoke about how she sees Kenya's relationship with the global North. Like Mpho Ndebele in Lesotho, Salome began with the value of African traditions that were undermined by colonisation:

> At the London School of Economics where I studied gender, they taught us about community organising. But in Kenya, that's exactly what white people told us *not* to do. In our original traditions, men and women had the same value, and communities were about support. There was care for all: taking food to others, and receiving it in return, loaning dowries. But once children were put in schools with Western education, people's attitudes changed in just a generation or two. That worked well for the colonisers. They needed people to do certain jobs. Even our food was better before colonisation. We used to make natural honey, our cows were fed on grass, and we ate yams for breakfast. The colonisers told Kenyans that was not 'civilised' and we should eat bread and use agricultural chemicals. Now people see that organic food is better. That's what we used to have. But after a hundred years of Western education, now it's very hard to convince someone who has a degree to go back home. Many Kenyans speak English better than their parents' native language. Colonial issues connect to everything. Now we need to adapt our education system to our present needs.

Salome also spoke about the context of most international work in Kenya. She regrets that most development projects focus on treating the symptoms of poverty – ill health, hunger, and children not in school – instead of addressing root causes. When Salome visited ATD in Europe, she was shocked to discover white people who were living in the streets:

> The reality was so different from the way the white community presents itself in Africa. If there is a government-to-government visit, you are only taken to see what they are proud to show. I was shocked to discover differences in terms of education. I thought all Europeans were educated, but Mary introduced me to families where four generations hadn't finished school. I visited ATD's Herblay project where families living in caravans were supported to move into a house. They needed support and training to use an electric kettle. I discovered that even health insurance wasn't for everybody in Europe; some were left out of the safety net. In the 1980s this was a real cultural shock. ATD brought me into Europe through the back door to see things you weren't supposed to see.

Following a visit to the Hamels in Dakar, Mary formulated her thoughts about privilege, whether linked to whiteness or wealth:

Philippe Hamel, centre, at an exhibition about progressive Senegalese voluntary work in 1986

© *Bruno Masurel, ATD Fourth World / Joseph Wresinski Centre*

Elisa and Philippe told us they often have the impression that they are not contributing to ATD. Empty-handed in a culture where they have to learn everything, they oblige us to think about our activism, our ambition to succeed, our desire to be out in front. They remind us where our true place should be – at the back, waiting even before asking questions, searching in the dark with only our senses to guide us.[22]

Because the Hamels had heard others say 'only Catholic charity work is organised', they decided to avoid relationships with Christian missionaries, knowing that their approach was a Western one. Instead, they got to know working-class Muslims to understand existing

Philppe and Elisa running an educational project for 'talibé' children
Provided courtesy of Philippe Hamel

Elisa Hamel at right
Provided courtesy of Philippe Hamel

solidarities in the community. This was very different from most of the NGOs around them. Mary said:

> They have renounced the temptation of more reassuring social relationships which are likely to lead them astray from their mission. To live in a country where one has neither family nor personal friends, nor even teammates who can help and dissipate your doubts and discouragement: this is a choice that we have the responsibility to recognise and reflect on as Volunteer Corps members. For such choices are no different from those we have long been confronted with in order to seek out people in the deepest poverty.[23]

Mary wanted ATD's work in Africa to remain in the spirit of its earliest work in Noisy-le-Grand: discreetly alongside people in the worst situations and anyone supporting them. Neccy and David Kikaya, a couple who met Mary on one of her visits to Kenya, confirmed: 'The trouble with voluntary organisations is their preoccupation with the pride of having answers and remedies. Little do we realise that actually the answers are there in the village. What is lacking is guidance. It is in this light that we were glad to be introduced to your needed approach of first seeking out the poorest and then building from there.'[24]

On one journey to Nairobi, Mary and her teammate Susie Devins were hosted by Mary's cousins. Susie remembers: 'We took the bus into town regularly, but from time to time, Mary's relatives loaned us their jeep. That's when we saw a giraffe nibbling on acacia thorn trees.'[25] Their purpose was visiting people who were part of the 'Forum on Overcoming Poverty' network of correspondence. Susie explains:

> Postal letters remained the mainstay of the Forum. By visiting, we realised how precious the letters were when people told us what the cost of a stamp or writing paper represented to them. Many Forum members aren't acting in a professional capacity to meet the poorest; they're like Mrs R., a cleaner who takes in ironing for other people and who knows what it is not to have what you need.[26]

Looking back today, the Hamels say of Mary:

Philippe (right) watches Henry Mendy (centre) carry out interviews of excluded young people in the south of Senegal (Casamance).
© Catherine Morel, ATD Fourth World / Joseph Wresinski Centre

Philippe (with camera) films interviews in Casamance to prepare International Youth Year.
© Catherine Morel, ATD Fourth World / Joseph Wresinski Centre

In countries where poverty is so widespread, she really wanted to understand the differences between poverty and extreme poverty. Mary also wanted to learn how people can become excluded in African communities. And she knew well that overcoming poverty requires us to act together with others, so she wanted to get to know the people standing by those who were rejected by society. Mary agreed with us that it was crucial to encourage these efforts because of the lack of means and support

Provided courtesy of Paul de St Croix

available for it. There's a saying in Senegal: 'If you help nine of the poor, you will become the tenth.' We wanted to push back against that.

Mary's approach was very gradual, making no comparisons, but simply noticing who in the shadows was supporting people in deep poverty. In this context, Mary questioned people widely to learn from the know-how developed in each community to build solidarity in the face of misery. Her 20 years with ATD had honed her awareness of how much there was to learn, everywhere, and of the fact that constant learning together was the way to nourish this movement for social justice.

Chapter 21

A Meaningful Foundation for Friendship in Sierra Leone

In 1984, Mary returned to West Africa. This time, she and Philippe Hamel visited Freetown, Sierra Leone, on the shores of one of the largest deep-water harbours, with a dramatic mountain backdrop. During the rainy season, thunder echoes among the peaks like a lion's roar – hence the country's name because *Sierra Leone* means 'lion mountain'. They aimed to meet and learn from people facing deep poverty, and also from their allies.

On this visit, Mary met Judith Grandi, co-founder of the Sierra Leone Society for the Welfare of the Aged. Judith helped people who

© *ATD Fourth World / Joseph Wresinski Centre*

had lost connections to community networks and were completely destitute. Mary was so struck by this work that she wrote about it for ATD Fourth World's internal reflective practice newsletter:

> I would like to tell the remarkable story of tenacious involvement in a place where human beings have been abandoned by their families; a story at once public and silent because, as in all places of most squalid misery, it is very difficult to open doors without wounding any further the sensibilities of the population and the authorities.

Judith Grandi, right, at the gates of the home for the incurably sick with one of the residents, James
Provided courtesy of Judith Grandi

Judith is English. When her husband was posted to Freetown for his work, Judith regularly visited three older women in her parish. Judith then left the country for five years. On her return, she discovered that one of these women, Annie Johnson, age 91, had been admitted to a home. Mary wrote:

Dating from colonial days, the home was built for the incurably sick; then occupied by incapacitated war veterans. Eventually it became a dumping ground for all types of marginalised persons whom a new law prevented from being on the streets. At the time, they refused to let Judith in without ministry authorisation. She insisted, saying that she was Annie's only family. Finally they let her in without authorisation. Judith has always been able to open even the most tightly closed doors, simply by refusing to go away. And this without any support from anywhere during four years.

That first day, Judith found Annie dying on the floor without anyone to wash or feed her. Around her were ninety men and women, equally abandoned, sick or suffering from various mental illnesses, human relations severed to the point where many were no longer identified by any name.

Judith recalls: 'In such a tight-knit society, it seemed almost worse than in more fragmented societies that no one knew their names. But Annie had outlived her children and everyone else in her family.'[1] Others in the home had not had children, or had disabilities that people feared. In the seven wards, some occupants had a straw mattress on an iron bedstead, while others did not even have a cloth to sleep on. The wash-rooms were not working. Mary's article continued: 'The atmosphere is silent, except when somebody speaks or cries out. For three weeks, Judith went there every day to look after Annie until she died. After her, the other residents asked, "Who will look after us when we die?" And so it was that her involvement with all the others began.'

Judith said: 'I began by speaking to each one of them to understand what they wanted of me. They were hoping for a relationship based on giving; but I explained that I had nothing to give except friendship.' That friendship began with asking their names, or choosing a name for those whose name had been forgotten. Judith visited regularly, sometimes offering mints, sugar, or medicine. She was also able to get some very ill residents hospitalised.

At the same time, she tried to encourage and give what help she could to the staff, given practically no means or supplies to carry out their work. ... At the kitchen, a little shed made of cement blocks, thick with smoke, the two cooks told her they were having serious problems with their eyes and chest because of the smoke.

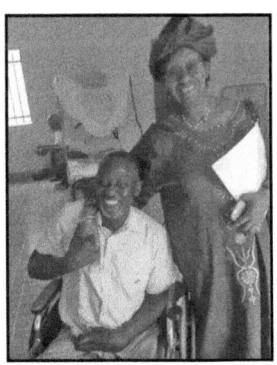

Gladys Jusu Sheriff, visiting the home

Provided courtesy of Judith Grandi

As a foreigner, Judith was distrusted by the administration, who did not want 'outside interference'. She agreed to keep the ministry informed of everything she did, but she refused to give up. Then a crisis struck: because of administration debts, suppliers refused to deliver any more food to the home. 'For five days, Judith took food to all those who were too frail or sick to go out to beg. Then, knowing that it couldn't go on, in desperation she turned to a friend to ask what to do.' This friend, Gladys Jusu Sheriff, a university librarian, consulted her husband, the country's Vice President. He advised setting up an association, which Gladys would co-sponsor. Judith insisted on every member of the association personally visiting residents in the home to get to know them as individuals. She said:

> I wanted them to understand that it isn't simply a question of giving money. I always believed that once they really got to know the people, they would not be able to forget them. ... [In this home], family links no longer exist. When solitude is too great, one even loses the sense of self and so one cannot relate to others. When I asked the name of each one and always referred to the person by that name to others, little by little a kind of network was built up: a man who is just a little bit sick is still able to assist someone worse off than himself. Now sometimes a friend in the next bed tells me someone's problem if he can't speak for himself. I try to encourage this solidarity. I think that the sense of others comes back when one realises that they have needs.

The association organised fundraising events, media broadcasts, and a day of prayer observed in all the city's churches and mosques. Judith witnessed a transformation, with increased respect given to the residents. Mary wrote:

> Our own visit to the home left no doubt that Judith knew each individual personally, knew each story and knew each pain, either visible or hidden, on the bodies or in the hearts of these men and women. ... Judith worries sometimes about the future ... [but] on the day of our departure, Judith was just on her way back triumphantly from the printers with the new statutes of the association. Her victory was to have succeeded in retaining the words 'social justice' in the text, which more cautious members had tried to delete.
>
> We left with the sense of having met a remarkable person whose encounter with suffering enabled her to go

beyond the bounds of the possible, in opening doors closed by others stronger and more powerful than herself. Our meeting was good fortune because wherever there is misery and wherever men and women are engaged in refusing to accept it, we want to be there to learn and to share.[2]

For me, one of the details that stands out in this powerful story is the cement-block kitchen 'thick with smoke [causing] serious problems with the eyes and chest' of the two cooks. When my family moved to Madagascar in 2005, many neighbours cooked outdoors in a pot balanced atop three stones. The charcoal aroma reminded me pleasantly of popcorn. But that smoke was lethal. For one of ATD's big events, I spent the day cooking for about 80 people with the help of my 15-year-old and two of her American School classmates: the daughters of a North African ambassador and of a wealthy Asian businessman. It was only their strong friendship with my daughter that led them to join me for a household chore that neither had any experience with. Valiantly, they joined us in chopping vegetables with dull knives; but when the oven smouldered too thickly, all of us took turns fleeing the kitchen to gasp for air, tears streaming down our cheeks. The World Health Organisation reports 6.7 million premature deaths a year caused by air pollution – including due to cooking with coal.[3] That sooty kitchen in Sierra Leone was just one of so many obstacles to people's well-being; and yet against all odds, Judith navigated the barriers, nurturing friendship and solidarity.

Judith, second from left, representing ATD Fourth World at a conference in Freetown

Provided courtesy of Judith Grandi

Mary remained in close touch with Judith and involved her in a 1987 UNESCO conference. To find potential contributors, Judith travelled up-country to a remote village. There, she interviewed Mustapha Yanka-Kanu, a disabled blacksmith who had set up an apprenticeship scheme for children with polio. Next, Mary asked her to interview the Revd Michael Samura, in Freetown. Judith recalls:

> He had grown up in the streets and was running a wonderful project for street kids. But the paper he originally sent to ATD was full of professional jargon because he wanted to be respected as a manager, not a former street kid himself. That's fair, of course; but Mary was looking for a more passionate and personal tone. So I interviewed him for a paper he called: 'Extreme Poverty and the Breakdown of Family Life: The Street-Boys of Sierra Leone.'[4]

After Mary's death, Judith fell out of touch with ATD. But in 2017, Judith noticed on Twitter a video I posted about Mary. She got in touch, and renewed her involvement with ATD, supporting us with several projects, including this book. Being about Mary's age, Judith helped me piece things back into the context of their generation.

Mary got to know Michael Samura during her 1984 visit to Sierra Leone's Boys' Society, founded for the 'rehabilitation of delinquent, rejected, or underprivileged boys'. Working mainly with children living in the streets, they ran urban residential centres, and a rural agricultural training centre. Mary wrote:

> Michael was a remarkable man, constantly on the move both physically and mentally. Having grown up living on the streets of Freetown, he knew everything there was to know about the dangers and temptations that children and young people are exposed to. The residential centres offered them shelter and a place to be listened to. But Michael also insisted on rebuilding links with their families, whatever the difficulty that led them to leave home. A true educator, he focused on what he called 'the inner heart' of his work: developing strong relationships with each boy and gradually offering small responsibilities to demonstrate trust. Once they could handle those responsibilities, Michael then developed their leadership

skills by encouraging them to pass on confidence to others. The boys described Michael as a driving force who motivated them to go further. Their eyes lit up during his inspired talks as he convinced them how hard they must work to develop the best in themselves. Knowing Michael's life story, they hung on his every word.

Mary's encounter with Michael sparked a plan to mark International Youth Year (1985) with a joint project. To prepare, Mary returned to Sierra Leone in March. She explained the challenges to Susie Devins on 25 March 1985:

> Dear Susie,
> … The representative of UNICEF seems to think that our volunteers will not be able to cope with the hardships of daily living here. I'm also working on the ATD UK annual report and the odd translation because it's urgent and no one else has time. In London, two different house fires killed two different babies our team knows. A third family has been in and out of court for the last four years and is about to lose custody of their two youngest children. It's very difficult to work sufficiently on the UK report while also preparing pages for UNICEF that have to be diplomatic so as not to embarrass the Sierra Leonean government but without being empty either (help!). The International Youth Conference in Geneva is creeping up fast, and our UK event for 'April Tools Day' has hardly begun to be organised (scream scream!). The mind boggles – but I suppose it's the same everywhere.
> Love to all, Mary[5]

I recognise Mary's frenetic pace: firing on all cylinders, keeping her standards high for a wide variety of challenges, with little help.

That December Mary returned to Freetown for a three-week workcamp, this time with Susie and seven other ATD members. They were of five nationalities and a variety of manual skills and professional experiences. The trip was funded by months of activities: auctioning donated clothing; selling raffle tickets; applying to the New England War Tax Resistance, which preferred supporting non-profit work to paying for military weapons.[6] The goal was to work with the Boys'

The goal of the work-camp was to improve the Boys'
Society agricultural training centre.
© ATD Fourth World / Joseph Wresinski Centre

Society to improve their agricultural training centre, which needed a gazebo for group discussions, a shed for the electric generator, and fencing to protect plants. Susie recalls:

> The boys were considered at risk in having left their families to try to survive in the streets doing odd jobs. They had no real skills. ... The director spent a lot of time trying to get to know their families, and to help them return home without being a financial burden on their family.[7] ... We didn't want to sit around talking: we wanted to do something with our hands, something that would leave the Boy's Society with something they wanted. But first we had to learn local building methods. For example, to make cement we

Michael Samura is second from left in the back row;
Susie Devins is second from left in the front row.
© ATD Fourth World / Joseph Wresinski Centre

collected lumps of laterite rock and banged them together to make sand. Then we hauled water from the well, which was exhausting in that heat and humidity. It brought home to us the struggle that many – usually children – go through every day to get water for their families.[8]

The ATD group included talented artists, so each day also included times for sketching, as well as playing games and singing. Jeanpierre Beyeler, who did not travel with Mary but is a painter, says: 'Mary wanted artists in the group because we're pragmatic. She never prioritised office work over manual work. She saw the point of both and always valued people who knew how to work with their hands.'[9] Mary explained:

> We took artists because drawing a scene or the face of someone in front of our eyes was one way of remembering and admiring what was beautiful. In our own countries, some of the families in poverty whom we knew well wanted to send the boys messages, so we made an album of their words and photographs and showed it to the boys.

The visitors from ATD Fourth World perform a skit
for the Boys' Society.
© *Mary Rabagliati, ATD Fourth World / Joseph Wresinski Centre*

'Drawing a scene was one way of remembering and admiring what
was beautiful.'
© *ATD Fourth World / Joseph Wresinski Centre*

During our work camp, we took lots of photos and used some to create another album to offer to the Boys' Society. We celebrated Christmas with them; and for New Year's we danced together at a moonlight picnic. We also made up a song to thank the boys and all those who welcomed us.

At the time, many non-profit organisations founded in Europe were funding development projects in Africa with a traditional top-down approach. European donors chose priorities and implementation methods while local communities had very little say. Mary's approach was the reverse. François Jomini, a young Swiss artist who travelled with Mary, says:

> This trip reversed my European perspective. At the time, I was sensitive to 'Third World' trends, and the prevailing idea of unilateral aid to establish economic justice. But ATD's angle of approach was new: you don't go to an African country first and foremost to help or deliver supplies but to *learn*. There was nothing routine about this work-camp; it was a creation of Mary's. When I looked for contributions to finance our trip from my friends and family, I had a hard time convincing some of them that the approach needed was not setting up a new project, but immersing ourselves in a new reality.

Fabienne Klein, a French artist who also participated, recalls:

Fabienne Klein
© *ATD Fourth World /
Joseph Wresinski Centre*

> We wanted to show that not all white people were rich donors. Our goal was rolling up our sleeves to help the boys with their own project. Mary thought the best way to show them our commitment to fighting poverty and exclusion in our own countries would be to create things together, learning from one another. We made sketches – of ourselves as well – as a way of learning to understand everyone around us. Every time we held a drawing or puppet-making workshop, large crowds of children joined us. Our focus on art was another way of challenging the usual practices from 'rich' countries.[10]

Although all of the ATD work-camp participants prepared their participation with people in poverty in their own countries, several were almost completely new to ATD. François found that meaningful as well:

> Mary took it upon herself to welcome into the delegation a young person like me, who wasn't yet very clear about just

how involved I wanted to be with ATD, and who could be off the mark. She took risks, took people as they were. Without making a big deal, she knew how to shake us up. For me, this experience spoke volumes because it enabled me to rub shoulders with ATD's Volunteer Corps, individuals united in a powerful adventure, one as meticulously prepared as a high-mountain expedition with a great deal of intelligence and friendship. I was amazed to see the high standards, fellowship, respect, trust, and humour that connected more senior participants with those of us who were inexperienced.

About the artistic dimension of this project, François said:

> I felt a little embarrassed that my school English was insufficient for conversation. Mary encouraged me to express myself through drawing, and to consider it seriously as a tool for action. If all I had were my eyes, then my art had to be as useful as the written and spoken word. I felt very respected for the simple fact of being able to sketch a few portraits of children and young people. Mary also encouraged me to pick up my guitar (despite me being a very mediocre musician), and I remember a moment that helped weld the group together just as our trip began. We composed a blues song to introduce ourselves to the Boys Club.
>
> This artistic dimension was one way we communicated. By including a cultural dimension, and not just a practical service, Mary put this project on a human level of people looking one another in the eyes. Mary made a point of ensuring that we had our bearings in order to get to know people in as sincere and honest a way as possible.

When Wresinski saw the group off, he told them: 'Know your place and never forget how much more they know than you do.' This lesson sank in the first time that François and Fabienne started drawing in the street. Suddenly a huge crowd gathered, clearly upset. Fabienne told François, 'Stop drawing, we'd better leave. If we were in a housing project in France, they'd already have punched you!' Then someone in the crowd explained that it was customary to meet with the local chief and brought them to his home. Once they introduced themselves

Karen A. Hart is at left;
François Jomini is in the back row, at right.
© *ATD Fourth World / Joseph Wresinski Centre*

and explained what they were doing, the chief authorised it and there were no problems. They had learned that before any kind of project, developing a relationship is the best starting point.

Karen A. Hart was an American painter in the group. She describes the adventure of their homeward travel:

> Leaving Sierra Leone, we got stuck at the airport. They got a better price for our tickets! The airport was not modern in the least and we were most bummed about the prospect of camping out there. Departing planes were only once a day, and getting tickets was questionable – they said they did not have any foreseeable open tickets. Anyway Mary just shook her head and said, 'Uh, no'. She disappeared and arranged for us to spend the night in a luxury hotel – all comped – and fly home the next day. I called her 'the Blade' cause she cut right through bullshit efficiently and with no fanfare. She had our backs and was a great leader.[11]

So Mary was not only a Rottweiler but also 'the Blade'!

One priority on Mary's mind was the role played in Sierra Leone by international institutions like those she met at the 1975 and 1980 world conferences on women organised by the United Nations. Philippe introduced her to the UNICEF representative there because of the relationship he had built in Senegal, where he recalls:

The UNICEF representative, Mr Audat, became a good friend of ATD. He agreed for ATD to look at a draft of their annual report because he wanted to know if their projects were reaching the poorest and making real change. He invited me to meet him in his office, where he let me in through a back door as he was coming back after a tennis game. He asked me to talk about concrete situations that he was not hearing about from his staff. For example, it made no sense that UNICEF stated that a vaccination campaign had reached '96% of children'. The truth is that this statistic corresponded only to places where health workers visited; while certain shanty-towns weren't counted because professionals didn't set foot there. So when Mary and I travelled to Sierra Leone, Mr Audat put us in touch with UNICEF there, which even offered us use of a car and driver so we could travel outside of Freetown to assess the state of children's schooling in certain villages.

Hearing about the remote places not counted in statistics that Mary and Philippe would have struggled to visit without support reminds me of transportation challenges in Madagascar. ATD's practice is to live, work, and travel as economically as possible, so our team in Madagascar – like most ATD teams – had no car. This made travelling outside the capital a major undertaking. Reaching a village in the far north, for example, could take a week, including a hike of several days over uncharted hills. In the rainy season, this trek involves slogging through mud and having adults in good physical health to carry luggage and small children. Even where roads exist, paving can be irregular at best. Any long journey is also likely to be broken up by police stopping vehicles to request 'tips' – called corruption by some, but a bit like a toll system to support badly paid civil servants.

Even in the capital, I was often startled by the pace of journeys, such as when a driver pulled our full jitney bus over to watch him have an open-air piss. Most taxis were ramshackle in the extreme with no seat belts. I rode in one where the wind-shield wipers did not work, so the driver occasionally stopped to swipe at the rain with a sodden rag. In another, when we turned a corner, the faulty back door swung open – with my 3-year-old daughter about to fall out of the moving car! Thank God, my oldest, 15 at the time, was next to her and had the lightning reflex to yank her back to the safety of a lap with no harm done. The driver seemed completely unfazed, pausing only a moment before barrelling ahead while I remained a basket case of nerves, agonising over our close shave with catastrophe.

So I imagine that UNICEF's well-maintained car made a significant difference to Mary's journey. She also read several UNICEF reports and wrote a 20-page paper for UNICEF. After noting her appreciation for some aspects of their work, she raised a long series of questions pushing them to go further in trying to reach children in the worst situations of poverty.

Overall, however, Mary's priority was not policy, but getting to know people working at the grass-roots. Philippe says: 'Before even thinking about advocacy, Mary felt we needed to take things one step at a time, to learn on the ground before taking a public stance. She wanted ATD to be recognised not just for having "ideas", but for our sustained action.'

About Sierra Leone, Mary concluded:

> We were wholly committed to it in our hearts; and we found the same commitment among the boys and members of the Boys' Society. We met people who cared about the children, loved their country, and wanted us to love their country too. We were welcomed into homes, which gave us a further opportunity to learn through the hearts and eyes of Sierra Leoneans themselves about the efforts being made to benefit the very poorest people. All this made it the most meaningful foundation for friendship. It taught us how to go about establishing a long-term presence elsewhere in

© ATD Fourth World / Joseph Wresinski Centre

Africa. We returned home certain that the Boys' Society and ATD Fourth World will continue to be a source of strength for each other.

Mary's original approach combined creative and practical endeavours, and attention to policy-making, along with intergenerational mutual learning drawing on the intelligence of people in poverty in Sierra Leone and Europe. She was designing a more equitable way to think about partnership between the global North and South.

Chapter 22

Palestine, Israel, and Sunrise over Mount Tabor: A Fractured and Disharmonious Land

By 1963, the year after Mary first set foot in Noisy-le-Grand, Wresinski knew he could count on her for the long haul. But he worried about burn-out among volunteers, most of whom fled the camp's squalor after a few weeks. To sustain Mary's motivation, Wresinski proposed a holiday for her in the Middle East with two other volunteers. The others had both joined ATD Fourth World at the very beginning, in 1957.

One was Francine Didisheim, who quit her job as a Belgian journalist to coordinate Wresinski's correspondence and act as his deputy. The other was a French woman, Bernadette Cornuau, an executive secretary at L'Oréal. Initially, she spent Sundays visiting Noisy-le-Grand to run children's activities. Although interested in Wresinski's work, she hesitated to join him full time because he was a priest while she was a diehard atheist. In 1961, he convinced her to help him found a Volunteer Corps for people of any belief or philosophy. Bernadette left L'Oréal to move into a trailer in La Campa, another shanty town on the outskirts of Paris, where she pioneered projects similar to those in Noisy-le-Grand. For meetings, Bernadette commuted from La Campa to Noisy-le-Grand using a beat-up Citroën 2CV. It was this car that Wresinski suggested the three women use for their holiday. Francine recalled how surprising it was for Wresinski to send the three of them away for so long: 'It was crazy of Père Joseph to send us here when we have so little money to get by on. But to him it was a necessary extravagance. He wants to widen our minds outside the camp. To build a Volunteer Corps that can keep its sanity, each of us needs to take a step back sometimes to get a sense of meaning.'[1]

Bernadette agreed:

> You could count on one hand the long-term volunteers. We couldn't be spared: I was working day and night, and so were Mary and Francine. But Père Joseph insisted we get a break from feeling closed off from society. He loved the beauty of Israel and was also deeply moved by the lives of Palestinians and the fact that they had lost their villages and were living in camps. He also wanted us to learn from the energy of nation-building: How were Israelis trying to create an ideal country? What compromises did they make? What might kibbutz community life suggest for us?[2]

So it was to be a working holiday – with useful purposes as well as well-deserved relaxation. Mary and Bernadette drove in the Citroën 2CV, while Francine, who had even less free time, joined them later by aeroplane. Crossing northern Italy, Mary and Bernadette drove to Venice, then boarded a ferry boat for the week-long sea crossing to Haifa. Bernadette said:

> I was sick as a dog on the ferry. Meanwhile, Mary was in fine form, dancing and making tons of friends. Many passengers were migrating to Israel, sight unseen, uprooting their lives to move to a place where everything had yet to be created. But arriving in Haifa, it struck us that the immigrants seemed to be categorised. Europeans mainly headed to the fertile Galilee in the north, where relatives or friends would welcome them. However, immigrants from other Middle Eastern countries or North Africa usually knew no one; they were sent south to tiny desert towns like Dimona and Beer-Sheva.[3]

By the time they arrived, they had spent most of their money on youth hostels in Italy. Left with a very small food budget, they ate mostly watermelons and tomatoes – except when they were invited to meals. Francine, who joined them in Tel Aviv, said:

> I was struck by the unsightliness of Tel Aviv, built in haste with shoddy materials. Harsh sunlight makes all the buildings look parched for fresh paint. Haifa is beautiful; there, however, we discovered a true shanty town. We've seen camps for triaging newcomers that reminded us of Noisy-le-Grand in their uniformity and sorrow. But the Haifa shanty town was different because it has been built by its own residents with whimsical variety under eucalyptus trees. We were welcomed by an older German immigrant. We communicated using her German and my Yiddish. She offered water and insisted on washing our feet in a shower improvised from a bucket of water on a raised plank and tipped by pulling a cord. She doesn't like Israeli rules, which is why she lives in the shanty town 'like all us pariahs'. Her greatest fear is being deported back to Germany where she has no one left. We also met a Jewish social worker from Morocco. She is baffled by the hatred between Jews and Arabs because she spent her childhood playing with Moroccan Muslims who were her best friends.

At left, Francine de la Gorce (née Didisheim) with Mary in Noisy-le-Grand

© *ATD Fourth World / Joseph Wresinski Centre*

Their itinerary included Nazareth, where they were befriended by Arabs who welcomed them overnight, insisting the guests sleep in their beds. They also visited several Jewish kibbutzim. They were struck by the challenges of growing crops on arid land while developing a new framework for family and community life. Bernadette wrote:

> In thinking of Noisy-le-Grand, I wondered: how can community life among us volunteers give families in poverty the strength it gives us? In the kibbutzim, we met people of strong ideals – but they are a kind of elite. ... The best part

of our trip was admiring the beauty of the landscape, and appreciating the hospitality shown by people in poverty.

Much of the hospitality they received was thanks to Mary's foresight on the ferry crossing when she collected addresses, which led to invitations across the country. One night, however, they had no invitation, as Francine described:

> We travelled to Mount Tabor to watch the magnificent sunrise. The Franciscan monastery has the perfect bird's-eye view; but meeting the brothers made me ashamed to have converted to Catholicism. When we arrived at sunset, a short monk took us on a tour of the church. When he learned that Bernadette is a non-believer, he got the notion to bless her. That exasperated Bernadette – and made Mary and me laugh. Then we told him we could not afford to rent a room as pilgrims do. We asked permission to lay our sleeping bags in the monastery courtyard. His superior gave a firm 'no'. So we slept outside, to the shock of the Arab labourers employed by the monastery. They consider hospitality a sacred duty and could not understand why we were put outdoors. Bernadette and Mary slept in the car, their feet sticking out the windows. I spent most of the night fighting off mosquitoes and worrying about snakes before finally I found a peaceful spot among the stones. The next morning I saw that I had slept beneath a stone engraved to mark the transfiguration of Christ.
>
> The short monk, embarrassed at having turned us out, invited us for breakfast with his community. That gave us the chance to sign the monastery guest book. As our home address, we wrote, 'Noisy-le-Grand Camp for the *Homeless*', heavily underlining the last word!

Bernadette added that sleeping outside had given them an advantage. 'Despite the long night, that morning, we had the ideal vantage point for the sunrise. The pilgrims sleeping at the monastery missed it because they came outside fifteen minutes late!' Mary agreed, writing to her brother: 'What a fabulous holiday! The sunrise over Mount Tabor is magnificent – the Christians know how to choose their sites!'[4]

Travelling onward from Mount Tabor, abruptly their journey took a startling turn. Francine explained:

> We decided to continue on a small road. Our map showed it running along the northern border of Israel before circling back down to the south. Was our map outdated or did we read it wrong? In any case, by 9 a.m. we found ourselves under the aim of Lebanese machine guns! Apparently the Israeli border guards were in an adjacent field and didn't notice us pass their checkpoint. ... It's true we passed signs marked 'Attention, Border Ahead'. But we never saw a border officer until, suddenly, we were stopped by Lebanese soldiers aiming at our wheels. Then Israeli guards ran up behind us shouting: 'Come back!' But it was too late. The Lebanese had us surrounded. And we were being given two contradictory orders. If we tried to turn and the Lebanese shot our tyres, what then? So we followed their orders.
>
> We were brought to an officer who told us to sit down. But immediately Mary stood up again saying: 'Sir, I want to go to the toilet.' We all looked at one another, a little afraid. Then the officer solemnly took a pass from his drawer and gave it to Mary, who was taken to the toilet by a soldier (armed, of course). This is Mary – a second earlier, the atmosphere was warlike, but now we were again treated like human beings.
>
> The officer interrogated us for a long time. He seemed nice and definitely liked French people. But Bernadette, the only French one among us, aroused suspicion because of her atheism. In this country, you are supposed to be Christian, Jewish, or Muslim. Still worse, Bernadette's passport had an old stamp from Leeds. The Lebanese confused British Leeds with Lydda, the Tel Aviv airport, and thought she had visited Israel more often than she admitted.

Suspicions worsened when soldiers discovered their voluminous trove of notes, and photos. Were they spies? Following the border questioning, a jeep-full of armed soldiers escorted them to Beirut for further cross-examination. The detour allowed them to admire beautiful villages from the road; however there was no question of stopping to visit.

The soldiers found Bernadette's atheism particularly troubling because the car was registered in her name. They were separated, and her interrogation lasted the longest. She recounted:

> Around 3 p.m., with me still under heavy questioning, Mary burst in and announced, 'I'm starving!' That changed the atmosphere completely. The officer cross-examining me invited us to dine in the officers' mess hall overlooking the Mediterranean. Over lunch, our conversation grew so relaxed that finally he believed that we met at a camp for the homeless in France. He even decided to make a donation to ATD Fourth World! We were quite proud of having brought him around to our way of seeing things.

Francine narrated the conclusion to this misadventure:

> Around sunset, we were handed over to the Israeli border guards by a UN officer who laughed, saying: 'It's usually goats or camels who wander carelessly over the border!' But the Israeli guards took the situation seriously and proceeded to interrogate us. They expected us to say we had been mistreated. But we were not – except that soldiers had confiscated or destroyed our photos, journals, and even our road maps and tourist guides.
>   That evening, we visited a German couple who had hosted us before. We laughed about our capture by soldiers; but our light-heartedness upset them. Sternly, they said that Israel and Lebanon were on the brink of war and this incident was serious. It's true that armed conflict threatens. However, as outsiders, it was hard for us to understand hatreds that made people interpret the slightest misunderstanding as a crime.
>   In any case, this trip made Mary, Bernadette, and me fast friends. It was crazy for Père Joseph to send us away with no one to replace us at work. But it was a really wonderful idea!

The three women long cherished their memories of this special voyage – and, as Wresinski hoped, all remained dedicated to ATD for the rest of their lives.

Mary's second voyage to the Middle East came a quarter century later. The invitation grew out of a 1972 UN conference on poverty where Dr Jona Rosenfeld, a social work professor at the Hebrew University in Jerusalem, was a presenter. He recalled:

> The meeting included young researchers who, like me, gathered to report on our studies of poverty.... Unexpectedly, after each presentation, a priest – who turned out to be Joseph Wresinski, the founder of ATD Fourth World – got up to say he had grown up in poverty and wanted to say something about his own experiences of poverty. Whenever he got up, he was shushed and had to sit down again, without any of the budding researchers willing to hear his contribution. I was upset by the way he had been treated. When the session finished, I joined him for lunch. ... Almost before I sat down, he told me, totally out of the blue: 'Families living in extreme poverty have something to contribute to the world.' I had no idea what he meant. It took me several decades of work and contemplation to truly understand what this very puzzling but meaningful statement was all about. It was an idea which I, as social worker and as a teacher of social work, had never thought about before. Since then, this idea has never left me.[5]

Over the decades that followed, Jona became an ally of ATD who wrote several books about our work.

Dr Jona Rosenfeld, third from right
© *ATD Fourth World / Joseph Wresinski Centre*

In 1987, ATD met another prominent authority from Jerusalem: Dr Mustafa Barghouti, president and founder of the Union of Palestinian Medical Relief Committees. On a visit to Europe, the French ministry for foreign affairs noted his concern about poverty and encouraged him to visit ATD's international centre. Based at Maqased Hospital in the early 1980s, Barghouti founded Medical Relief because so many of his patients needed to be rehospitalised soon after being discharged. He began making house calls to refugee camps and rural villages to learn more about conditions undermining health. Determined to reverse the situation, he recruited other doctors to support long-term care through outreach, mobile clinics, and primary care centres. Although the doctors were at first accused of political agitation, their work became widely accepted and grew into a network serving the entire West Bank and Gaza. Barghouti called ATD 'unique because it does not aim to find solutions for families but rather to reintegrate them into society'.

Wresinski planned a trip to learn from both Palestinians and Israelis fighting poverty – but he died before this was possible. So in 1989, Mary and Bernadette returned together to the land they explored decades earlier. This time there was no question of a holiday; as senior members of a movement that had just lost its founder, it was an important moment for them to continue developing the relationships that underpin ATD's work. Jona asked them to meet with social workers 'to show them your way of being and acting. You have a new approach that has an impact by improving the lives of the very most

Bernadette Cornuau, at left
© *ATD Fourth World / Joseph Wresinski Centre*

disadvantaged families and populations – the ones whom no one else knows what to do with.'

One goal of this journey was to make known two publications:

- *The Wresinski Report: Chronic Poverty and Lack of Basic Security*, was the translation of Wresinski's 1987 blueprint for government policy, written when he was a member of the French national Economic and Social Council. The report explained generational poverty and laid out detailed policies for overcoming it.
- The second publication – *Emergence from Extreme Poverty*, by Jona – applied a social work analysis to explain how ATD's approach made it possible for people in deep poverty to take on civic responsibilities and become full partners in the life of their communities. In presenting this book, Jona said: 'I was lucky to meet Joseph Wresinski. By creating ATD's archives, he and Mary have been telling the history of families who had no voice in history. The most important thing is that ATD's volunteers allow these families to move them. Professional distance is the worst enemy of meaningful social work.'[6]

In addition to book talks, Mary and Bernadette visited a 'second-chance school' for young people who had dropped out. This was where Jona's wife, Ruti, worked. Mary was struck by the teachers' creativity, motivation, and high qualifications.

Mary and Bernadette also reconnected with Dina Wardi, who spent a month in France with ATD in 1988. Dina introduced them to her colleagues saying: 'It is clear that ATD's one goal is to liberate the poorest and most excluded families from poverty. As a professional, I find very interesting how ATD creates a real partnership between these families and the Volunteer Corps.'

During a conference of the Israeli Association of Social Workers, Mary and Bernadette ran a workshop on human rights and the World Day for Overcoming Poverty. Jona explained to a journalist why he invited them:

> We have many social interventions, but they haven't prevented very poor people from growing up in our midst – and social workers don't know how to handle them. There

is an illusion that everyone here is taken care of, and that makes it difficult for people to listen to what some of the poor are saying. The insult that poverty is still in our midst is very hard for us to take.[7]

Mary was impressed by several of the social workers they met: 'Some of them are exceptional. They go above and beyond what their profession calls for. They take risks to go places that others avoid and to do what no one else dares to.'[8] However, the dialogue at the book talks often frustrated her. She wrote:

> Although we did make positive connections – and also sold a number of both the books we were promoting – the atmosphere around us was too admiring. When people admire you, they keep you at a distance. They don't feel personally engaged by what you are saying. Most of the social workers we met doubt that they could ever reproduce our approach. They have excellent university qualifications; and yet they feel helpless faced with the families in the worst situations of poverty.
>
> The approach they were taught is to try to solve problem after problem. Wresinski showed us a more effective way forward: to understand that all people in poverty share a fundamental connection with one another; to foster this connection by bringing them together to speak out; and by acting in solidarity with their common struggle for a better future.

As they travelled across the country, Mary turned her attention to the conflict between Palestine and Israel. She wrote:

> The atmosphere here reminds me of South Africa or Northern Ireland, where everything is focused on the conflict, and where we must ask many questions to understand the history. ... It's a real opportunity to discover a country from the bottom up, by meeting people who live in deep poverty. With them, it becomes clear how urgent it is to make peace, and how nonsensical territorial and political conflicts can be. It is also with them that we discover how some people

make daily efforts to live peacefully with others. There are many peace movements here; but do any of them begin with people in the worst situations of poverty?[9]

Bernadette added:

> The president of a peace movement here told us, 'We don't have time for the poor now.' And yet it's easy to imagine what will become of children in poverty if they remain abandoned today. Already, their health is damaged by polluted water. … I'm most struck that, on both sides of the conflict, people are ready to pay a heavy price for their sense of identity. It is vital to them to identify as part of the Palestinian people, or as part of the Jewish people. For me, this confirms the importance of ATD's work with families in poverty to be able to gain their own sense of identity and belonging, whatever their nationality.[10]

Their journey continued to the West Bank, the Gaza Strip, Bedouin encampments in Israel, and elsewhere. In Mary's report, she wrote:

> They say that when God made the world, He put nine tenths of all the beauty into Jerusalem, leaving only one tenth for the rest. It's true, this city – which we missed seeing in 1963 – is a marvel, not only for its holy places, but for its hills and stone architecture. We were also enchanted by the Negev Desert, the ancient fortification of Masada, and the Golan Heights in the north-east, on the borders of Lebanon, Syria, and Jordan. Everything is in bloom now, and the plant life is a feast for the eyes.

Since 1963, industrialised agriculture had exploded, with massive irrigation systems to defy the desert droughts. Mary also noted growing unemployment and tightened public budgets. These changes fed a national debate about whether Israel had become an 'industrialised' country or remained a 'developing' one. Travelling to Jenin in the West Bank, Mary saw Palestinians subjected to economic penalties and home searches. She wrote:

© ATD Fourth World / Joseph Wresinski Centre

Palestinians are deprived of freedom. Mosques have been closed to avoid large gatherings of people. The schools have been closed for sixteen months now, compromising children's entire future. In small villages, they have nothing to do but herd livestock. In one West Bank town of about two thousand people, water access is limited to a few cisterns for domestic use. Not a drop of water is allowed to be used for gardening or farming. Almost 80 percent of the town's residents are unemployed. Because gardening is not allowed, they really have no way at all to occupy their time. Most young people move away before the age of 30, and the few who stay often spend their whole lives in debt.

She also observed frequent but unannounced curfews trapping people in close quarters all day long and also for weeks on end, shutting down both shops and schools while military patrols enforced that everyone remained locked inside. When Mary was travelling to the village of Zababdeh, she needed to drive through Jenin during a curfew period. At the military roadblock, she was told to turn back. A Palestinian passenger in the car, Sister Hortense, did not dare speak to the Israeli soldiers. But when Mary explained that they were going to visit Father Manuel Musallam, a Christian priest 15 km past Jenin, she was waved through – unlike most other vehicles that were turned back, including one that was driving the Latin Patriarch to Jerusalem to seek medical care. Mary wrote:

It is hard to describe how shockingly eerie the curfew atmosphere was. For a good five minutes we drove through a city of 130,000 people without hearing a single noise or seeing a single person. Even the windows were deserted. It seemed like a ghost town. Later, it was explained to us that during curfews people can be shot for showing themselves, even at a window. What must it feel like for children and families cooped up together in these conditions, and in such heat? People we met in the West Bank spoke of frustration with the curfews; but we were even more struck to hear them say that their very identity has been lost because their native village, or that of their parents or grandparents, has been renamed or no longer exists.

In Zababdeh, Fr Musallam told Mary that the only children allowed to attend school were kindergarteners. His church ran a creative kindergarten with a project for families to record details of their heritage as a way of maintaining their sense of identity despite their dislocation.

Entering Gaza also proved challenging. People warned Mary that it might be impossible, and when she got to the checkpoint, she was told that no civilians could enter. However, Mary – as usual! – argued. She not only asked the soldier to ask his commanding officer, but she followed him into the mess tent, surprising all the soldiers who were having breakfast. The superior officer explained that no journalists were allowed into Gaza; so once Mary convinced him that they were not journalists, she and Bernadette were let through. Mary wrote:

> The total disharmony of Gaza City is extreme. Many roads are damaged. Most buildings are run down. Several have been demolished with explosives by the military, and the rubble left in place. We also saw curfews in Gaza, sometimes locking in the residents of just one street at a time. Most striking is the graffiti everywhere. The military paints over it with huge streaks of black. Entire streets have had every wall plastered with vast waves of black to prevent any future graffiti, which looks sinister indeed.

Once in Gaza, Mary learned from her host about her nursing in a paediatric clinic, where she saw many infants suffering from diarrhoea, which she considered caused by the psychological stress of frequent military aggression and constant fear weighing on the whole family. Mary also heard about a 12-year-old boy beaten by soldiers so badly that he was hospitalised, because he had continued bicycling when told to stop. Mary wrote:

> Hearing this helped us understand a Palestinian family we met in East Jerusalem. There, schools remain open, but the parents told me they are too afraid of trouble to let their 10 and 8-year-old sons attend. Soldiers are posted on their way to and from school, and the parents worry about violence. Their mother told us, 'I don't know how to explain anything about politics. But I know that Israelis too fear for their children. For all of us, it's unbearable. We carry our suffering deep inside.'
>
> In the camps, the jumble of shacks in various stages of construction make it look like a shanty-town. The worst place we visited was the sprawling Al-Shati refugee camp. The children here are growing up in a Kafkaesque universe. That's reflected in their drawings, which show the horrors of daily life. The young people have no memory of anything different. They have never even set foot in Jerusalem. One woman explained that they are no longer allowed to walk along the seaside. She described the atmosphere as one of 'unending mourning'.

At the same time, Mary was impressed with Gazans strong sense of solidarity and mutual help. Teenage girls in particular were active in people's committees where they made sure neighbours could access food, clothing, and health care. They visited hospital patients and prisoners, and also home-schooled children. 'We saw one school that is half empty, but that does manage to continue teaching some children by keeping them well hidden from view of the military. The families we visited certainly live in poverty, but it seemed to us that the strong current of neighbourhood solidarity protects them from feeling completely abandoned.' Back in Israel, Mary met some people involved in Jewish-Arab peace initiatives. For instance, Jona's wife Ruti was part of the Women in Black movement launched in 1988 to protest the human rights abuses of Palestinians.

She also met Jewish Israelis living in poverty. Despite social protection policies, some could not manage to access these benefits, and some felt stigmatised by them. Those who were already in debt lost access to benefit payments for their children. As Mary and Bernadette had observed on their 1963 ferry trip, immigrants from places like North Africa, Libya, Ethiopia, Syria, or Iraq were more likely than European immigrants to be living in the most dangerous zones where armed conflict was a constant risk and where there was scant employment or access to public services.

> Some immigrants still recall that on their arrival they were driven in trucks from the seaport directly to uninhabited places in the desert where they were given nothing but tents and tools to start their new life. The next generations in these 'development towns' live in crowded housing projects where drug abuse and violence are rampant and life is an uphill battle. Another sign of exclusion is that, although military service is required of all young people, some are rejected for being illiterate, or excused because of an 'unstable' family situation.

Mary visited several nomadic Arab Bedouin families. Here, too, there were differences, with some living in beautiful tents and welcoming many guests, while others were quite isolated in the desert, struggling to meet their basic needs:

> They may even be ostracised by other Bedouins, as happened to one family whose son was accused of a crime. One family, whose ancestors came to Israel from the Sudan two hundred years ago, were enslaved at the time. Today, they continue to use a name which means 'slaves'. Even more striking is the fact that they are unable to detail their family's history. Traditionally, it is a point of pride for Bedouins to be able to name their 'seven fathers' by reciting seven generations of their genealogy. Those who cannot do so feel ashamed.

Mary and Bernadette travelled with photos of families in poverty in the UK and France. In the desert town of Dimona – a place with shuttered industries, high unemployment, and a dwindling population – one father grew distraught looking at their album. He said, 'I've been out of work for months now. I'm afraid that we'll end up as badly off as they are.' His wife added, 'We have too many worries. This torments me all day long.' Mary commented:

> Discovering how painful life is for this family renewed our sense of connection to all families who, despite their suffering, find ways to keep going and even to make us welcome in their lives. In the north, Atlit is another of these 'development towns' founded specifically to house the immigrants with the least education or resources. This kind of social engineering ensures that entire cities are completely disadvantaged culturally and economically, with no openings for more dynamic residents to invest in the whole community.

Throughout Israel, Mary met young people who – like the teenage girls in Gaza – helped out wherever they could. Some volunteered to spend a few years living as a group on very little money in underdeveloped zones to foster local solidarity. One such group in Atlit had jumped into many tasks: running children's activities, fixing wiring, helping teenagers job-hunt. Mary was struck that they received no training or opportunities to reflect with others about poverty. One of the young people told her, 'At first, I came thinking I would show people how to live better. But I've realised that these families have things to teach me too.' A similar youth project in Beit She'an on the border of Jordan had an approach that Mary described as having 'no pretension to do-gooding'. Located in the most run-down housing amid rampant drug traffic, arguments, noise, and begging, the young people looked for jobs like gardening, housework, or waiting tables. Pooling their earnings, they aimed to contribute to a sense of community. Mary reflected:

> Neither youth group speaks explicitly about people in the worst situations of poverty; however, it seemed to us that this concern is part of a national spirit of solidarity behind their projects. These young people are trying to live up to a powerful ideal; however society has not been able to come together to overcome poverty and protect the rights of all. Even the Little Sisters of Jesus have split into two communities: one

© ATD Fourth World / Joseph Wresinski Centre

for Jews, the other for Arabs. Young Israelis and young Palestinians believe in the same ideals of freedom, justice, and peace. All aspire to own land and to feel secure in their identity. They want all children to be safe, to be able to learn, and to have the same chances in life. They could all join forces as part of the same generation, ready to transform the world; and yet the political situation here causes them to hate one another, to lash out, to kill one another. Everyone here is terribly afraid that the country could descend into a civil war like Lebanon's.

And yet, there is more here than hatred, fear, and war. We met many people, both Palestinians and Jews, who are searching for peace and trying to keep hope alive against all odds. Being here and seeing how terribly disharmonious life is in Gaza has made us even more keenly aware of how vital it is for all people to be able to have harmony and beauty in their lives.

Mary's first trip to the Middle East was part of Wresinski's plan to prevent burn-out and to keep his most reliable team members motivated. The observations of her and her companions are not only a fascinating historical record; they also draw clear lines and parallels into the present. In a place deeply riven by conflict and disharmony, Mary sought out people who were doing their utmost to promote social justice. As ever, she would try to bring what she learned through these encounters into furthering the cause of overcoming deep poverty.

Part VI

Forging Legacies

Chapter 23

Upheaval

Mary's plan was eventually to leave ATD Fourth World's international centre in France and move to Nairobi to set up an English-speaking network similar to the one the Hamels were running from Dakar. She enrolled in a course to learn Swahili and applied to a secretarial training programme in Kenya with the idea that finding a local job would make it possible for her to move there. She arranged with the All African Conference of Churches to be able to share their post office box and office space.[1]

In 1983 however, Mary was diagnosed with the cancer that claimed her life nine years later. Anneke van Elderen says, 'That fear was living in her.' During the Sierra Leone work-camp, Niek Tweehuijsen, one of the participants, recalls: 'One day, Mary was rushing with us to an appointment when suddenly she collapsed in the middle of the street. She hardly missed a beat, but we were very worried because she never held back. She just kept running around, meeting as many people as she could. She had an incredible temperament and capacity for work.'[2] Fabienne Klein, who also remembers that day, adds: 'I think she tried to hide her exhaustion as much as possible.' Karen A. Hart says: 'Mary was solidly brave with little fuss

Niek Tweehuijsen (left), during the Sierra Leone work-camp

© ATD Fourth World / Joseph Wresinski Centre

about it. I was at the hospital when she got wheeled into surgery the first time. Still brave.'

I first met Mary in 1986, the year after that work-camp. On arriving at the international centre for training, I was assigned to live in the same group house as Mary. Although she began chemotherapy a few months later, I agree with Fabienne: in front of me, she carried on as best she could. Though we couldn't help but glimpse the terrible toll of the disease, she made herculean efforts to spread joy. One evening, Mary saw that I was stressed out from frenetic overwork and promptly decided that we should head for Paris, an hour away. She swept me into a cosy bistro where people hand-rolled cigarettes while carrying on full-throated arguments about politics and literature. Mary kept me laughing all evening and treated me to French onion soup, its lacy drapery of melted cheese giving way to broth made sweet with caramelisation.

Instead of moving permanently to Nairobi, Mary remained at ATD's international centre near reliable health care and lifelong friends. But in between medical treatments, she continued to advance ATD's work in Africa, namely by organising the 1987 UNESCO seminar. Michèle Gérardin was a housemate of Mary's and mine. Like me, she was newly joining ATD's Volunteer Corps. Her main responsibility was corresponding with teachers and children for our Tapori Children's Network. However, having previously worked as a nurse, at home she used her professional skills to support Mary through chemo. Michèle recalls:

Michèle Gérardin
© *Jeanpierre Beyeler, ATD Fourth World / Joseph Wresinski Centre*

> Mary didn't want to give up on anything: not her life, her work, or her health. She tried everything – but without actually following through on any of it. She started a macrobiotic diet, then the Kousmine Method –

I remember that one: it promised to cure cancer if you gave up booze, red meat, full fat, and all processed foods.

> – but next thing you know, she'd be in a restaurant ordering wine and steak! She didn't really accept the idea of chemotherapy, so she refused to stop working even when she had another round of treatments. Then she tried unblocking her chakras, but she didn't stick very long with that either.[3]

Mary in June 1992, five months before her death
© *Pierre Klein*

Susie explains: 'Instead of working together for and with Mary, the chemo people and the alternative medicine people pooh-poohed each other's methods, which was frustrating.'

Michèle became close friends with Mary and felt committed to remaining nearby to help with laundry, cooking, and lots of healthcare paperwork. But Mary considered it selfish to keep Michèle nearby instead of letting her discover new horizons. Only at Mary's absolute insistence did Michèle finally move reluctantly to the Indian Ocean island of Mauritius, where ATD was just starting up.

When Mary was no longer up to travelling, she remained a guide and counsellor for others. When Michael Samura asked her advice about expanding the Boys' Society skills-training project, she worried that young people trained to repair typewriters were slowly losing out as offices switched to word processors. She responded:

> Bravo for this project – but be careful about the participation of the most disadvantaged. All the youth served, and particularly them, should have the chance to get on top of the economy and not stay beneath it. Do more to describe and evaluate how the Boys' Society carries out its objectives

so others can learn and thereby benefit more children and youth.[4]

Answering a letter from Michèle, she wrote:

> I'm glad you're getting to know people doing something meaningful, sometimes with no resources other than themselves. That's the idea of the Forum: around the world, people work miracles out of nothing. How lucky we are to seek them out and pool our experiences with theirs. Even though our efforts are small, together we are building a worldwide movement. Investing in people is the most important.[5]

In Europe and North America, Mary often asked people about the worst situations of poverty and how community efforts left some people behind. She explained to Michèle how she later adapted:

> In Kenya, I started to see what people refused to accept. I understood that you cannot ask directly. (Still worse, depending on the local language, it can sound as though we are looking for the 'weakest' people.) Instead, we can ask: 'In poverty, how do people defend their dignity?' and 'Who is supporting people in deep poverty?' It's important not to force anything. ... Personally, I think the greatest opportunity is travel. This allows us to learn, reflect, and question ourselves. But we must take care not to turn into researchers looking to put others under a microscope. You need to find the right approach for meeting different people so that each of them can be on equal footing with you to decide how to tell you about what they do.[6]

While Mary never put others under a microscope, I think her reflection about the Volunteer Corps deepened over the years. Wresinski aimed for Volunteer Corps members to live in harmony to model for others peaceful relations with neighbours. In an open letter to other senior Volunteer Corps members, Mary reflected:

> I've never found team life easy because we aim to fight on the side of families others exclude, families we ourselves may

> struggle to accept. It is demanding to change the hearts and priorities of everyone, beginning with ourselves. For me, the Volunteer Corps remains as difficult as when I started. And yet I consider our living together very important because it's where we learn: the continuous personal transformation that each of us needs, and which takes place through shared daily life. This allows young people to experience the exacting nature of our commitment. It is equally important for older ones, like myself, not to stagnate or to shut ourselves off with work responsibilities. Welcoming new people brings us back to the world and to people in poverty so that we never become impervious.[7]

In the Noisy-le-Grand camp, all volunteers lived crammed together, wedged into bunk beds with scant privacy. When I joined ATD, however, there was enough space in its international centre for someone of Mary's seniority to have her own studio flat as some of her peers did. This made it all the more striking that she chose to live alongside several of us newly arrived interns, even as she grappled with cancer. I'm touched to realise that she imposed this on herself to avoid 'stagnating', despite how hard she found team life.

Before joining ATD, I spent four years at my college newspaper, *The Cornell Daily Sun*. For the second two years, I was an editor responsible for training and managing newer reporters. I did my best to motivate them – which meant that if I wanted to gripe about staff spats, I vented only to friends outside of *The Sun* staff. A few months after meeting Mary, I once asked if she found it hard to live with so many of us who were just starting out for fear that we would not understand the context of things she might want to complain about. Her dumbfounded reaction told me that I had touched a nerve. That's when I promised that if she ever wanted to harangue against a teammate – or all of ATD – I would take it with a grain of salt. Her belief in spending time with newer people to avoid shutting oneself off has taken root in me. If I spend too long interacting only with my closest long-term peers, I get impatient and hunt for people who have never heard of ATD or simply start to chat with those who are fairly new to our work.

In a speech to fellow senior Volunteer Corps members about our 'unity', I see Mary's realism about the challenges:

© Luc Prisset, ATD Fourth World / Joseph Wresinski Centre

> There were confrontations that could have divided the Volunteer Corps; but despite everything, we've remained united. ... It's very important that we don't hide behind stirring words or good intentions such as 'the poorest transform us' or 'the most excluded people are our common reference'. No one is here to judge the sincerity of those words; but we need to tell each other how they affect our lives.[8]

Mary considered it important to 'stick it out' alongside people in the worst poverty:

> as a challenge to society as a whole, to ourselves, and to the families who were our full partners from the beginning. ... They ask us to be honest about our limits and honest with ourselves about things we may not want to hear. ... Our unity is not easy. We are constantly shaken up. The poorer people are, the more they may upend our plans and disturb the things we thought we could rely on. This leads us to constant confrontations and self-doubt – which we find umpteen ways to avoid. For all of us, these are hard issues to discuss with our teammates. ... I'll end by quoting Père Joseph about the connection between the unity of the Volunteer Corps and the unity of people in poverty: 'Families need the friendship that unites us in order to believe that tomorrow they too will be able to show others the love in their hearts despite the poverty that continually snuffs out their attempts to show it.'[9]

Chapter 24

Dissonance and the Black Forest

Joseph Wresinski died in 1988, just after marking ATD Fourth World's 30th anniversary. In the following decade, ATD spiralled into attempts to perpetuate his legacy in ways that made many young people flee. Mary, who seemed eternally young and always connected with young people, did her utmost to steer ATD towards a more constructive approach.

For eight years, she had been part of a small group of 'Co-Founders' of ATD convened

Mary, with Joseph Wresinski
© ATD Fourth World /
Joseph Wresinski Centre

by Wresinski.[1] These twelve people all joined him early on and had leading roles. The group's first meeting took place in 1980 in south-west Germany at the home of Mary's teammate Erika van Weldt, who was dying of cancer. This location, in the Black Forest Mountains, led others in ATD to later refer to them as the 'Black Forest Group'. Erika's family lived in Bierbronnen, a tiny farming village of picturesque gabled roofs. Jeanpierre Beyeler, another of the group's participants, says: 'Each of us saw in the group what we wanted to see. Wresinski never created any structure for it. He simply wanted to think with us informally. It was only after his death in 1988 that we began to have a more formal structure as "the Black Forest Group".[2]

The main question Wresinski hoped to resolve with this group was ATD's future leadership. Inviting Mary to Bierbronnen, he wrote: 'This group will think about the perspectives of our movement for the twenty years to come.'[3] As the founder, he was consulted about virtually all decisions. But in 1980, he envisioned stepping away from this daily stewardship at the international centre in order to move to the global South, some place where slow postal mail and expensive telephone rates would make communication difficult.

Most members of ATD trusted Wresinski's judgement because of his childhood in abject poverty and his vision of a worldwide movement encouraging people to 'take justice to heart'. In Mary's words: 'He gave meaning to whatever we did. Families in poverty trusted him. It wasn't peaceful; they argued with him all the time. But people felt that his ideas were sound ones that could push people to achieve more than they thought they could.'[4]

At that first meeting, it was challenging for most of the Black Forest Group to imagine new leadership. They admired Wresinski and relied on him for security. Mary, however, felt differently: 'From the time that each of us has a certain amount of experience, we're not always wondering what Père Joseph would do in our shoes. Personally, I feel quite free.'[5] At the same time, she connected her sense of freedom

The Black Forest Group, from left: Bernadette Cornuau, Huguette Bossot Redegeld, Hélène von Burg Beyeler, Alwine de Vos van Steenwijk, Gabrielle Erpicum, Francine de la Gorce, Mary, Eugène Notermans, Jeanpierre Beyeler, Claude Ferrand, and Eugen Brand
© ATD Fourth World / Joseph Wresinski Centre

to an ethos of co-responsibility: 'We learn together as teammates, confronting one another every day. That's how we learned from the beginning in Noisy-le-Grand – and it was usually the intensity of our team life that drove away those who chose not to stay. Being present to your teammates takes courage.'[6]

One issue the group discussed extensively was the standards for recruiting and training new Volunteer Corps members. They agreed on high standards, but were wary of making rigid rules, which could be counterproductive – perhaps even cult-like. Instead they hoped to foster diverse views about ATD: it needed to be demanding to best serve people in deep poverty; however, codifying this rigour would prevent creativity and renewal.

Mary addressed the question of standards in an open letter to senior Volunteer Corps members when some wanted to measure the sincerity of each volunteer's commitment to ATD. Mary saw that question as an inappropriate distraction from more important goals. She wrote:

> I'm not comfortable questioning anyone's sincerity. Who knows what's in a person's heart? ... For me, the word 'commitment' does not mean feeling 'devoted' as a goal in and of itself, but rather that we are committed to creating *change*. ... We shouldn't end up running some kind of confessional; and if we're truly honest, all of us must admit we have failed to measure up to everything we want to achieve and to become. ... I'd rather simply believe in my own sincerity and that of others in order to focus instead on the work at hand.[7]

Susie Devins (American) remembers Mary's approach standing out, particularly because in the 1980s, French was virtually the only language used at ATD's international meetings. Susie says: 'The French way of speaking seemed too vague. Mary's frank way of speaking was most welcome to people like me.' It is indeed vague to imagine 'measuring devotion'. To Mary, the priority was instead about useful work that makes a difference and feeling united toward a common purpose:

> The commitment we make must always remain freely chosen, which requires each of us to have the time and freedom to deepen what motivates us to drive forward ...

Susie Devins
© Luc Prisset, ATD Fourth World / Joseph Wresinski Centre

and to trust and communicate with one another. ... In that context, we must create opportunities for activists who live in poverty to develop their own ways of expressing their motivation and developing their skills and talents.[8]

Some Black Forest Group members continued to worry that ATD would fall apart without Wresinski at the helm. Mary insisted, 'I disagree that we're not capable.'[9] Like Mary, most members of the group had already founded teams, either in new geographic places, or by tackling research or advocacy challenges. By the 1980s, in most cases, the daily running of these teams had in turn been taken over by newer members of the Volunteer Corps. This sparked new questions about the role of people with long seniority stepping back from projects they created. Mary said of the younger generation:

> They are completely responsible for the projects they are running. At the same time, we have an influence. And it can be helpful for them to have people to think with when they need advice. All of us need to think with others, because nothing ever guarantees that we make the right decisions. Also, team leaders may sometimes supervise people with whom they just don't get along. This is why we need to change teams regularly, so that a personal issue does not prevent a team from taking advantage of what each member can best contribute.[10]

Some in the Black Forest Group worried about generational divisions within ATD. Younger Volunteer Corps members accused them of being set in their ways. Huguette recalls that, hearing these accusations: 'Mary took the time to listen to young people who were upset. She would invite them to take a walk and talk things over. She always had a strong character and her own point of view; but also a very frank straightforward way of wanting to understand their point of view. That made her very authentic.'[11]

When the Black Forest Group was invited to submit a publication to a French journal series about human rights, their first outline began with accusations made against them by younger volunteers, framing the publication as a rebuttal. Mary strongly advised against this negative discourse, writing dryly:

> That's certainly an original approach! But there are also many positive things we hear from young people about the Volunteer Corps. Why not include those along with some of their concerns? I'm quite sure you could write about the Volunteer Corps without turning it into a strict list of rules and regulations. After all, every one of us is only human – with a little streak of madness for attempting the impossible!

Mary's thoughts about generational differences, reminds me of my own experiences changing teams. At 19, when I joined ATD, I sometimes chafed under heavy-handed team leaders who seemed to distrust anyone young. A decade later however, I found myself behaving similarly. Shortly after leaving ATD's youth centre where I had edited the monthly newsletter, I received the new team's first newsletter issue. Instead of sending an encouraging note, my first reaction was to nitpick, hunting for errors and wondering why they changed my approach. It took a few days for the penny to drop: I was about to turn 30 and would need active efforts not to become inflexible!

In Black Forest Group discussions about teamwork, Mary voiced acute awareness of the challenges:

> In so many teams, each one feels alone. It's natural that we panic, faced with the constant crises of poverty. And our group isn't the response to every need. But we should

> create a better atmosphere. You have some volunteers who are not running grass-roots projects because they are in an office writing a ton of letters and feeling distant from what motivates them. Others have the privilege of working closely with families in poverty – but they too can feel very frustrated if they're not involved in a team dialogue to develop their understanding of impossible situations. This is why we need to collaborate as teams: by trusting one another enough to communicate, sharing our difficulties, and also moments of joy.[12]

Jeanpierre agreed. About annual gatherings of senior Volunteer Corps members, he said:

> They need to be times of warmth. In daily life, we seek out the harshest situations of poverty and we are rigorous about how we structure our work. We need to make sure that daily life is warm and kind. Coming together once a year is a chance to discover one another, deepen friendships, and shower one another with the kindness that keeps you going from one year to the next.[13]

Jeanpierre remembers Wresinski looking to Mary in particular as a confidant:

Jeanpierre Beyeler
© ATD Fourth World / Joseph Wresinski Centre

> He had strong personal relationships with each of us. But with Mary, he really trusted her common sense. She had a strong sense of the identity of people in poverty and also of our Volunteer Corps – but without being dogmatic about anything or taking sides. At one of our general assembly sessions, he referred to Mary as his 'other self'. He and Mary had a kind of osmosis between them. He had big ideas about what could move us forward; and she had a concrete sense of what was possible. There was a communion of spirit between them.[14]

Mary spent much of 1987 organising the UNESCO seminar that brought together Michael Samura, Salome Muigai, Judith Grandi, Mustapha Yanka-Kanu, and many others. To celebrate ATD's 30th anniversary, the year was marked with conferences, publications, and events, all leading up to a giant festival inaugurating 17 October as the first World Day for Overcoming Poverty. Mary was pleased about the UK mobilisation for this event. When the Minister of State for Employment visited Frimhurst, Mary rejoiced:

> For once, press coverage is speaking not about 'social problems' but simply about efforts made by families to have their dignity recognised and to gain the means to lift themselves up. ... It's most interesting that several articles describe Frimhurst as a project of national and international interest because of the training given there to disadvantaged people.[15]

When Mary promoted 17 October to social justice leaders, civil rights leader Coretta Scott King responded, writing: 'I am proud to join with you in the struggle against poverty around the world. The agony of the poor impoverishes the rich.'

In January 1988, following the great strains of the anniversary events, Wresinski was hospitalised for a heart operation. Members of the Black Forest Group remained at his bedside. He imagined the year ahead as a sabbatical one for the whole of ATD on the biblical model of forgiving debt and leaving fields fallow. At the same time – perhaps anticipating that his life might be drawing to a close – he was full of future plans. To Mary, he spoke about the need to be more

After 17 October became an annual tradition, during the 1989 commemoration Mary welcomed United Nations Secretary-General Javier Pérez de Cuéllar (left) to the Plaza of Human Rights and Liberties in Paris.
© Yannick Lefeuvre, ATD Fourth World / Joseph Wresinski Centre

strategic about promoting ATD's publications. Mary agreed – though argued about what to prioritise. His recent major achievement was authoring a report on *Extreme Poverty and Social and Economic Insecurity*, adopted as a blueprint for government policy by the French Economic and Social Council. He imagined publicising this everywhere; but Mary cautioned him that the report would not be as meaningful in countries where ATD had not led research on a national scale, and particularly outside of Europe where government anti-poverty policies needed to be very different from France's.[16]

Five weeks after this conversation, on 14 February 1988, Wresinski died at the age of 71. Susie reflects: 'Mary, who had lost her own father, was especially close to him, even though she never hesitated to argue with him. His death was very hard on her.' Mary took the lead in publishing a special issue of ATD Fourth World's newsletter to memorialise him and to share messages from people he influenced.

In a letter to Judith Grandi, Mary wrote:

> Père Joseph's sudden disappearance was a great shock, but we haven't had any time at all to stop and grieve. His death mobilised everyone, and especially Susie and myself who had the job of pulling together all the messages that flowed in from around the world and putting together a journal in five languages. Now we're sending it out and catching up

with letters that have been accumulating. Being so busy has, I suppose, been what we needed to keep going during these first few weeks. In fact, I think we will feel the loss more later. But the spirit is strong here, and there's no reason to believe it will ever be otherwise.[17]

Just after putting out the newsletter, Mary was asked by the Black Forest Group to take on responsibility overseeing ATD's French national newsletter, with the idea of making it progressively more international, building on the unity presented in the special issue.

In the following weeks Mary welcomed Dina Wardi for her month-long visit to ATD. At the end of the month, Dina reflected: 'It is striking to see how a movement begun and inspired by one person is so open and non-dogmatic without any shadow of personality cult. The commitment is to all people living in poverty.'[18] But despite what Dina observed, some Volunteer Corps members had grave qualms about the future without Wresinski. As the Black Forest Group prepared to speak to the general assembly of the Volunteer Corps that August, Jeanpierre Beyeler wrote about this uncertainty:

> You can feel the fear of losing our unity ... because of our diversity and our differences; but we have to leave that attitude behind. So much the better that we are so different – long live diversity! ... We build our unity on a conviction. ... Poverty has caused all of us to take a moral stand in one way or another. Each of us chose freely to act in order to say no to poverty. ... Alone, nothing can be done. So the Volunteer Corps becomes a source that sustains a lifelong project. ... Our diversity is increasing with more volunteers from the developing world. So we need to invent new ways to remain a school of freedom, where each of us deepens our own path, giving us the means to situate ourselves in such a diverse corps.[19]

At that general assembly, Mary made a speech about the common convictions uniting ATD, such as writing regularly about the daily experience of poverty as part of a search for understanding and to avoid 'the trap of abstract concepts and preconceived ideas'. She added that in addition to the experience of poverty, it was critical to question people in poverty about their views of the world and of public policy. About challenges, she said:

> Many of you speak of failures: ... not having managed to reach the hospital before a very poor man died; ... not having been able to prevent a mother addicted to drugs from humiliating herself ... And yet, I don't think these moments *are* failures if they remind us that we must always begin again if we hope to measure up ... [and] that we have no reason to judge or accuse one another of not being committed enough. What right have any of us to sit in judgement? Isn't the only difference between us and others that they did not have the opportunity to meet someone like Père Joseph, to meet a movement that would trust us? ... In [every] country, isn't the reality the same? ... Always learning to become discreet and patient, trying to learn, starting from scratch, learning again to be humble and take what comes; or perhaps taking on responsibility in a way that means one's personal ambitions must be put on hold.
>
> Having common convictions isn't a master key. On the contrary: our convictions unsettle us, pushing us toward slammed doors, humiliations, and indifference – sometimes even within our teams. This is normal, and we know it. But it's important to say that if we are lucky enough to share belief in an ideal for humanity, then we also have the responsibility to work toward it despite having no tools.
>
> What is it that we want to tell others about? We are a movement of action and of reflection, but we also have a way of life and a point of view. By this, I mean the way that others look at us which could lead to society taking on the goal of overcoming poverty for the well-being and joy of all. And by 'us', I mean all of us together. Who among us could pretend, even after ten, twenty, or thirty years to measure up? We absolutely must safeguard the precious part of what we have received from Père Joseph: the knowledge that all people, whatever their background or their beliefs, must find a place among us, and also that we need all people for this societal project.[20]

In 1989, the Black Forest Group took stock of ATD's development since Wresinski's death. Mary was concerned about getting stuck in the past. Looking back, I realise how lucky I was to have met ATD in the vibrant and dynamic era of Wresinski's lifetime. For those who joined just after his death, it was very hit or miss. Some were in teams led by someone as daring and forward-looking as Mary. But many, unfortunately, had team leaders who felt rudderless and bereaved without Wresinski. They were trying to keep everything going in precisely the way that they imagined he would have done – a recipe for inertia.

Wresinski's death changed the nature of the Black Forest Group. In 1987, I remember Mary explaining it as something informal and meant to evolve: 'Others will join it at some point, and those of us in the group might leave at any time.' However, some in the group felt that they carried a lifelong responsibility to ensure that ATD would not splinter apart. Jeanpierre Beyeler said, 'We fell into the trap of absolutely wanting to defend our points of view when on the contrary, what was needed was calmness to discern what the Black Forest responsibilities should be in this new period without Père Joseph'[21] To the group, Mary said: 'For ATD's future, we must not stick rigidly to doing things as before. Our history is an anchor; but we must invent new approaches. With people in poverty, we must undertake innovative projects. About the Volunteer Corps, how will we remain open to all?'[22] She had a long-term vision and often told the group: 'Nothing will work if we can't even get along with one another'. Jeanpierre feels that it was Mary's struggle with cancer that enabled her to reach this attitude of wisdom.[23]

An unfortunate tendency of those who wanted ATD frozen in amber was to talk constantly about Wresinski, and to glorify only his good points while glossing over his temper (which rivalled Mary's!). Although he was a visionary man with extraordinary accomplishments, unceasingly singing his praises can drive people away. Personally, the more I feel I'm hearing a sales pitch, the more suspicious I become about what's hidden behind the glorification. Mary said: 'If others are to understand Père Joseph through us, it must be through our ways of living and being. Not everything can be communicated in words. It is like getting to know families in poverty: our physical presence can demonstrate our sincerity.'[24]

These different ways of respecting Wresinski's legacy existed across ATD and within the Black Forest Group. They tried to fill the vacuum in leadership left when he died. And they were all mourning a founder they had loved dearly and drawn daily inspiration from. In this context, the group was rife with tensions. Susie recalls that Mary 'stepped up to define a future and to keep the peace' within the Black Forest Group. Following one Black Forest meeting, Mary wrote: 'Our daily working relationships are not easy. But spending several days together to meet in the Netherlands has helped us to progress slowly toward wisdom and understanding our responsibility. May we keep trust and hope!'[25] Two years later, she added, 'We've managed to stick together because we were determined together to put in the work. … We've resisted, and at least we didn't break anything.'[26]

The pre-existing tensions between the Black Forest Group and younger members of the Volunteer Corps persisted too. During preparations for the 1990 General Assembly, Mary said: 'If one of us from the Black Forest makes a speech, it should simply be as a volunteer rather than in the name of our group. Perhaps we are seen too much as leaders or decision makers. All of us are volunteers.'[27]

Despite ATD's internal challenges, the Black Forest Group needed to remain attentive to the wider world. In February 1991, off the southeast coast of Africa on Reunion Island, riots protested unemployment of more than 30% and a lack of training programmes. Mary proposed that ATD's team there seek out the young people in the worst situations to interview them about their lives and their thoughts. At the same time, she suggested that teams in other parts of the world carry out similar interviews to learn more about the aspirations of young people in poverty.[28]

Mary's note to the Black Forest Group in advance of their 1991 meeting recalled what Wresinski had asked of them shortly before his death: 'to help move things forward by thinking, appreciating, making proposals; but definitely don't grind things to a halt'. Mary continued:

> For my part … as a member of the Black Forest Group, I have a status/responsibility that is more or less expected/appreciated – and even confused – by others. This means that, like it or not, I am always, at all times, seen as 'a Black Forester'. Have we fully appreciated this fact? Aside from the way others see us, Père Joseph used to tell us, 'At least this way you can't walk out the door.' Within this group, we can evaluate how we experienced becoming those who the founder asked to guarantee certain things. Of course we

have a long way to go, but it seems to me that we are entering better into our responsibility in this sense today – even if some of us continue to flounder in trying to carry it out.[29]

Perhaps the Black Forest Group's most challenging responsibility was creating a leadership structure that would allow for creativity and strength. In addition to continuing projects initiated by Wresinski, they needed to develop new ways for ATD to function with its members spread out over an increasingly diverse range of countries. They also faced the question of how Wresinski's memory should be honoured. Three members of the group – Claude Ferrand, Gabrielle Erpicum, and Eugen Brand – had been asked by Wresinski in 1987 to prepare to take on ATD's leadership. When he died, they became ATD's General Secretariat. Three years later, Mary's note expressed concern about how this was playing out:

> It's particularly urgent that we think about the General Secretariat. We are responsible, not for the details of their decisions, but for their well-being and harmony – I would even say for their happiness. We share their responsibility for the future. They have shared out their working responsibilities; but I don't yet see them collaborating in harmony.

At the time, this was not visible to me as a relative newcomer. However in 2008, when I joined ATD's International Leadership Team alongside Eugen, I learned that unfortunately, his years in the General Secretariat were utterly discordant. Despite respecting one another, the three of them had fundamentally different approaches, and no clear way to resolve differences of opinion. Mary continued:

> Disharmony is more than a question of how a team functions. It is also a question of personalities and each person's pathway in life (their path with Père Joseph, as part of ATD, and in the world). It comes down to human relationships. Like others, I feel somewhat lost and disoriented before this fundamental quandary – all the more so because each of us in the Black Forest Group struggles not to assert our own passions and convictions before focusing on the trajectory of ATD as a whole.

How shall we move forward? It seems to me that we could at least try to better understand the difficulties in this situation, without judging or undermining any of them, and taking as much time as necessary. To carry out our responsibility requires great wisdom. Regrettably, wisdom cannot be special ordered! ... I plan to check myself often. What we need is quite different from directing strategic policies. It's a tall order; but I am confident that we can rise to the occasion.[30]

Responding to Mary's note, Jeanpierre expressed concern that ATD's formal governance structures were becoming 'choke points'. He argued that ATD should offer freedom:

With the magnitude of Père Joseph's approach, I always knew that I wasn't boxed in by the present. Young people who join us do not want to be boxed into an organisation where everything has already been planned. They wouldn't stay with us. They want to create, not to sacrifice themselves. ... Diversity is the antidote to uniformity. ... Père Joseph created the foundations and broad strokes of our movement. We can innovate, but on condition that we stop being afraid of losing our unity at every curve in the road. In our search for security, we've been trying to pin down Père Joseph's thinking and to extricate his principles of action. But above all he wanted a Volunteer Corps made up of people who feel free to make a wholehearted commitment.[31]

At the same time, any international organisation needs a decision-making structure. Jeanpierre wrote:

As Mary said, 'each of us makes the effort not to impose our own passions and convictions in order to focus on ATD as a whole.' ... We need to widen our lens to look at the whole of this movement, at the poorest people, and at the world, so that we're not always looking through the same filter. ... but we also need to know that there is a place where it's possible to judge and discern, where the efforts are tenacious to unriddle and anticipate the world, and to avert the tragedies that the poorest people fall prey to. This is the role of our General Secretariat, and it's the only kind of governance I can imagine among us. It requires a great deal of kindness, insight, intelligence, and maturity. Maybe this reliance on one another … without freezing us in place can become a sign of liberty where we take things on ourselves so that others can develop.[32]

Reading their exchange today, I think they had the right handle on things. We continue to grapple with tension between our individual passions as opposed to overall common ambitions across ATD. Our goal – proving that the world is better off when valuing and supporting the unique contributions made by people in deep poverty – is uncharted territory. We need to maintain moral guardrails and to coordinate strategies together; but often the initiatives of individual members of ATD fuel our forward momentum. When tensions arise, it's unhelpful to shut down one side or the other. Eugen often used an approach described by Mary: 'At least try to better understand the difficulties, without judging or undermining anyone, and taking as much time as necessary.' Time is our most precious tool; it's by investing the time to fully hear out people we disagree with that we sometimes unlock unexpected hidden ways forward.

Jeanpierre's words resonate strongly for me: no bottlenecks and no boxing people in. We can't move forward without creativity. As we experiment with new approaches, we need the widest possible lens to ensure that we never do harm. After reading this exchange, I phoned Jeanpierre to ask him how he looks back now on those first years after Wresinski's death – which were also the final years of Mary's life. He said:

Eugen Brand

© *Philippe Sarazin, ATD Fourth World / Joseph Wresinski Centre*

> Père Joseph's death paralysed us for a long time. But Mary never criticised anyone. Even when she disagreed with their ideas, she knew that an idea is never more important that what it allows people to achieve. She had affection for each of them as people, beyond our work. By then, Mary knew she was dying and it softened her; at the same time, she remained very lucid and sure of herself,

Mary, with Susie Devins
© *Luc Prisset, ATD Fourth World / Joseph Wresinski Centre*

always stubbornly determined. During the years of her illness, she never stopped working, and she continued travelling as long as she had the strength. I learned a great deal from Mary about the fragility of humanity. In those same years, my family was shattered at discovering that our daughter had a serious illness. In poverty too, many people have very fragile health. Mary brought peace and balance. She loved people so much.[33]

Chapter 25

Doubt, Religion, and Beliefs

From the earliest days of ATD Fourth World, some people urged Wresinski to declare it a Catholic or Judaeo-Christian movement. However, among the very first to join his work, some – like Bernadette Cornuau – were atheists who would never join a religious organisation. Wresinski firmly defined ATD as being for those of any belief or philosophy to learn from people in deep poverty. He wrote to Mary: 'We must have among us people who do not believe in God. The poor need them; they need to be with us; and we need them. How can we reconcile what seems irreconcilable? … Is it possible? Seemingly not. But if we really seek, who knows?'[1]

Was there a way to reconcile the different convictions among members of ATD? There was no precedent for an organisation that

© Daniel Gingras, ATD Fourth World / Joseph Wresinski Centre

was not purely secular or religious. Mary said: 'ATD's choice to remain open to all – whatever their personal beliefs or motivations – is not without its difficulties.'[2] Mary once said of her upbringing: 'Where I come from, we were prejudiced against Catholics. It must have been the same for the Catholics against the Anglicans. We're all raised with the idea that what one's family and community taught us is true. But I learned that you have to think things out again.'[3] Even after joining a priest in his life's work, Mary rarely discussed religion. In some ways I think she saw religion as a perfunctory backdrop to life – an approach that seems to me quite British.

In France, asking someone's religion is inappropriate, particularly in the public sphere where the doctrine of secularism bans all religious signs. The US is the polar opposite. The word 'God' is emblazoned on coins, in courtrooms, and in the oath of public office. For many Christians, overt religiosity is extremely common. I have regularly passed complete strangers who offered to convert me – once when a woman noticed my 3-year-old's hearing aids and rushed over to promise that if I started praying in her church, my daughter's hearing would be restored. Things are trickier for minority religions; and my parents – both atheists – grew up during the McCarthy era when their views were interpreted as endorsing 'godless Communism'.

But in Britain – where the colonial legacy includes long history with Hindu, Muslim, and Sikh citizens – the most common approach seems to be to calmly 'live and let live'. In *Watching the English,* Kate Fox comments:

> We English are probably the least religious people on Earth. ... George Orwell wrote that 'the common people are without definite religious belief, and have been so for centuries.' ... The Church of England is notoriously woolly-minded, tolerant to a fault, and amiably non-prescriptive. ... Whether or not one believes in God tends to be sidestepped. It's not quite in good taste.... The Archbishop of Canterbury bemoaned the fact that 'a tacit atheism prevails.' ... The key word was tacit. We are not a nation of explicit unequivocal atheists. Nor are we agnostics. Both of these imply a degree of interest in whether or not there is a deity – enough either to reject or question the notion. Most English people are just not much bothered about it.[4]

Doubt, Religion, and Beliefs 295

This was how Mary lived most of her life. But in Africa, she saw how explicit and vital religious beliefs are. For ATD Fourth World to welcome everyone, religious or not, Mary began thinking differently about how we should situate ourselves organisationally.

Colin Barham, who lived with Mary in Frimhurst, recalls: 'I was never aware of Mary's religious beliefs. She kept them to herself, even when discussions of a philosophical nature were sometimes the topic at the end of the working day.'[5] After Mary moved to London, she lived with Ursula Jomini, who recalls:

> Mary was open-minded. Among the various people who passed through, I remember conversations about Catholicism, Hinduism, the Russian Orthodox Church, and Kenyan voodoo practices. Occasionally Mary and I stepped inside a church, just to sit in silence for a while. At Christmas once, we went to mass at St Paul's Cathedral. And she took our team to St Martin-in-the-Fields Church in Trafalgar Square, because their concerts were beautiful, and also because they made homeless people so welcome. Then there was Mary's work with Quakers on behalf of South Africa. But Mary and I didn't often speak about religion.

Anneke – quite different from Ursula – recalls:

> Mary didn't like religious institutions. Her connection with Père Joseph made her think differently, but she hardly ever attended his masses. Sometimes we were invited to collect donations at churches. She put her glad-rags on but she didn't go to mass; she'd stand at the door shaking the basket as they came out. People would say, 'Oh, you mean charity for the deprived?' She hated that and always told them, 'We don't like that word'.[6]

Mary's conversations took a different path with Stephen Baker who eventually left ATD for a vocation as an Anglican priest. He said:

> My memory is that she had a faith; but I have little to no proof of this. You can misread signals. My partial guess is that to her God was a part of life – but I don't think she

had very much time to think about it.[7] ... [Also,] I think she was often irritated by Christians who did not put into practice her understanding of 'Christian socialism'.[8]

In the Noisy-le-Grand camp, during a meeting about volunteers choosing to live on low salaries, Wresinski connected this choice to his own belief in Jesus Christ. Mary pointed out that atheists could share the same ideal of simple living: 'Even a person who does not believe in God usually believes in goodness.'[9]

The stigma attached to the bleak camp meant that residents felt unwelcome in the churches of the adjacent middle-class town. Thanks to a donation from Charlie Chaplin, Wresinski organised the residents – including Muslims, Hindus, Jews, Christians, and atheists – to build an interdenominational stone chapel in the same shape as the corrugated metal 'igloo' homes. Jean René Bazaine designed its stained-glass window. This chapel became a place for the community to share special moments together, and to seek solace from crisis.

An interdenominational chapel built in the camp,
funded by a donation from Charlie Chaplin
Provided courtesy of Margaret Bourgein

When living in New York, Mary heard that the French Government might bulldoze all the igloos to make way for a housing development – without guaranteeing rehousing for any camp residents. She wrote:

> I'm wondering about the chapel and its destiny during the reconstruction. You should prevent its demolition, so it can

remain a permanent testimonial to the presence of the poor and their evictions. We must remember their evictions not only from this camp but from every field, block, or town where they have ever been pushed out to make way for others. It was for these thousands of people that this chapel was created; it ought to remain in place until every last one can have a permanent home.[10]

For Mary herself though, the path towards renewal was more about human connection than a chapel. When living at Frimhurst, she wrote:

Inside the chapel, with a view of the window designed by Jean-René Bazaine
Provided courtesy of Margaret Bourgein

> Things have been hard for everyone this winter. The cold lasted so long that it felt like we were all hibernating bears. The snow was so heavy that it broke several of our loveliest trees. It was quite sad seeing them crushed to the ground. Still worse, for four months now, not a single new family has arrived. Several families were scheduled to come, but at the last minute they lost courage. People here take it as a personal affront. We must be careful that life does not become boring. And when we volunteers feel as bored as the families, we try to avoid them, which of course only makes things worse.
>
> Last month, I went to the conference at ATD's international centre. I felt, again, how much strength we draw there. With only yourself to count on, it's too hard to renew ideas and energy. Quickly, you feel that the families and the work are weighing on you. I'm increasingly convinced that truly progressive work is possible only when you have a way to renew yourself, whether through a religion, philosophy, or something in that vein. Otherwise, we close in on ourselves. For self-protection, we end up opposed to progress. This is why it's important that we are a movement of people together.[11]

Leading ATD in the UK, Mary discovered the diversity of interactions families in poverty had with religious communities. In 1978, she organised a Fourth World Evening discussion on the theme 'Religion is part of life'.[12] The guest speaker was an Anglican bishop because Mary wanted people on the margins of society to discuss with a church leader their experiences of feeling they didn't belong in religious institutions. Her invitation urged the participation of 'those of us who feel our needs have not been met by churches, whatever our beliefs'. Mary summed up the ensuing discussion: 'The majority of people in poverty believe in God; but not in churches. There is too big a gap between the wish to be part of God's family and the locked doors, the refusal of baptism, and the lack of understanding.'

Once, Mary was invited to address Faith and Light, a network of Christian communities composed of people with intellectual disabilities, their families, and friends. Explaining her belief in what she described as 'an inner presence' to people in poverty, she said:

> To describe to you my own experience of living amongst the poorest families, I want to show the difficulties I have had to go beyond a purely physical presence among them, without knowing them, in order to reach a real inner presence which can be a quite different state. To live this kind of presence among the poorest is the most difficult of all because it is possible to live with them without knowing them. To know them, we have to put them within us and that is not an easy task, certainly not for me. My experience is not more important or more worthy than anyone else's,

© ATD Fourth World / Joseph Wresinski Centre

but it is real and I hope to illustrate how, in reality, the first battle in overcoming exclusion is within oneself.

This 'inner presence' was Mary's response to the challenges of living in Frimhurst where:

> [Residents] are ... resentful of and often very hostile to those who presume to help them, certain that they are failures and ... anyway all the world is against them. ... Their growing confidence enabled them gradually to say what was on their minds – not only to confide in me, but also to vent on me their frustration and anger with the world. So I could be, and was, shouted at, mocked, treated by the families as though I was a doormat, insulted, called all the names I knew, and a few more.

Mary described feeling 'exhausted and fed up, dreading the next day, the next confrontation' to the point of wondering why she didn't quit:

© *ATD Fourth World / Joseph Wresinski Centre*

> This question is one I've asked myself more times than I can count ... because to stay at Frimhurst, I have to know why. There can be only one answer: the hopes [these families] carry within them for themselves and their children, and the message they carry for humanity. To succeed in going inside [to reach an inner presence], I have had – and still have – to change myself, to look with different eyes, listen with different ears, think, feel, pray differently. It means a complete transformation of myself, something that I had not reckoned on when I accepted the invitation to go and 'live' at Frimhurst. In that respect, it didn't really matter whether I lived there or not. I could be as present anywhere. In fact, our presence which involves living cheek by jowl may be an illusion, a total deception: unless we have put those to whom we seek to be present into our thoughts; unless when we think about the world we are also including

them; unless when we fight or pray for justice and freedom, we are fighting and praying not for ourselves but for the justice and freedom of others who are denied it; unless when we pray, we pray not for ourselves but for them.

Presence, in this sense, is something within us. It is not our job or activity or location, but it is a profound solidarity with the others so that everything which concerns them concerns us vitally. To be present is to put those who are outside within us; to be unable to live unless they are within us.[13]

This speech of Mary's is food for thought. To some extent, I think of the idea of 'inner presence' as inherently Christian. In Judaism, we are more focused on actions: we can't ask forgiveness from God unless we first atone by reaching out to people we have hurt to make things right with them. But when Mary speaks about literal presence, which is of course a concrete action – that 'cheek-by-jowl' proximity with families in poverty who sometimes shouted at or mocked her – I flash back to the years when my children were young.

Living in Brooklyn, we spent many evenings and weekends with families in poverty for ATD activities. During one beach outing, my tired and cranky 3 year old threw a tantrum. Several parents in poverty, most of whom had been raised with harsh discipline, were sure a good walloping would put an end to it. I never spanked my children; but nor did I ever find a solution to tantrums. That day, other parents – particularly Mrs N. – berated me for being too lenient. Unsure of myself to begin with, I was miserable and humiliated at this evidence of my ineptitude both as a parent and also in my role with ATD. I see our work as improving relationships; but communication is barely even possible when a toddler is screeching away.

I sometimes found that literal presence very oppressive. Did it somehow transform me 'to listen with different ears, think, feel, pray differently', as Mary put it? One of my Brooklyn teammates was Babette Ayassamy, a brave woman who grew up in poverty in France and first got involved with ATD as a teenager. Soon after my family moved to New York, she took me to visit Mrs N., whose children were regulars at ATD's Street Library project. We spent an hour or so chatting in her kitchen, ostensibly about changing welfare policies – but when we left, I confessed to Babette that I hadn't managed to make sense of much at all. My main impression was of wild incoherence.

Mrs N. expressed herself so differently from others I knew that I got completely lost (and the darting throngs of roaches didn't help). But Babette, despite being new to the United States, had keys that helped her understand far better.

Over the years, being mentored by Babette and others, I have indeed learned to look, listen, and think in new ways. Mrs N. also grew in the ways she expressed herself, later presenting ideas at our discussion groups in ways that even the uninitiated could understand. I'm still not sure about 'inner presence' because to me the idea of prayer makes sense chiefly in terms of how we behave towards others. But I feel very strongly about another intangible word: belonging, particularly as the antidote to social exclusion. Perhaps it's a form of spiritual practice to build a shared sense of belonging to the ATD community for people as different as Mrs N. and I are? Whatever our inner beliefs might be, we are connected by a sense of shared purpose that gets us through the moments when we are exhausted and fed up.

Chapter 26

'Faith in Life; Faith in People'

In 1980 the challenge 'to reconcile what seems irreconcilable' faced a new challenge. On her deathbed, Erika van Weldt voiced a strong request. Huguette explains: 'There was a confrontation. Erika was deeply Catholic and wanted us to start saying that ATD Fourth World was religious and inspired by Catholicism. She considered our roots Catholic. Père Joseph insisted that he would never agree.' Jeanpierre adds, 'He lost his temper, saying, "Out of the question!"'[1] Huguette says: 'He was respectful of Erika, but I was impressed by his clarity, firmness and vision on this issue. For him, ATD had to remain open to each and every person, no matter what their beliefs.'[2] Wresinski's word was final: ATD was not a Catholic or even Judaeo-Christian organisation.

Another of Wresinski's convictions was that world leaders should think together with people in poverty. This is why ATD organised delegations to meet with the Secretary-General of the United Nations on five occasions. In 1982, it was Pope John Paul II who received an ATD delegation of 50 young people in poverty. Not all members of ATD were comfortable with the idea of a non-religious organisation sending delegates to the Vatican. Mary, however, agreed with Wresinski, who wrote to her, 'This is a unique opportunity for young people to meet a man who represents hope for more justice, more fairness, and more love amongst all people.'[3]

In inviting teenagers to join this delegation, Mary felt it did not matter whether they practised any religion. Instead, she sought out young people 'who are clearly concerned by others and thinking about how best to serve others'.[4] The delegation, from three continents, included Muslims, Protestants, Buddhists, and Catholics, Babette among them. The six British delegates included one from Belfast, where the conflict between Catholics and Protestants was at its height. He explained that his family home was burnt down with a petrol bomb because they hadn't moved away from a previously mixed area. He added that foreign newspapermen paid children to throw stones at the army so that they could get good photographs.

A delegate from the outskirts of London said:

> People think we young people are all ruffians. Police ask you to move on. Where I live, the road has a bad reputation. When people ask where I live and I tell them, they don't want to know me. At church, no one listens to our problems. Everybody thinks you're around to make trouble, so we're always told to go away. Maybe visiting the Pope can change the way they look at us.

As the British cohort got to know delegates from other countries, one who struggled at school said, 'I've learned I'm not the only person who can't read and write. We've experienced the same things as what the others say. This gives me an outlook on life to be more aware of the world, knowing my country's not the only one that has troubles.'

Of the pope, they discovered that he was 'quite normal, really, and more friendly than other priests. The atmosphere was electric because the comradeship was good.'[5] The pope told them that the church is 'for the poor'; but a 17 year old from London contradicted him: 'It's not true. In church, you've got to be well dressed. If you just go like that, you're ashamed, or you feel out of place.' Others agreed: 'When you're poor, you don't go to church because you haven't got the clothes. Everyone's looking at you.' The pope encouraged them to 'continue helping the poor to fight against misery'.[6] They appreciated the chance to meet him, saying 'He cares what happens to people. It makes you feel important when you've lived what we have. It brings our hopes up again.'

Mary felt that their dialogue was meaningful to non-Christians as well. She said: 'The pope's words to ATD's delegation weren't just for Christians or religious people. It was clear that there were people who do not share his faith. When the pope told them, "Bringing people together in gatherings is a good way to overcome poverty", he wasn't speaking about Christians. He was speaking to everyone.'[7]

In the 1980s, Mary was spending more time in Africa where she was impressed by the commitment of some of the European sisters and priests she met, writing:

> For long arduous years, often in great isolation, [they] have dug themselves into Africa ... accepting the conditions of a difficult climate, economic and political regime without any preconditions or guarantees. ... Whether or not we question the way of life and work of some of them, we cannot forget the gaunt figures of certain priests, marked by years of privation, yet ... prepared to entirely rethink their way of working, their place in the country, their presence amongst the very poorest.[8]

Her reflection about questioning their 'way of life and work' reflects her highly critical view of certain projects. But what impressed her was people 'prepared to entirely rethink' everything – which echoes her own journey towards an inner presence where she listened 'with different ears'.

The 'irreconcilable' question resurfaced in 1984 when a Catholic sister who was a member of the Volunteer Corps proposed that, within ATD, she form a religious congregation. Mary had two reactions. On the one hand:

> We are now present in more Muslim communities, especially in Africa, where people feel their history is imbued with a special kind of spirituality. I'd like to put this sister's request in a more universal context. What I understand from the people of Africa, Asia, and Latin America is that, in order for us to make a commitment to moving forward together, it is important to go beyond action, particularly in the relationship of humanity to God. Perhaps a religious initiative – as long as it involves only those who choose it – would help us to think about what is meaningful in the lives of people in the worst forms of poverty.

However, remembering Catholic sisters in the Frimhurst team, she added:

> I noticed that, while they did find their place at the sides of people in poverty, they had trouble living there and forming a community with others. This is because of their nostalgia for basic ecclesial community life, or sometimes because they are afraid of families in poverty. In either case, they do not feel 'at home' in the place they have chosen to be. Perhaps this is why they need to form their own community.[9]

Wresinski opposed the proposal, speculating that it stemmed from the uncertainty associated with ATD's Volunteer Corps. The sister and her supporters, he said, 'want to ensure their fate. They are troubled by not knowing how to explain to outsiders quite what they are doing' in the Volunteer Corps. Mary was not convinced, arguing: 'If we want to develop an understanding of people on other continents, it's urgent that we develop our spirituality, beginning with what is meaningful in the lives of people in the worst forms of poverty.'

However, Wresinski remained dubious, citing certain middle-class people interested in praying with people in poverty. He said:

> There are hysterical people who use the poorest people to compensate for their own psychological weaknesses. They are capturing 'their poor'. They divvy up religiosity in the same way that they once spread soup kitchen hand-outs. Only the Volunteer Corps can guarantee that these groups avoid gushy sentimentality and excessive piety.[10]

Jeanpierre agreed: 'Spirituality is essential; but not a congregation. That would only be the response to a search for security. You can't create something new based on a question of defining your status. The danger of hysteria comes when form goes before content, and when people lose touch with reality.' Today, he adds: 'Père Joseph understood that our work together was bigger than any religion.'[11]

Jeanpierre (who is Swiss) remarks: 'French people are deeply attached to secularism. One day that exploded for ATD.'[12] This explosion occurred after Wresinski's death when the Black Forest Group was confronted by several members of ATD's Volunteer Corps running projects to deepen their personal Catholic faith by evangelising families in deep poverty and inviting them 'to collaborate in hastening the coming of the kingdom of heaven' or 'to take a positive look back at their lifetime of poverty to discover the traces of presence of God as creator and saviour'.[13] In fact, these projects had been launched as personal initiatives; the request made of the Black Forest was to legitimate the projects as part of ATD. Following long discussions, Bernadette concluded:

> Their approach is not fair to families in poverty who believe in the whole of ATD, but are being coerced only into spiritual groups and not even invited to events like the World Day for Overcoming Poverty. ... Families in poverty have a right to our whole movement. That's what the indivisibility of human rights is about. ... Almost all those who talk about religion express it as their *personal* need to have religion more present in the Volunteer Corps; they don't speak about how the Volunteer Corps can create more freedom for families in poverty, or how that goal would be helped by bringing religion into the Volunteer Corps.[14]

Bernadette spoke of coercion because building these projects on a foundation of relationships forged by ATD might lead people in poverty to believe that those relationships could not continue outside of Catholicism.

By now, Mary's view, while still sympathetic to 'a spiritual dimension in our work' and 'nourishing our motivation', was that certain choices were situated outside of ATD. She wrote:

Mary, with Jeanpierre Beyeler
© Michel Lansard, ATD Fourth World / Joseph Wresinski Centre

> We must untangle this before it affects the unity of the Volunteer Corps. ... It is our responsibility to ensure ... the place where families in deep poverty can gain in freedom based on all their aspirations and the different dimensions of their lives. ... The projects that have already begun will continue *outside* of the Volunteer Corps. We should clearly answer that there's nothing for us to accept or refuse because the choices have already been made independently of the Volunteer Corps. ... We have a responsibility to shape projects *together* because what is spiritual touches on each person's reason for being. It can challenge the very nature of the Volunteer Corps. ... We can't expect the Volunteer Corps to bear the weight of all of our choices and desires, our personal baggage, our follies and weaknesses. If that were the case, we would lose our ideal of embodying the suffering and hopes of families in the worst poverty. Each of us must ask whether projects we want to carry out actually originate with the Volunteer Corps and with families in poverty or should be carried out elsewhere.[15]

In that same spirit of preserving ATD's unity across differences of belief, Mary opposed Alwine de Vos' campaign for Wresinski to be beatified.[16] Jeanpierre stresses that Wresinski's priority had been for ATD to be accessible to all people:

> He never wanted this movement to be linked in any way to the Catholic Church so that the commitment he invited people to make could be open to all. Hence his determination to have ATD recognized as an international non-governmental organisation fighting for the rights of the poorest people. As a builder, he built a chapel in Noisy-le-Grand, then in Pierrelaye, and elsewhere. Each time, he recruited artists to decorate them. I think his faith and spirituality are connected to the beauty and harmony that he constantly sought to offer people in deep poverty. These chapels stand as testimonies of his personal spirituality and fidelity to the Catholic Church. He never confused spirituality with a commitment to a religion.[17]

After Michèle Gérardin left Mauritius to join ATD's team in Haiti, she asked Mary how she 'managed with the question of faith and churches'? Having grown up in France as an atheist, Michèle was surprised to discover that Creole culture and language were so steeped in belief that there was no way for her to express unbelief. Mary responded:

> Faith is very personal. Each of us has the right to believe whatever we wish. You're right that when I'm surrounded by Catholics I often defend Protestantism purely from a spirit of contradiction; and also that I sometimes attend Catholic mass just because I feel like it! Years ago, when I was fairly new to ATD, I met a little old lady who told me that only Catholics could truly aid the poor. I was furious; but since then I've learned that truth lies elsewhere. The world of humanity and of God is so much bigger than any one religion or moment in history. Today, I really don't mind what people say. And if families in poverty believe in God, that's their right.[18]

In 1989, ATD had another opportunity to meet the pope. Again, some members of ATD were opposed, arguing that this was inappropriate for a non-religious group. Before deciding, the Black Forest Group sought advice from non-Christian friends: Saco Kassé, a Senegalese Muslim; Dina Wardi, who was Jewish; and the Baha'í International Community's UN representative.[19] All encouraged this step as a way to make known and understood Wresinski's anti-poverty work. In this spirit, the Black Forest sent a large, diverse delegation, including members of ATD from every continent, and Forum correspondents from India, Nigeria, and Uruguay.

Mary continued to stress the importance of spiritual issues. When families in poverty travelled from Paris to Wresinski's tomb in our international centre, Mary ensured that their welcome included words inspired by Muslim traditions in case some visitors were Muslim. The minutes of a Black Forest meeting noted:

> This year, of course most teams will mobilise around human rights. But Mary thinks we should also develop a deeper understanding from families in poverty on the theme of 'spirituality': the meaning they see in life, their values,

'Faith in Life; Faith in People'

In 1989, Mary joined a second ATD Fourth World delegation received by Pope John Paul II.

© Folkert van Galen, ATD Fourth World / Joseph Wresinski Centre

thoughts that hearten them, and things they express through daily gestures. Bernadette gave the example of a man who is trying to purchase his trailer rather than rent it because owning the trailer could give his children security. It is not enough to interview families without also thinking about their actions and what those actions might mean to them. Mary reminded us that this is how we should always develop our understanding, without assuming too quickly that we already have a definition of the word 'spirituality'.[20]

During that meeting, about a year before Mary's death, she was keenly aware of her own mortality. Anneke says: 'She was afraid. She said, "I never thought I would believe in anything; but you try to find different ways to cure yourself."'[21] Jeanpierre reflects:

> To this day, Mary's feelings about religion remain a mystery for me. She didn't speak openly about it at all; but at the same time she was very free. We just didn't talk about religion. Before she died, she tried alternative medicine. Following the encouragement of several of us who were close to her, she agreed to have her chakras aligned; she went with Gabrielle to Lourdes; and she met with a healer in London. She tried different diets, but wasn't strict about any of them. Chemotherapy and

radiotherapy didn't heal her. But she prepared for the end. All her filing was done. Then in June 1992, she decided to come for a day to visit Noisy-le-Grand, where I was working with a team of artists from ATD to prepare an event marking our movement's 35th anniversary. On the 27th October, the night before she died, she told me I needed to leave. She was incredibly clear-sighted, with a life force rooted in her soul.[22]

When asked what is most important, I've heard some people in poverty speak about God. One feels that her church is the only place where she can break silence around challenges her family faces. Some see in religion a hope for their teenage children to break free of drugs and gangs. Positive religious connections can make an enormous difference in the lives of many people. Other people in poverty – like some who spoke to John Paul II – do not see hope in religion. They may have been told by a religious leader that their suffering is due to their sins. A woman in Switzerland – unable to save her sons from despair, drugs, and violence – asked, 'How can I face God when I couldn't save my children?' In Guatemala City, I visited a woman living in a makeshift shanty towards the top of a steep ravine, the air heavy with the stink of sewage. She told me that her every effort had failed, and asked: 'Has God cursed me?'

For others in poverty, religion is a point of contention. Religious charity can be linked to coercion and extremism – or simply making recipients feel unworthy. Lenore Cola, an ATD activist in Harlem, told me:

> Religions put pressure on: 'We can do this for you, but you have to do this.' When you go to church as a donor, you sit up front proud, bragging about what you did. Your name is all over. … Jehovah's Witnesses force their beliefs on you. One person started doing that at the Fourth World House. We argued every time. So we just had to stay away from the subject of religion.

I'm thankful that Mary, Huguette, Bernadette, Jeanpierre, and others reinforced Wresinski's decision that ATD is not religious. At the same time, Mary's sensitivity to the 'spiritual dimension' reminds me of my stint volunteering at Martha's Table. The 40-year-old employee in charge was burnt out, on the verge of a nervous breakdown. Later, when I discovered ATD, one of the things that struck me was Mary's care for her teammates, supporting each of us to sustain our motivation over decades.

Discussing this can be challenging. The very term 'burn-out' is one ATD avoids because of its association with privileged top-down efforts. But fighting the horrors of social injustice requires struggling against fury or despair for all, including people born into poverty. Some feel strengthened by religious beliefs; others are driven forward by beauty and culture, values, or non-religious spirituality. Yet words can be treacherous. I was moved by one friend's poetic phrase that ATD 'is what makes my heart sing!' However, another friend, equally engaged in ATD, but more prosaic in nature, is not comfortable speaking about 'singing' hearts.

As difficult as it is to pin down Mary's innermost beliefs, she drew strength from the community she co-created. I agree. Whatever challenges emerge, I'm more motivated if at least two people are on the same side. The late Moraene Roberts, an ATD activist in poverty, practised paganism. Asked about it, she quoted Sun Bear, an author born on the White Earth Indian Reservation in 1929:

> When humans participate in ceremony, they enter a sacred space. Everything outside of that space shrivels in importance. Time takes on a different dimension. Emotions flow more freely. The bodies of participants become filled with the energy of life, and this energy reaches out and blesses the creation around them. All is made new; everything becomes sacred.

That description of sacred space evokes what many of us experience on the World Day for Overcoming Poverty. By gathering to commemorate it, we show each other that people in poverty contribute something meaningful. We resist exclusion and stigmatisation by creating a sense of belonging for all. Sacred space can also be found

Moraene Roberts
© *Eva Sajovic*

© Daniel Gingras, ATD Fourth World / Joseph Wresinski Centre

in different visions of beauty. Poverty damages health and puts people in harmful situations. But together, we can collaborate on creating music, art, theatre in ways that enhance each person's sense of agency, identity, and intuition. This can also bless creation.

People in poverty deserve to be joined by those of all beliefs; and everyone should get the chance to think together with people in poverty. There's no clear road map for ATD's approach. But our roots and soul are in building links with people who have been excluded from many aspects of life, including from places deemed sacred. People who may have felt they belong nowhere can transform society by creating sacred spaces for all to feel sustained.

As Mary put it in an interview with the Catholic newspaper *La Croix* in 1989:

> It's a spirit that is in [the poor], that makes them get up and face a new difficult day, a spirit that keeps them from going under. That's what faith is: keeping your head above water. … It's important for everyone, whether they believe or not, to keep faith in life and in people. When people in poverty see a 20-year-old girl arrive in their shanty-town, a girl who earned a good living elsewhere and decided to come live with them, those who believe in God may think He is smiling on them. But for everyone, whether they believe or not, there is more hope.[23]

Chapter 27

Some of my Best Friends are Journalists

Mary's enduring legacy includes the prodigious wealth of her own writing, as well as her efforts to open up the work of ATD Fourth World to the gaze of the media, academics and a wider public. Members of ATD often feel betrayed by journalists like the one who painted Mary as a martyr 'saving drunkards and derelicts'. Many tabloids mine trauma for impact in what's termed 'poverty porn'; they focus on failures rather than aspirations and steps forward; or they play to stereotypes, condemning 'skivers and scroungers' in the UK, or 'welfare queens' in the US.

© ATD Fourth World / Joseph Wresinski Centre

Journalists can also shoehorn people into hurtful assumptions about appearances. When a London ATD member agreed to welcome a reporter in her home, she spent hours tidying up – only for the journalist to declare that it didn't 'look poor enough' for the photo-shoot and should be made to seem dishevelled. On another occasion, ATD brought people in poverty to meet the UN Secretary-General. A BBC journalist skipped the main event but then offered to interview me and Gina Russell, from New Orleans. Gina's family was going through very hard times then, struggling to make ends meet. Her kids' school didn't have enough textbooks to go around, and rain leaked into the classrooms. She felt a duty to speak out about poverty but was anxious about this meeting at the Geneva Palace of Nations. After the journalist rushed us into a side room, he began: 'This conference is about poverty, so why don't you don't look poor?' Maybe this boorish man was trying to provoke a sassy female response, but Gina – who had actually borrowed clothes to feel she was dressed appropriately for the prestigious venue – then became so deeply flustered that she didn't open her mouth for the entire interview. The irony is that the journalist actually *aimed* to speak to someone in poverty but didn't realise that his high-handed premise had hamstrung him.

Given ATD's discomfort with journalism, another irony is that our full name includes 'Fourth World' which originates from the term 'Fourth Estate'. In English, 'Fourth Estate' has described journalists; while for ATD 'Fourth World' means people in deep poverty. We are often asked if this references the 'Third World'; but in fact ATD began using the term long before 'Third World' became widely used. 'Fourth Estate' originated during the French Revolution, when three 'estates' claimed a voice in the new consultative assembly: the clergy, the nobility, and 'commoners'. This last category was meant to include all wage-earners and peasant labourers. However Louis Pierre Dufourny de Villiers, a merchant, declared that a 'Fourth Estate' included people too poor and powerless to have a voice, even in the Third Estate.[1] In his 1789 book, *Les Cahiers du Quatrième Ordre*, he wrote about day labourers, the infirm, and the indigent. Two centuries later, Wresinski saw clearly that Dufourny de Villiers was speaking about people like those in the Noisy-le-Grand camp, whose voices were completely unheard. In English, however, Dufourny de Villiers' legacy evolved from his work *reporting* about people in poverty, leading us to deem that journalists are the 'Fourth Estate' that deserves a role in democracy.

My personal connection to journalism was somewhat accidental. My college room-mate wrote articles for *The Cornell Daily Sun*, so I joined her. Although writing remained my passion, I never considered working in journalism. I was more interested in joining social change on the ground than in neutral reporting. When I joined ATD, Wresinski was delighted by my newspaper experience because he dreamed of getting journalists on the side of people in poverty. But when he sent me to interview Mathilde Aparicio, who grew up in the Noisy-le-Grand camp, I realised that my approach was all wrong. At *The Sun*, when new trainees joined us, we taught them to control an interview. In mock scenarios, we asked them to investigate an official who was hiding something. Unless they took just the right tack to questioning one of us (in the role of the duplicitous official), they would never uncover the scandalous nugget that would make or break their article. Preparing to meet Mrs Aparicio, I realised that I had no idea how to *release* control of a conversation and to prepare the terrain for someone in deep poverty to express their own ideas without feeling the need to be led by my questions.

It turned out that Mrs Aparicio was by then an old hand at being interviewed and very comfortable telling me exactly what she thought. But since then I have often met people in poverty who have never before been asked their opinions, and who need substantial encouragement to speak their mind. Having had their words used against them, they need time to build up trust in others, as well as confidence in themselves. They may feel an undue obligation to respond to a question, even when it violates their personal boundaries. Also, they often lack opportunities to talk issues over in a safe space while developing their thinking.

So this is a big part of ATD's work: long before public speaking, we create safe spaces for people who share similar experiences of poverty. As peers, they think about setting and protecting their own boundaries. We use techniques like photo-language, where each participant chooses an image to use as a metaphor before diving into conversation. This gives everyone time to choose their own words before being influenced by others. In participatory research, we aim for people in poverty to co-develop the questions we will explore together. This approach is diametrically opposed to my training to never let an interview get out of my control. I often need to check myself if that reflex kicks in.

Another issue with my training is that traditional journalism is designed to extract information from a more or less passive subject for the journalist's own purposes – which may remain hidden behind the journalistic demeanour of complete neutrality. ATD's ethos is the polar opposite. Our aim is to create a context where all goals can be co-created together with people experiencing some of the worst situations of poverty. Ideally this means designing together not only the questions but the purpose. Even when this is not possible (for instance when timescales are too short), now I aim always to put aside any pretence of neutrality. If I'm going to ask someone in poverty a question, in addition to protecting their freedom not to answer me, I also want to be vulnerable myself by telling them about my own experiences and views. So in fact, most 'interviews' I now do as part of my work with ATD are really two (or three) way conversations.

But I continue to value investigative journalism as a profession essential to a healthy democracy – all the more so in this era of unfounded accusations of 'fake news' and of the deep fake content created by artificial intelligence. Many of the friends I made at *The Sun* have spent their lives in journalism. One, the talented and perceptive Marc Lacey, won a Pulitzer just five years out of college, and is now managing editor of *The New York Times*. This means that when others in ATD might run down the media, I'm the one inclined to say #NotAllJournalists.

Mary's frustrations with the media went beyond the 1964 *Daily Mail* article. That same year, she was profiled in three other media outlets, all describing her simply as a young 'Guildford girl' making an inexplicable choice to live amid the homeless. The first profile was 'The Future is Yours', a French documentary made for RTF Television by Françoise Dumayet. The airing of the documentary was followed by a two-page profile of Mary in *Télé 7 Jours* magazine:

> Mary lives in the camp at the end of a dirt track. Conditions are primitive. Like other volunteers, Mary takes her turn with all chores: emptying dustbins, delivering mail and looking after toddlers. Volunteers sleep in a dormitory, eat in the refectory; it is the rule of community life. Sometimes Mary is unhappy. But she always keeps her smile. Père Joseph, Mary and the others are interested only in the great business of humanity. She says, 'Yes, I'd like to get married. But if I do, I shall continue to work here.' Mary speaks without bitterness of the difficulties of a young girl without money: 'I earn 200 francs a month. Of course it's hard to window-shop in Paris and be unable to buy anything. But if I earned ten times as much I should spend it just the same. What I miss most perhaps is going out. It is difficult to go to the theatre. And we only have one car for all of us. I should love to travel, to keep up my piano lessons, and to realise my dream, which is to play the organ. But the important thing is that I not give up this work.'[2]

The following month, a Surrey newspaper published an article titled 'Guildford Girl (22) Helping the "Lame Ducks" of Paris'. The article included passages translated from the *Télé 7 Jours* article, along with added information from Mary's mother:

> Mary was last home in December, when she said she could not stay for Christmas, as that was the time she was specially needed in the camp. The families there need to feel wanted and the only people to offer them affection were the helpers and the camp commander, Père Joseph. A scientific survey is being made of them, and Mary is taking a course of psycho-sociology at the Sorbonne. ... She feels it is important that the frequently maligned young people of today be recognised as the hard-working youngsters they often are. ... Mary has no social life, and only a very occasional visit to a theatre. Her mother is sure she is happy. 'She has always taken the side of the persecuted', she said. 'Many of her friends were "lame ducks" even when she was small.'[3]

A different newspaper cutting led Mary to again express her exasperation with journalists. When ATD sent children from Noisy-le-Grand for a holiday in England, an article in the *Daily Telegraph* and *Morning Post* called the children 'bewildered and woebegone'.[4] Mary fumed: 'The English are no better than the French for this kind of ridiculous article.'

To fight back, Mary did plenty of her own writing. On top of that, she was the first to index the writings done by all camp volunteers. When she was 21, Wresinski asked her to develop an archive of these daily reports so as to hone understanding of poverty and contribute to academic research. From Wresinski's arrival in the camp in 1956, he kept a journal documenting obstacles of poverty, as well as acts of courage and fellowship. However, frequent fires destroyed his early notes. Mary's archive needed protective metal filing cabinets. One of the igloos was particularly large and housed a thrift shop. Because this was the only building in the camp that could be locked shut, Mary started her work in the back of this igloo where a lone padlock could protect second-hand clothing donations and also the highly confidential reports. Mary coordinated the work of all volunteers, assigned to spend four hours a week helping in the archive, as well as the work of 60 friends of ATD outside of the camp who typed up the handwritten reports. Gabrielle describes the bitter cold in this

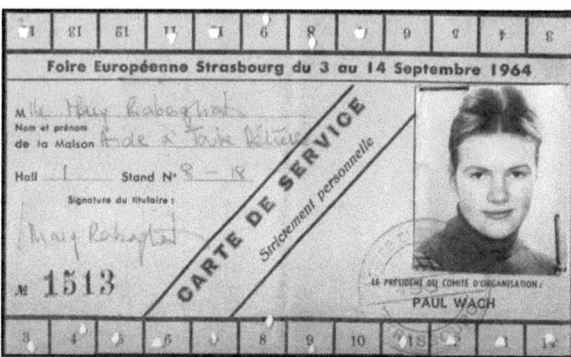

Provided courtesy of Paul de St Croix

makeshift office: 'In the winter, when we worked in the office at night, we used old newspapers to wrap up our feet. Then we'd stick our feet into crates to try to keep from shivering. I used to hope donors might bring us soft crocheted blankets instead of the rough army ones.' Mary remembers that the work was tiring 'but when we were fed up, we'd throw a disguise party or something'.[5]

While Mary enjoyed writing and threw herself into collaborating with Prof. Labbens and later Prof. Weissman, she remained reluctant about public speaking. Her initiation to public events came in 1964 when Wresinski took her along for two weeks to the European Trade Fair in Strasbourg, the first-ever time ATD Fourth World entered the public arena. They asked each fairgoer to donate a single French franc. Mary recalled:

> An architect designed a beautiful stand displaying photos of Noisy-le-Grand. But when Père Joseph saw it hidden in an overlooked corner, he had us take it apart to set it up more visibly. So off we went, carrying the wooden slats. Completely unauthorised, we set it up right in the middle of the crowd. Furthermore, Père Joseph insisted that we buttonhole official visitors to the fair. He literally pushed me nose to nose with a British minister to invite him to our stand! It was not subtle, and perhaps not effective. But whatever our methods, it's important to meet people in unexpected places where we can shake up ideas.[6] It was mostly children who wanted to look at our photos – while

parents pulled them away. For our 'One Franc' campaign, many children emptied their pockets to donate. We collected a million francs.[7]

In 1966, a few months after her return from the US (where she had been compelled to deliver a speech for Wresinski), her next opportunity to address a group came at a Sorbonne Law School international colloquium. Mary needed the urging of an older teammate to ask for the floor. In her report about the event, Mary wrote:

> I was dying with fear to speak up. But an idiotic woman who called herself 'a teacher of maladjusted children' said that 3-year-olds are already so 'deformed' by meanness that they throw their shoes at the teacher's head. Other speakers said that overcrowding leads to delinquency and criminality and that people need to 'make an effort' not to be 'anti-social' and to afford better housing. So I told them that in Noisy-le-Grand, despite the overcrowding, we've created an atmosphere where people feel at home. There are six hundred teenagers in the camp, and not a single gang or criminal.[8]

Mary's outrage at the maligning of people in poverty drove her not only to overcome her shyness but to develop a method for people in poverty to do the same. In the 1970s, Speakers' Corner in Hyde Park seemed to her the perfect opportunity. In theory, this makes sense. Since the 1870s, Speakers' Corner has been the world's foremost place for unfettered speech. Marx and Lenin spoke there, and it is open to anyone who cares to turn up with a soapbox to stand on and who can shout loudly enough for passers-by to hear. But to me Mary's idea boggles the mind because Speakers' Corner was and remains a place where bellicose throngs heckle fanatic speakers. Almost all speakers are men, and some onlookers make a point of coming every week specifically to interrupt and hound their least favourite speakers.

Mary's idea about Speakers' Corner was to always go with several of the parents in poverty who had lived at Frimhurst. Ursula recalls:

> Once people decided to become activists with ATD, we invited them to regular meetings in our centre. It was clear to Mary that we shouldn't stay comfortably among

ourselves. We needed to get out the front door and dare to take on the public gaze. We had to denounce injustice and tell others what it was like to live in poverty – and Mary wanted us to invite criticism. Before going, we'd prepare as a group to decide what message we wanted to get out and practice presenting. At Speakers' Corner, Mary would start, but often several activists in poverty would speak too. Whenever it got 'hot', with nasty heckling, Mary would jump back in to handle it.[9]

Anneke found Speakers' Corner very off-putting:

> Men there make a sport of heckling, so you have to expect it. And some were prejudiced against people in poverty too. Most of us hated going there. But Mary insisted. When people in poverty became activists, Mary would encourage them to speak there. Some activists became very good speakers. After we left, she'd help us learn to keep the upper hand in lively discussions. Mary liked rows because that was the start of a discussion where you could reflect on the heavy things that life was throwing at you.[10]

During the debriefings, Ursula says that Mary tried to help ATD members understand society's judgemental attitudes about poverty, and how better to frame things to be understood instead of bullied. Stephen Baker was not a fan of this activity either, but explains his participation:

> Mary clearly expressed how we should prepare ourselves. A neat presentation was a minimum to even begin to represent ATD. Then she expected me to stand up and prattle away – but I'm an introvert! Neither was I eloquent! I was very new and very young. The fact that I did stand on that bloody box shows the extraordinary confidence I had in her. I wasn't in terror of her. There was something in her that I trusted.[11]

Over the years, Mary grew more and more comfortable speaking up. Following Mary's significant investment in the International Year of the Child, in 1982, at ATD's annual international planning meeting, Wresinski complimented Mary: 'The new ATD UK newsletter is an upheaval in our international publications, it's a discovery!' Mary responded: 'It took us five years of gestation to finally deliver it, and we may not manage to put out another issue!'[13]

In 1982-84, Anneke collaborated with Mary to help a mother of three write her life story. Pauline lived at Frimhurst in 1977. Although all her children were eventually removed into care, she made great efforts for them to remain a family. Mary reflected:

> Pauline lost custody of all her children, despite having lived at Frimhurst, despite (or because of) us volunteers who didn't manage to prevent society from playing its dirty game. But Pauline doesn't consider her life a failure – despite the suffering that will never leave her – because she discovered a movement of volunteers and of other families like hers. This discovery made it possible for her to find meaning in her life. Because of everything she endured and also thanks to her trusting friendship, she is going to help improve the chances of other families.[14]

Anneke recalls:

> Mary was very demanding because she wanted us to get Pauline's story right. She thought the supposedly 'scientific' case studies of the time were too distantly analytical. She gave me a lot of support for the first draft; and then she dug in to edit every page herself. Because Pauline was in conflict with social services and went to court many times, Mary wanted her book to be irreproachable and impossible to attack. Most of Pauline's official papers were lost during long hospital visits. So Mary started from scratch to research the facts, and then she verified everything with Pauline.[15]

This life story was published as a 45-page booklet under the title: *Pauline, Families of Courage*.[16] The book received positive reviews in *Community Care*, which noted how important it is for professionals to learn what it feels like to be their client, and in *Social Work Today* which said: 'It is particularly hard for social workers to recognise violence towards themselves as a sign of maternal love or an indication of deep distress and need for help. Pauline's story should be valuable material for use in training social workers.'[17] Mary acted on this idea, asking Anneke to bring the book to social work classes in universities. Anneke recalls it having been unusual at the time for universities to have outsiders speak to students, but to this day, running anti-poverty practice training for social workers remains central to our work.

Mary took to heart the conversation with Wresinski just before his death about the importance of ATD's publications. Even more than previously, she threw herself into this work. She and Jeanpierre got the idea for a 36-page booklet, *Father Joseph Wresinski, Founder, ATD Fourth World Movement.* Knowing that many people in poverty felt particularly bereft, they designed this booklet to fit in a pocket for those who wanted to keep it close to hand. Printed in five languages, it presented a short biography, and quotes from Wresinski, illustrated with simple sketches.

In the wake of 17 October 1987, as this became an annual event, people in poverty around the world used this opportunity to speak about their struggles and aspirations. In 1989, Mary collated these testimonies into a book called the *Fourth World Chronicle of Human Rights,* funded by UNESCO and the French Prime Minister's National Consultative Commission on Human Rights.[18] I helped with the proofreading and layout of the book's abridged English version and a subsequent edition covering 1990-91. By then, I was in ATD's team in Washington, DC. In one letter to me, she wrote, 'I've had to take a lot of time off "sick" so things have accumulated';[19] still, she'd managed to send me a sheaf of handwritten notes for this project.

During Mary's travels, she also made a point
of interviewing people for ATD Fourth World's publications.

Provided courtesy of Paul de St Croix

© ATD Fourth World / Joseph Wresinski Centre

Seeing writing as a crucial role for ATD, Mary told a volunteer in Haiti:

> The lack of means for bare survival there is unacceptable. Reading your letters, I'm constantly wondering how society understands our message. In writing about poverty, we have an enormous responsibility. None of this suffering must be in vain. You feel helpless; so do I, because if our message is not understood, none of this work does any good. I'm not pessimistic though; on the contrary. But being realistic about challenges keeps us humble and motivates us.[20]

For Mary, publications shaped ATD's legitimacy. In a multi-year collaboration, a professor shadowed ATD to explain its effectiveness in social work terms. However, the resulting publication was so complimentary that a rival academic reacted: 'Great – but not believable.' Frustrated, Mary railed that the book should have included more about confrontations between volunteers and people in poverty. She concluded that ATD should expand its rigorous evaluations from structured projects to day-to-day conversations 'to show how something that doesn't seem to succeed may later yield progress after all'. Although it's challenging to see breakthroughs in daily life, 'still the volunteers making routine home visits to families … are creative. … That laborious head-on contact with families is both impossible and also possible. … We should evaluate to showcase it.'[21]

At the 1990 Paris annual book fair, ATD ran several events about Wresinski's life and legacy. However, Mary felt that these events went badly because ATD had so little experience introducing him to the public. The following year, she proposed instead that the most public part of ATD's book fair event, set in the children's museum of La Villette, focus on children's workshops. About Wresinski, she curated smaller events hosted in ATD's French national centre, in another Paris arrondissement, to allow for semi-private experimentation.[22]

Mary disliked when ATD communications simply quoted people in poverty without making clear their broader message. She also criticised a lack of coordination among ATD teams, leading to contradictions about prioritising among needs to translate and publicise books. For ATD's annual internal planning, Mary dedicated a full day to harmonising the messages of future publications.[23]

Today in ATD's publications catalogue, Mary's name doesn't appear because of the collaborative nature of the way she worked. And yet her communications accomplishments were massive: daily writing; founding the archives; abundant correspondence, reports, and newsletters; public speaking and mentoring of activists to find their own public voices; and painstaking editing of *Pauline*, *Children of Our Time*, and three *Fourth World Chronicle of Human Rights* volumes, among others. I love her incisive voice and was motivated to write this book to share it more widely.

© *Luc Prisset, ATD Fourth World / Joseph Wresinski Centre*

Some of my Best Friends are Journalists

© *Jeanpierre Beyeler, ATD Fourth World / Joseph Wresinski Centre*

Conclusion: 'Mary Helped Us Discover Our Strengths'

When Mary died in 1992,[24] condolences arrived from people from all walks of life, from the House of Lords to UNESCO's director-general to people in poverty, one of whom said: 'When I first arrived at Frimhurst, I felt so alone and unwanted. I didn't trust anyone, and I didn't like anyone. But Mary … showed me a new way to look at life. I began to feel like a person who could stand on my own two feet. That gave me the strength to move forward … [and] take chances.'[25]

Provided courtesy of Paul de St Croix

Conclusion: 'Mary Helped Us Discover Our Strengths'

Mary Totham, at Frimhurst
© *ATD Fourth World / Joseph Wresinski Centre*

Another person in poverty, Mary Totham, said at Mary's funeral in St James's Church, Westminster:

> I didn't make life easy for Mary. I've been in children's homes all my life and people told me I was no good. When people in charge wanted me to do something, I often was against it. So when I arrived at Frimhurst, I brought all the parents out on strike against Mary. Because of all my rudeness, Mary didn't need to talk to me – but she took the time to do it, and I felt free to talk to her. Mary didn't talk down to me, and she never turned her back on me. Once Mary asked me to read something about our work standing on a soap box at Hyde Park Speakers' Corner. I was so frightened; but she stood by me. She was as nervous as I was! We had a good laugh together when we had done it. Her joy was infectious. She helped us discover our strengths in a way that saved us our dignity.[26]

Sir Peter Bottomley also spoke at the funeral where he compared Mary to a Salvadoran human rights activist: 'Like Oscar Romero, Mary found the saintliness in other people. She could get ordinary people to do extraordinary things often, and that's where extraordinary talent comes from.'

In 1990, remembering the early years of ATD Fourth World in Noisy-le-Grand, Mary wrote to Michèle:

> At the time of course, none of us carried any weight in society. We had no impact at all on laws, institutions, or public opinion. Père Joseph would say, 'I haven't managed to do a thing for the families. Nothing ever changes.' He wasn't being humble; it was the reality. No one listened to us. We were ridiculous and others made fun of our efforts. On top of that, whenever people in poverty were seized by despair, they would shout at us: 'What good are you? You've never given me a thing. You're no help at all.' Now, we reminisce about those years with starry eyes – but that's not what we said at the time.[27]

After being called ridiculous in France, Mary's civil rights efforts in the United States led only to her immediate arrest. In Frimhurst, people in poverty argued constantly with Mary and the general public considered ATD 'dreamers and lunatics'. She must have questioned herself constantly. Yet she always found reasons to push forward. Her letter to Michèle continued:

> You mustn't try to measure yourself against some validated standard of efficiency. On the contrary: we all have to accept that sometimes all we can do is keep going. We can take on ourselves people's suffering … to help survivors feel trust and hope, and to make sure that those who die in poverty haven't suffered in vain.

Despite the challenges, Mary's committed her whole life to building a movement which places itself squarely beside those who live in poverty and, with them, fights social injustice. She was asked many times why she stayed.

In the 1989 *La Croix* interview she said:

> I believe in God, but don't associate Him with any particular church. Wresinski did not open my eyes to an Anglican, Catholic, or Muslim God, but rather the God of all those who are crushed by poverty. That's where the truth lies. …
> *For you, this truth is…?*
> Truth is being able to enter the world of human misery and to do something there for the poorest people and, of course, with them. When you love that much, when you

Conclusion: 'Mary Helped Us Discover Our Strengths'

are happy to be there, there is no need to have any particular religious label attached to you. In fact all people should further their understanding of their own faith. ... The sign that we are trying to understand our faith is this labour of love and joy with the poorest people.

You say 'joy'?

Without that, you cannot stay. In fact if there is no joy involved, it is worthless. ... Somehow, people deprived of everything are able to be creative and maintain a joy for life when they realise they can change something. As soon as you know you are capable of changing something, even when things are at their worst, you can overcome sadness. I never would have believed that on my own. All I would have seen was failure, instead of seeing what poor people can do. Believing in them helps the poor, not crying with them.

You spoke about a labour of love. Which love? ... You're hesitating?

To say 'I love them' or 'they love me' does not go deep enough. They taught me that we are the same, and that is the great truth of love. I come from a very different background. I should feel distant from them and they from me. But no, ... one discovers that we're all part of humanity – all children of God if you prefer; for me, it's the same. You discover humanity when you can love everywhere. ... We can be generous, we can change and create change. When we get behind suffering and egotism, all the way to what's human, then we are where love is.[28]

© Isabelle Williams, ATD Fourth World / Joseph Wresinski Centre

In 1986 she spoke with nine young people who grew up in poverty and lived at Frimhurst as teenagers. They challenged her to say what she had achieved and learned. She responded:

Alone, I don't think I'd have been able to achieve anything. We do something because there are others around us. And because I've been with a group of people who've tried to achieve things together, we've kept Frimhurst going. ... I've learned that everybody has something important to say and contribute, in spite of difficulties. Some people talk in a way you can't understand immediately. They may have had less education. But education doesn't show anything. Underneath it, I've discovered that they have a lot to teach me about being a good human being. They've also taught me that we all can do much more than we think we can. In a more ordinary job, I probably would never have realised this. We all tend to think, 'Oh, I'll never be able to do this.' But if you have a go, you realise that you can. Just as every one of you has done things that you didn't think you could.

Kicking herself for her temper, and sometimes behaving like a Rottweiler, Mary was also a charming dynamic woman full of charisma and authenticity. One of her cousins recalls: 'I was struck by her inner serenity, her wonderful sense of humour and her ability to make you feel you were the only person in the room.'[29]

Mary was determined not to lead a shallow life. She used to say, 'It's no use opening doors unless you also push people to walk through them.' That's how she mentored people in poverty to hold their own in the fray at Speakers' Corner. Her legacy was also opening a pathway for ATD Fourth World to push past its founder's death in order to innovate once again. I was lucky to discover the organisation during Wresinski's lifetime because in the aftermath of his death, as Eugen Brand puts it:

> Most of the gigantic personalities in the Black Forest Group spiralled into in-fighting over titles and spheres of influence. They were smothering the approach Mary brought. ATD could have splintered into a federation of off-shoots: some religious, others based on different methodologies of action, all destabilising one another. Sometimes when people need to feel reassured, they fall into the trap of trying to repeat the past forever. But we're never done learning new things, and Mary knew that.[30]

The approach Mary brought is described by Karen A. Hart, who was quite upset after having to witness a teammate being chewed out by another team member. When Mary came for a visit a few days later, Karen remembers:

Mary was the only one who had the ovaries to grab the bull by the horns and let me process some of it out loud, which I never would have done with someone less strong or truthful. Mary's unsentimental sentimentality at that moment was one of the most respectful and fearless actions I have ever seen – to be brave enough to get in there.

Karen A. Hart

© *ATD Fourth World / Joseph Wresinski Centre*

Susie describes Mary as 'the adult in the room who rose up above the worries to look further down the road'.[31] ATD did not fully emerge from that era of conflict and paralysis until seven years after Mary's death. But those who helped thrash the way out – Eugen and Susie foremost among them – were mentored and inspired by Mary. Her unshakable conviction was that ideas and strategies, in and of themselves, are never more important than what they allow to happen; and that there is a constant need to go back to the basics of getting to know new people and becoming sponges to drink in what they have to offer. I think that, like Mary Totham, many of us discovered thanks to Mary our own strengths for joining in and persisting in this movement of social justice.

Mary, with Susie Devins

© *ATD Fourth World / Joseph Wresinski Centre*

© *ATD Fourth World / Joseph Wresinski Centre*

When visiting Mississippi, Mary wished for 'a real revolution among people who tasted the cookie and were not prepared to let it go'. Overcoming poverty and social injustice *do* require an ongoing transformation, one centuries in the making – and surely a long road is still ahead. But whatever may come, Mary showed us how to continue this work. As she said: 'When you're stuck in the misery of poverty, joy matters even more.'

Acknowledgements

Advice, assistance, and early editing support from: Irit Aizik, Moya Amateau, Naomi Anderson, Stephen Baker, Colin Barham, Leslie Bell, Fran Bennett, Paige Bowers, Anne Champagne, Francesca Crozier-Roche, Régis De Muylder, Nicholas Edwards, Judith Grandi, Patricia Heyberger, Gwennaelle Horlait, Jessica R. Kaliski, Kathy Kelly, Gill Main, Seymour Mike Miller, Eloise Morrison, Nisreen Muzayen Al-Najjar, Elizabeth Naumann, Amalia Paraskevas, Peggy Simmons, and Gertraud Trivedi.

Research support from:

- **the Joseph Wresinski Archives and Research Centre** in Baillet, France, particularly Sophie Razanakoto, Nathalie Barrois, Axelle Brodiez, Elisa Hamel, Marie Jahrling, Honorine Kouamé, Chloé Najera, Jacques Ogier, and Paule René-Bazin; as well as Nathalie Bénézet, Dominic Bernas, Magdalena Brand, Gabrielle Erpicum, Daniel Fayard, Rosana François, Dylan Moglen, Béatrice Noyer, Sarah Ortega, and Bruno Tardieu;
- **Mary Rabagliati's relatives**, particularly Paul de St Croix, Duncan Rabagliati, Alastair Rabagliati, Margaret Bourgein, Julia H. Moss, Margaret Rabagliati Wood, Peter Akehurst, John Bourgein, Raymond Bourgein, Dorothy Bourgein, Alden Irons, and Charlotte Vesey;
- Professor David Piachaud of the London School of Economics;
- Mary Morrow of the Selma-Dallas County Public Library Reference Department;

- **and Mary's friends, classmates, and teammates**: Judith Stone Abbs, Josephine Alumanah, Paul Arneson, Françoise Barbier, Huguette Bossot-Redegeld, Fanchette Clement-Fanelli, Bruno Couder, Jean-Michel Defromont, Geneviève Defraigne-Tardieu, Susie Devins, Eileen Donovan, Hyacinth Egner, Pierre Espinasse, Roger Gordon, Pauline Grace, Judith Grandi, Karen A. Hart, Penny and Tony Heath, Rosemarie Hoffmann, Ingrid Hutter, François and Ursula Jomini, Fabienne Klein, Salome Muigai, Francoise Sleeth, Jean Tonglet, Niek Tweehuijsen, Stuart Williams, and Anneke van Elderen.

Many of the quotations included in this book were written in French and translated into English by the author who assumes responsibility for any errors or inaccuracies.

For more content about Mary Rabagliati, please scan the following code:

(https://www.lutterworth.com/product/joyful-revolution/)

Notes

Chapter 1

1. Interview of A. Van Elderen by D. Skelton, 4 March 2018.
2. Joseph Wresinski Centre: Archives, YB03 Fonds Chrono Provisoire, Interview with M. Rabagliati by 'Hibernation' group, 11 May 1990.
3. Joseph Wresinski Centre: Archives, 1030/02/01, Letter from M. Rabagliati to S. Devins, 3 April 1985.
4. Joseph Wresinski Centre: Archives, 2AV557-E-2ARCH-0065, interview of M. Rabagliati by Maître Titinga Pacéré, 1991.

Chapter 2

1. Interview of A. Van Elderen by D. Skelton, 26 May 2019.
2. Interview with Margaret Rabagliati Wood, 18 September 2018.
3. Kate Fox, *Watching the English: The Hidden Rules of English Behaviour* (London, Hodder, 2004), p. 436.
4. *Dorchester Collection Magazine,* 10 February 2017.
5. Interview with M. Rabagliati Wood, 18 September 2018.
6. Francis Green and David Kynaston, "Britain's Private School Problem: It's Time to Talk", *The Guardian*, 13 January 2019. [Available at: https://www.theguardian.com/education/2019/jan/13/public-schools-david-kynaston-francis-green-engines-of-privilege]
7. Obituary 'Mrs. Priscilla Bright McLaren', *Sheffield Daily Telegraph*, 6 November 1906. [Available at the British Newspaper Archive.]
8. Personal archives of Paul de St Croix, an undated note by Sandra de St Croix, née Bourgein, about her childhood recollections.
9. Personal archives of John Bourgein (a nephew of Sandra de St Croix).
10. 'The Airmen's Stories – F/Lt. A. C. Rabagliati', The Battle of Britain London Monument. [Available at: http://www.bbm.org.uk/airmen/Rabagliati.htm]
11. Letter from Margaret Bourgein to D. Skelton, 8 July 2019.
12. Personal archives of P. de St Croix, an undated note by S. de St Croix about her recollections.

13. Personal archives of P. de St Croix, letter of 3 November 1992 from Ann Robinson to S. de St Croix.
14. Personal archives of P. de St Croix, an undated note by M. Rabagliati about her childhood recollections.
15. Personal archives of P. de St Croix, an undated note by M. Rabagliati about her childhood recollections.
16. Moira House School later became known as Roedean Moira House.
17. Joseph Wresinski Centre: Archives, 0375-22, letter from Judith Stone to ATD following M. Rabagliati's death, November 1992.
18. Letters from Judith Stone to D. Skelton, 28 March 2025 and 5 April 2025.
19. Personal archives of P. de St Croix, letter from Mona Swann, principal of Moira House School, Eastbourne, to Sandra de St Croix, 22 July 1957.
20. Letter from P. de St Croix to D. Skelton, 23 June 2019.
21. Personal archives of P. de St Croix, transcript of a speech by Sandra de St Croix at a celebration for M. Rabagliati, 4 December 1983.
22. André Sève, 'Mary, volontaire à ATD Quart Monde', *La Croix*, 21 December 1989. The same interview was later published in Sève's book *Le Manteau de Martin: 43 dialogues sur le partage* (Paris: Centurion, 1991).
23. Letter from Paul de St Croix to D. Skelton, 18 September 2018.
24. Interview with Margaret Rabagliati Wood, 18 September 2018.
25. Letter from Duncan Charles Pringle Rabagliati to D. Skelton, 10 April 2018.
26. Paul Langan, 'Enigmatic Ilkley Politician Remembered in Special Lecture', *Ilkley Gazette*, 19 April 2007. [Available at: http://www.ilkleygazette.co.uk/news/1338943.Enigmatic_Ilkley_politician_remembered_in_special_lecture/]
27. Priscilla Bright McLaren, "Assaults upon Women by Men", *The Women's Signal: A Weekly Record and Review for Ladies*, 16 February 1899. [Available at the British Newspaper Archive: https://www.britishnewspaperarchive.co.uk/viewer/bl/0002232/18990216/018/0003]
28. The Medical Register, The General Council of Medical Education and Registration of the United Kingdom (London, 1879); Catriona Blake, *The Charge of the Parasols: Women's Entry to the Medical Profession*, (London: Women's Press, 1990); and Janet Gottschalk, *She Stepped Out of Her Class: The Life and Times of Agnes McLaren*, (London:Medical Mission Sisters, 2001).
29. Letter from Dr Jo Stanley to D. Skelton, 22 August 2018; London Gazette, 1 January 1934.
30. 'Dying Woman in Honours List Never Knew of New Year's Award', *Daily Express*, 4 January 1934,
31. Letter from Dr Jo Stanley to D. Skelton, 22 August 2018.
32. Caroline Brown & Mark Hunnebell, *Ilkley and the Great War*, (Gloucestershire: Amberley Publishing, 2014), chapter 4.

33. Letter from Dr Jo Stanley to D. Skelton, 22 August 2018.
34. *Ilkey Gazette* of January 1934 as cited in Dr Jo Stanley's research.
35. Jim Greenhalf, Jim, 'Daring Raid Stunt Inspired Iconic James Bond Moment in Goldfinger, *Daily Telegraph*, 18 February 2015. [Available at: http://www.thetelegraphandargus.co.uk/tahistory/featuresnostalgiapasttimes/11801711.Daring_raid_stunt_inspired_iconic_James_Bond_moment_in_Goldfinger/] and Jeremy Duns, 'Dutch Courage', Debrief: The Online Playground of Spy Novelist Jeremy Duns, 21 April 2010. [Available at: https://archive.is/d4e2]

Chapter 3

1. Interview of H. Bossot Redegeld by D. Skelton, 20 June 2018.
2. Interview of A. van Elderen by D. Skelton, 26 May 2019.
3. Quotes of Mary Rabagliati in this chapter come from the Joseph Wresinski Centre: Archives, 0110/50, ATD Fourth World seminar on knowledge and action, 25 July 1990; 0138-XV56, Fourth World Evening about the history of ATD Fourth World, 13 October 1983; Interview with M. Rabagliati published by *La Croix*, 21 December 1989; Interview with M. Rabagliati conducted by young people in poverty at Frimhurst, 8 March 1986; and archives of 1962: 1C-19B, 'Foyer feminin, reflexions de Mary qui fait ses premiers pas comme responsable.'
4. ATD Fourth World – Addington Square: Archives, Genevieve Coste, 'Mary "la Volontaire"', *Tele 7 Jours*, March 1964.
5. N. Bourgein, 'Student Snapshot', 1964.
6. Joseph Wresinski Centre: Archives, speech by M. Rabagliati to a general assembly of allies of ATD Fourth World, 1 November 1989.
7. Joseph Wresinski Centre: Archives, Interview with Mathilde Aparicio by Etienne Boespflug, 2 July 1976.
8. Bernard Jahrling and Jean-Michel Defromont, *Pierre d'Homme* (Pierrelaye, France: Editions Quart Monde, 2004).
9. M. Bourgein, 'Student Snapshot', 1964.N.
10. Jahrling and Defromont, *Pierre d'Homme*.
11. Interview with Gabrielle Erpicum, 6 February 2019.
12. De la Gorce, Francine, *Un peuple se lève*, (Paris: Editions Quart Monde, 1995), p. 14.

Chapter 4

1. Joseph Wresinski Centre: Archives, 0259-WC69, activity report by Mary Rabagliati covering December 1989 to February 1990.
2. Joseph Wresinski Centre: Archives, speech by M. Rabagliati to a general assembly of allies of ATD Fourth World, 1 November 1989.
3. M. Bourgein, 'Student Snapshot', 1964.N.

4. J. Wresinski, *Ecrits et paroles aux volontaires, (Luxemburg: Editions Saint Paul-Quart Monde, 1992)*, volume I, pp. 81-88 citing a meeting of volunteers in May 1962.
5. Interview with Gabrielle Erpicum, 6 February 2019.
6. Joseph Wresinski Centre: Archives, Interview with M. Rabagliati by 'Hibernation' group, 1989.
7. M. Bourgein, 'Student Snapshot', 1964.N.
8. Joseph Wresinski Centre: Archives, 1C-19B, Foyer Feminin, May 1962.
9. Personal archives of Paul de St Croix, an undated letter from Mary Rabagliati to her family, circa April 1964.
10. Joseph Wresinski Centre: Archives, Ecrits quotidiens, M. Rabagliati, Noisy-le-Grand, 19-27 November 1962.
11. All names of camp residents in these reports have been changed to protect their privacy.
12. Joseph Wresinski Centre: Archives, letter from M. Rabagliati to G. Erpicum, 6 October 1964.
13. Joseph Wresinski Centre: Archives, letter from M. Rabagliati to G. Erpicum, 6 October 1964.

Chapter 5

1. Wresinski, *Ecrits et paroles aux volontaires, 1960-67*, volume I, p. 152.
2. Interview of H. Bossot Redegeld by D. Skelton, 20 June 2018.
3. Letters from N. M. Bourgein to D. Skelton, 8 and 15 July 2019.
4. Wresinski, *Ecrits et paroles aux volontaires*, volume I, pp. 228-30, citing a meeting with volunteers on 3 December 1963.
5. Wresinski, *Ecrits et paroles aux volontaires* (Luxemburg: Editions Saint Paul-Quart Monde, 1992), volume I, p. 37. Available in French only.
6. Wresinski, *Ecrits et paroles aux volontaires*, volume I, pp. 219-22, from a letter read aloud at a meeting of volunteers, autumn 1963.
7. Wresinski, *Ecrits et Paroles aux Volontaires*, volume I, pp. 219-22, from a letter read aloud at a meeting of volunteers, autumn 1963.
8. Sève, 'Mary, volontaire à ATD Quart Monde'.
9. Wresinski, *Ecrits et paroles aux volontaires*, volume I, pp. 93-95.
10. Wresinski, *Ecrits et paroles aux volontaires*, volume I, pp. 81-88, citing a meeting of volunteers in May 1962.
11. Wresinski, *Ecrits et paroles aux volontaires*, volume I, pp. 120-21 citing a meeting of volunteers in summer 1962.
12. Wresinski, *Ecrits et paroles aux volontaires*, volume I, p. 137, from a letter to Maria W. on 7 December 1962.
13. Joseph Wresinski Centre: Archives, YH40, 'La différence entre les pauvres vus avant, et les familles de Noisy-le-Grand', undated.
14. Tracy Shildrick and Jessica Rucell, Jessica, *Sociological Perspectives on Poverty* (York: Joseph Rowntree Foundation, June 2015), p. 15. [Available

at https://www.jrf.org.uk/report/sociological-perspectives-poverty, accessed 3 August 2019]
15. Joseph Wresinski Centre: Archives, YH40, 'La différence entre les pauvres vus avant, et les familles de Noisy-le-Grand', undated.
16. Personal archives of Paul de St Croix, letter from M. Rabagliati to her parents, 20 November 1964.
17. Joseph Wresinski Centre: Archives, Interview with M. Rabagliati by E. Boespflug, 2 September 1976.
18. Letter from Penny and Tony Heath to Tom and Shaeda Croft, 18 February 2017.
19. Joseph Wresinski Centre: Archives, Interview with M. Rabagliati by a 'Hibernation' group with C. Egner, D. Robert, and J. Toussaint, November 1985.
20. Wresinski, *Ecrits et paroles aux volontaires,* volume 1, p. 278 in a letter written to M. Rabagliati from Bangalore in March 1965.
21. Wresinski, *Ecrits et paroles aux volontaires,* volume 1, pp. 194-201, citing a meeting of volunteers on 8 October 1963, and p. 214, citing a meeting of volunteers with a group of Jesuits in November 1963.
22. Joseph Wresinski Centre: Archives, 0330-XV87, speech by M. Rabagliati to the Faith and Light European Region Meeting in Llanelli, UK, 21 September 1978.
23. Joseph Wresinski Centre: Archives, 0375-22, Letter from M. Rabagliati to Michèle Gérardin, 5 March 1990.
24. Joseph Wresinski Centre: Archives, 1068/13/1.3, Black Forest Group meeting, 1 February 1992.
25. Joseph Wresinski Centre: Archives, Interview with M. Rabagliati by a 'Hibernation' group with C. Egner, D. Robert, and J. Toussaint, November 1985.

Chapter 6

1. Letter from S.M. Miller to D. Skelton, 21 March 2017.
2. Joseph Wresinski Centre: Archives, Interview with M. Rabagliati by 'Hibernation' group with C. Egner and J. Toussaint, November 1985.
3. Graham Hodges, 'Lower East Side' in Kenneth T. Jackson (ed.), *The Encyclopedia of New York City* (2nd ed. New Haven, CT: Yale University Press, 2010), pp. 769-70.
4. F. Clement-Fanelli, *Taking a Country at its Word: Joseph Wresinski Confronts the Reality and Ideals of the United States* (Landover, MD: Fourth World Publications, 2006).
5. Personal archives of Paul de St Croix, audiotaped letter from V. Fanelli to M. Rabagliati, September 1983.
6. M. Rabagliati and E. Birnbaum, 'Organizations of Welfare Clients', in H. Weissman (ed.), *Community Development in the*

Mobilization for Youth Experience (New York: Association Press, 1969), p. 103.
7. A. Fried, 'The Attack on Mobilization', in H. Weissman (ed.), *Community Development in the Mobilization for Youth Experience* (New York: Association Press, 1969), p. 137.
8. Personal archives of Paul de St Croix, audiotaped letter from D. Kronenfeld to M. Rabagliati, September 1983.
9. Personal archives of Paul de St Croix, audiotaped letter from D. Kronenfeld to M. Rabagliati, September 1983.
10. Joseph Wresinski Centre: Archives, letter from M. Rabagliati to A. de Vos van Steenwijk, 14 August 1965,
11. Emmanuel Jovelin, 'L'enseignement du travail social en Europe: La reconnaissance par l'université en question', 2006, [Available at: https://www.cairn.info/revue-informations-sociales-2006-7-page-120.htm, accessed on 8 August 2017]
12. Joseph Wresinski Centre: Archives, 0375-7, YC54, letter from M. Rabagliati to J. Wresinski, 24 October 1965.
13. 'Schtick' is a Yiddish expression meaning behaviour or comments that a person is well known for.
14. Letter from C. de León to D. Skelton, 14 March 2017.
15. Joseph Wresinski Centre: Archives, 0375-7, letter from M. Rabagliati to J. Wresinski from New York, 23 March 1966.
16. Letter from S.M. Miller to D. Skelton, 21 March 2017.
17. Joseph Wresinski Centre: Archives, 0375-7, letter from M. Rabagliati to J. Wresinski from New York, 23 March 1966.
18. 'Northern Lawyer for Rights Group Jailed in Alabama', *New York Times*, 17 November 1966. [Available at: https://timesmachine.nytimes.com/timesmachine/1966/11/17/82157721.html?pageNumber=34, accessed 11 August 2019]
19. Joseph Wresinski Centre: Archives, Interview with M. Rabagliati by 'Hibernation' group with C. Egner and J. Toussaint, November 1985.
20. Joseph Wresinski Centre: Archives, 0375-7, letter from M. Rabagliati to J. Wresinski, 24 October 1965.
21. Joseph Wresinski Centre: Archives, Letter from M. Rabagliati to Beverly, 14 January 1967.
22. Joseph Wresinski Centre: Archives, 1AV043A-1AV043C (audiotapes), 'Evaluation voyage USA', 1967.

Chapter 7

1. 'Desire Projects', Wikipedia. [Available at: https://en.wikipedia.org/wiki/Desire_Projects#History, accessed 26 August 2019]
2. Audio recording of Dolores Huerta, Farmworker Movement Documentation Project, UC San Diego Library. [Available at:

https://libraries.ucsd.edu/farmworkermovement/medias/oral-history/, accessed 8 August 2019]
3. Clément-Fanelli, *Taking a Country at its Word*, p. 27.
4. Amy Sonnie and James Tracy, *Hillbilly Nationalists, Urban Race Rebels, and Black Power: The Rise of Community Organizing* (Brooklyn, NY: Melville House Publishing, 2011); and letter from P. Simmons to F. Clément-Fanelli, 22 July 2021.
5. Interviews with G. Erpicum, March and June 2018.
6. Rabagliati and Birnbaum, 'Organizations of Welfare Clients', pp. 135-36.

Chapter 8

1. Joseph Wresinski Centre: Archives, 1030-04-01.
2. Joseph Wresinski Centre: Archives, 1030-43-2.
3. Joseph Wresinski Centre: Archives, 1030/04/01.
4. Joseph Wresinski Centre: Archives, 1030/43/02, Letter from M. Rabagliati to Mr. Philip Bryers, 19 March 1974.
5. Joseph Wresinski Centre: Archives, 1030/43/02, Letter from Ellen Cumber to M. Rabagliati, 6 March 1975.
6. Joseph Wresinski Centre: Archives, 1030/43/02, Letter from S. Devins to M. Rabagliati, 25 February 1985.
7. Joseph Wresinski Centre: Archives, 1030/43/02, Letter from T. Kotze to M. Rabagliati, 5 May 1976.
8. Joseph Wresinski Centre: Archives, Report by M. Rabagliati, February-March 1983, 1030/04/04.
9. Joseph Wresinski Centre: Archives, Letter from M. Rabagliati to J. Wresinski, 6 March 1983, 1030/04/04.
10. Gavin Evans, 'Obituary: Phyllis Naidoo, Activist Who Sought to End Apartheid', *The Independent*, 24 April 2013.
11. Joseph Wresinski Centre: Archives, Letter from M. Rabagliati to J. Wresinski, 6 March 1983, 1030/04/04.
12. Joseph Wresinski Centre: Archives, Report by M. Rabagliati, February-March 1983, 1030/04/04.
13. Joseph Wresinski Centre: Archives, Letter from M. Rabagliati to J.P. Lescour, 21 July 1983, 1030/43/02.
14. Elin Martínez, 'South Africa's Children with Disabilities Need the President's Attention', 25 April 2019, https://www.hrw.org/news/2019/04/25/south-africas-children-disabilities-need-presidents-attention and https://www.facebook.com/SocialDevelopmentZA/photos/today-we-join-the-sidinga-uthando-self-help-group-to-paint-another-house-purple-/1177580018990554/
15. 'Martin Kalisa – Deputy Director – ATD Fourth World', ATD Fourth World, 2021, https://www.atd-fourthworld.org/who-we-are

/organization/international-leadership-team-atd-fourth-world-international/martin-kalisa/

Chapter 9

1. M. Rabagliati, 'Racism and the Fourth World', *Fourth World Journal*, 12, March 1980.
2. Letter from U. Jomini to D. Skelton, 11 April 2018.
3. Joseph Wresinski Centre: Archives, 0138-XV53, Fourth World Evening, 14 February 1980.
4. Joseph Wresinski Centre: Archives, 0138-XV53, Fourth World Evening, 13 March 1980.
5. Joseph Wresinski Centre: Archives, 0138-XV53, Fourth World Evening, 8 May 1980.
6. Suyin Hayes, 'The Enduring Lessons of the Battle of Cable Street 80 Years On', *Time Magazine*, 3 October 2016, https://time.com/4516276/cable-street-battle-london-east-end-80-years/
7. Joseph Wresinski Centre: Archives, 0138-XV49, Fourth World Evening, 11 November 1976.
8. Joseph Wresinski Centre: Archives, 0138-XV53, Fourth World Evening, 13 March 1980.
9. Joseph Wresinski Centre: Archives, 0138-XV49, Fourth World Evening, 11 November 1976.

Chapter 10

1. Valeriya Safronova, 'Catherine Deneuve, Others Denounce the #MeToo Movement', *New York Times*, 9 January 2018. https://www.nytimes.com/2018/01/09/movies/catherine-deneuve-and-others-denounce-the-metoo-movement.html
2. "Kills Girl of 17 as She Tries to Aid Him", *New York Times*, 6 May 1912, https://timesmachine.nytimes.com/timesmachine/1912/05/06/100533817.html?pageNumber=20
3. adrienne maree brown, *Pleasure Activism: The Politics of Feeling Good* (Chico, CA: AK Press, 2019), p. 16.
4. J. Wresinski, 'In the Vicious Circle of Violence', 1970. https://www.joseph-wresinski.org/en/young-boy-caught-in-the-vicious/
5. Wresinski, speech, 17 February 1971.
6. Joseph Wresinski Centre: Archives, Ecrits quotidiens, M. Rabagliati, Noisy-le-Grand, 19-27 November 1962.
7. All names in these confidential writings have been changed.

Notes   343

Chapter 11

1. Joseph Wresinski Centre: Archives, 0115-FRA-Detection-1955_1985-DS, R1B099 X076, letters from M. Rabagliati to J. Wresinski, 18 February, 25 February, and 7 March 1963, and also short excerpts from her reports of January and February 1963, written in Lee Crescent, Birmingham.
2. Letter from Colin Barham to D. Skelton, 27 March 2018.
3. A method by which a woman keeps track of her cycle to know when she is less fertile.
4. Joseph Wresinski Centre: Archives, Série C-Noisy, G. Erpicum, 'Reunion Action: Faut-il aborder la question contraception avec les familles?'
5. Joseph Wresinski Centre: Archives, Série C-Noisy, Erpicum, 'Reunion Action'.
6. Joseph Wresinski Centre: Archives, Interview with M. Rabagliati by E. Boespflug, 2 September 1976.
7. Jean Labbens, *La condition sous-prolétarienne, l'héritage du passé* [The Sub-Proletarian Condition: A Heritage from the Past] (Paris: Editions Quart Monde, 1965), p. 96. In French only.
8. Joseph Wresinski Centre: Archives, Interview with M. Rabagliati by E. Boespflug, 2 September 1976.
9. Joseph Wresinski Centre: Archives, Daily writings, M. Rabagliati, 1965.

Chapter 12

1. Joseph Wresinski Centre: Archives, Daily writings, M. Rabagliati, 1965.
2. Joseph Wresinski Centre: Archives, *0375-22*, letters from M. Rabagliati to Michèle Gérardin in Haiti, 12 February 1988 and 11 January 1990.
3. Francine de la Gorce, *L'espoir gronde: Noisy-le-Grand 1956-1962* (Paris: Editions Quart Monde, 1992), p. 247.
4. Joseph Wresinski Centre: Archives, Interview with M. Rabagliati by E. Boespflug, 2 September 1976.
5. Joseph Wresinski Centre: Archives, letter from M. Rabagliati to G. Erpicum, late 1966.
6. Joseph Wresinski Centre: Archives, Interview with M. Rabagliati by E. Boespflug, 2 September 1976.
7. Joseph Wresinski Centre: Archives, YB03 – Fonds Chrono Provisoire, Interview with M. Rabagliati by 'Hibernation' group, 11 May 1990.
8. Personal archives of Paul de St Croix, letter from M. Rabagliati to her parents, 11 July 1967.
9. Letter from U. Jomini to D. Skelton, 11 April 2018.
10. Letter from G. Adriaensens to D. Skelton, 15 April 2018.
11. Thomas Reese, 'Humanae Vitae: Sex and Authority in the Catholic Church', *National Catholic Reporter*, 20 July 2018. [Available

https://www.ncronline.org/news/opinion/signs-times/humanae-vitae-sex-and-authority-catholic-church, accessed 16 August 2019]
12. Wresinski, *Ecrits et paroles aux volontaires, mars-mai 1967*, volume II, (Luxembourg: Editions Saint Paul, 1996), pp. 86-87 and 99.
13. Wresinski, *Ecrits et paroles aux volontaires*, volume II, pp. 136-37.
14. 'Viol conjugal: ce que dit la loi française', E-Santé website, 28 November 2018. [Available at: https://www.e-sante.fr/viol-conjugal-ce-que-dit-la-loi-francaise/actualite/615619, accessed 16 August 2019]

Chapter 13

1. Joseph Wresinski Centre: Archives, 0269-INT-FondsChronoMvt-1954_2005-DS, Interview with M. Rabagliati in 1989 by the 'Hibernation' group.
2. Joseph Wresinski Centre: Archives, 0138-XV56, morning meeting in Addington Square with M. Rabagliati about the history of ATD Fourth World in preparation for October 1983 Fourth World Evening.
3. Interview of H. Bossot-Redegeld by D. Skelton, 20 June 2018.
4. Interview of S. and I. Williams by N. Anderson and M. Hogan, 30 May 2017.
5. Michael Lambert, '"Dumping grounds for … human waste": containing problem populations in post- war British public health policy, 1945–74', in *Publics and their health: Historical problems and perspectives*, Eds. Alex Mold, Peder Clark and Hannah J. Elizabeth, (Manchester: Manchester University Press), 2023, p. 55.
6. Michael Lambert, '"Problem families" and the post-war welfare state in the North West of England, c. 1943-74'. Unpublished PhD, Lancaster University, 2017.
7. Lambert, doctoral research.
8. Joseph Wresinski Centre: *Archives: 0107-INT-doc_GBR-CHE-BEL-1967_1979-DS*, notes by M. Rabagliati following a meeting with other recuperative homes, 18 May 1968, Manchester.
9. Lambert, doctoral research.
10. Letter from M. Lambert to D. Skelton, 3 April 2025.
11. Lambert, doctoral research.
12. Interview with S. and I. Williams by N. Anderson and M. Hogan, 30 May 2017.
13. Joseph Wresinski Centre: Archives, 0138-XV49, ATD Fourth World Evening, 9 December 1976.
14. Quotes from M. Rabagliati about Frimhurst come from: Joseph Wresinski Centre: Archives, VIDC-2012-022011, BBC 'Film about Frimhurst', 1974; *0135_309*, International ATD annual report, June 1970; 0110/50, ATD Fourth World seminar on knowledge and action, 25

July 1990; Interview with M. Rabagliati by Etienne Boespflug, 2 September 1976; 0255-EUR-GBR-Frimhurst-London-1965_2001-DS, The Frimhurst Journal, No. 2, July 1969 and No. 3, March 1970; 0255-EUR-GBR-Frimhurst-London-1965_2001-DS, letter from M. Rabagliati to Gabrielle Erpicum, 28 April 1973; 0138-XV49, ATD Fourth World Evening, 9 December 1976; 0330-XV87, speech by M. Rabagliati to the Faith and Light European Region Meeting in Llanelli, UK, 21 September 1978; and Interview with M. Rabagliati by Etienne Boespflug, 2 September 1976.

15. Joseph Wresinski Centre: Archives, 0110/50, ATD Fourth World seminar on knowledge and action, 25 July 1990.
16. Joseph Wresinski Centre: Archives, 0303-XL50, letter from M. Rabagliati to H. von Burg and J. Beyeler, 19 November 1968.
17. Joseph Wresinski Centre: Archives, 0255-EUR-GBR-Frimhurst-London-1965_2001-DS, *The Frimhurst Journal*, 2, July 1969.
18. Joseph Wresinski Centre: Archives, Film footage from 1974 excerpted from Pathway Films Camberley by A.J. Dalley and D.J. White, ARPE, with commentary by Peter Bayly.
19. Joseph Wresinski Centre: Archives, 0107-INT-doc_GBR-CHE-BEL-1967_1979-DS, 'In Practice', *Community Care*, April 1977.
20. Interview of V. and P. Bottomley by N. Edwards and D. Skelton, 27 July 2018.
21. Joseph Wresinski Centre: Archives, 0303-XL50, letter from M. Rabagliati to H. von Burg and J. Beyeler, 19 November 1968.
22. Joseph Wresinski Centre: Archives, 0303-XL50, letters from M. Rabagliati to H. von Burg and J. Beyeler, 12 July 1969 and 3 March 1970.
23. Joseph Wresinski Centre: Archives, 0330-XV87, speech by M. Rabagliati to the Faith and Light European Region Meeting in Llanelli, UK, 21 September 1978.

Chapter 14

1. Joseph Wresinski Centre: Archives, 0303-XL50, letter from M. Rabagliati to H. von Burg and J. Beyeler, 4 December 1969.
2. Joseph Wresinski Centre: Archives, 0255-EUR-GBR-Frimhurst-London-1965_2001-DS, *Frimhurst Journal*, 2, July 1969.
3. Joseph Wresinski Centre: Archives, 0255-EUR-GBR-Frimhurst-London-1965_2001-DS, *Frimhurst Journal*, 2, July 1969.
4. Joseph Wresinski Centre: Archives, 0255-EUR-GBR-Frimhurst-London-1965_2001-DS, *Frimhurst Journal*, 2, July 1969.
5. Joseph Wresinski Centre: Archives, 0303-XL50, letter from M. Rabagliati to H. von Burg and J. Beyeler, 19 November 1968.

6. Joseph Wresinski Centre: Archives, 0303-XL50, letter from M. Rabagliati to H. von Burg and J. Beyeler, 4 December 1969.
7. Joseph Wresinski Centre: Archives, 0255-EUR-GBR-Frimhurst-London-1965_2001-DS, *Frimhurst Journal*, 2, July 1969.
8. Joseph Wresinski Centre: Archives, 0138-XV56, Fourth World Evening about the history of ATD Fourth World, 13 October 1983.

Chapter 15

1. Joseph Wresinski Centre: Archives, 0303-XL50, letter from M. Rabagliati to H. von Burg and J. Beyeler, 26 November 1970.
2. Joseph Wresinski Centre: Archives, 0303-XL50, letter from M. Rabagliati to H. von Burg and J. Beyeler, 26 November 1970.
3. Joseph Wresinski Centre: Archives, speech by M. Rabagliati to a general assembly of allies of ATD Fourth World, 1 November 1989.
4. Joseph Wresinski Centre: Archives, 0255-EUR-GBR-Frimhurst-London-1965_2001-DS, meeting with J. Wresinski, 4 March 1973.
5. Joseph Wresinski Centre: Archives, letter from J. Wresinski to M. Rabagliati, 25 October 1964.
6. Joseph Wresinski Centre: Archives: letter from M. Rabagliati to J. Wresinski, 24 October 1965.
7. Joseph Wresinski Centre: Archives, 0303-XL50, letter from M. Rabagliati to H. von Burg and J. Beyeler, 12 July 1969.
8. Phyllis Willmott, 'Russell [*née* Stewart], Katherine Frances [Kit]', *Oxford Dictionary of National Biography*, 23 September 2004. [Available at: https://www.oxforddnb.com/view/10.1093/ref:odnb/9780198614128.001.0001/odnb-9780198614128-e-70246;jsessionid=3C45C25AD87274353B3F01B45036D99D, accessed 19 August 2019]
9. Personal archives of Paul de St Croix, letter from Kit Russell to Sandra de St Croix, 29 October 1992.
10. Joseph Wresinski Centre: Archives, 0303-XL50, letters from M. Rabagliati to H. von Burg and J. Beyeler, 12 July 1969 and 3 March 1970.
11. Joseph Wresinski Centre: Archives, 1068/4/1.6, 'Ce que les familles attendent de notre Volontariat', speech by M. Rabagliati at ATD Fourth World's General Assembly of senior Volunteer Corps members, August 1983.
12. Joseph Wresinski Centre, Archives: letter from M. Rabagliati to Gabrielle Erpicum, 23 August 1971.
13. Joseph Wresinski Centre, Archives: 0255-EUR-GBR-Frimhurst-London-1965_2001-DS, letter from M. Rabagliati to Gabrielle Erpicum, 17 May 1973.
14. Interview of F. Bennett by D. Skelton, 29 June 2018.
15. Letter from Paul Arnesen to D. Skelton, 24 June 2017.

16. Joseph Wresinski Centre: Archives: 0255-EUR-GBR-Frimhurst-London-1965_2001-DS, *Frimhurst Journal*, 3, March 1970.
17. Interview of S. Baker by D. Skelton, 22 June 2018.
18. Interview of S. Baker by D. Skelton, 22 June 2018.
19. Letter from Colin Barham to D. Skelton, 27 February 2018.
20. Joseph Wresinski Centre: Archives: 0255-EUR-GBR-Frimhurst-London-1965_2001-DS, *Frimhurst Journal*, 3, March 1970.
21. Film about Frimhurst, 1974.
22. Film about Frimhurst, 1974.

Chapter 16

1. Joseph Wresinski Centre: Archives, 0138-XV56, Fourth World Evening about the history of ATD Fourth World, 13 October 1983.
2. Interview of F. Bennett by D. Skelton, 29 June 2018.
3. Joseph Wresinski Centre: Archives, 0138-XV56, Fourth World Evening about the history of ATD Fourth World, 13 October 1983.
4. Joseph Wresinski Centre: Archives, 0110/50, ATD Fourth World seminar on knowledge and action, 25 July 1990.
5. Interview of Isabelle and Stuart Williams by Mark Hogan and Naomi Anderson, 30 May 2017.
6. Interview of F. Bennett by D. Skelton, 29 June 2018.
7. Joseph Wresinski Centre: Archives, 0375-22, letter from Mimi Parnell to Stuart Williams, 21 November 1992.
8. Interview of V. and P. Bottomley by N. Edwards and D. Skelton, 27 July 2018.
9. Joseph Wresinski Centre: Archives, 0110/50, ATD Fourth World seminar on knowledge and action, 25 July 1990.

Chapter 17

1. Joseph Wresinski Centre: Archives, 0375-22, letter from Judith Stone to ATD, November 1992.
2. Jo Tunnard, *UK Children OK?*, (London: UK Association for the International Year of the Child, 1979), pp. 13.
3. Letter from J. Stone to D. Skelton, 5 April 2025.
4. ATD Fourth World, *Children of Our Time*, pp. 20, 32, 76, and 94.
5. Joseph Wresinski Centre: Archives, 1030/34.
6. Joseph Wresinski Centre: Archives, transcript of interview of Reggie J. Chapman on 'Directions 1981', a Public Affairs Programme of WYLB Radio in cooperation with the A Philip Randolph Institute.
7. Joseph Wresinski Centre: Archives, transcript of interview of Reggie J. Chapman on 'Directions 1981', a Public Affairs Programme of WYLB Radio in cooperation with the A Philip Randolph Institute.

8. Letter from S. Williams to D. Skelton, 26 June 2017.
9. Interview of F. Bennett by D. Skelton, 29 June 2018.
10. Interview of A. van Elderen by D. Skelton, 7 March 2018.
11. Interview of A. Van Elderen by D. Skelton, 26 May 2019.
12. Letter from U. Jomini to D. Skelton, 11 April 2018.
13. Interview of H. Bossot Redegeld by D. Skelton, 20 June 2018.
14. Interview of F. Bennett by D. Skelton, 29 June 2018.
15. Letter from U. Jomini to D. Skelton, 11 April 2018.
16. Interview with A. van Elderen, 7 March 2018.
17. Joseph Wresinski Centre: Archives, 0269-INT-FondsChronoMvt-1954_2005-DS, Interview with M. Rabagliati in November 1985 by a 'Hibernation' group of H. van Breen, A.-M. Caron, C. Egner, D. Robert, and J. Toussaint.
18. Joseph Wresinski Centre: Archives, 0138-XV54, Fourth World Evenings, 1980.
19. Joseph Wresinski Centre: Archives, 0138-XV55, Fourth World Evenings, 1981.
20. Joseph Wresinski Centre: Archives, 0138-XV51, Fourth World Evenings 1978.
21. Interview with A. van Elderen, 7 March 2018.
22. Interview of S. Baker by D. Skelton, 22 June 2018.
23. Geneviève Defraigne Tardieu, *L'Unversité populaire Quart Monde : La construction du savoir émancipatoire* [The Fourth World People's University: The Construction of Emancipatory Knowledge] (Paris: Presses universitaires de Paris Ouest, 2012). Published in French only, but a draft English translation is available on request.
24. Joseph Wresinski Centre: Archives, 0269-INT-FondsChronoMvt-1954_2005-DS, Interview of M. Rabagliati in November 1985 by a 'Hibernation' group of H. van Breen, A.-M. Caron, C. Egner, D. Robert, and J. Toussaint.
25. Joseph Wresinski Centre: Archives, 0138-XV49, Fourth World Evening, 11 November 1976.
26. Unemployment rate in the United Kingdom from March 1971 to January 2024, https://www.statista.com/statistics/279898/unemployment-rate-in-the-united-kingdom-uk/
27. Joseph Wresinski Centre: Archives, 0138-XV56, morning meeting in Addington Square with M. Rabagliati about the history of ATD Fourth World in preparation for October 1983 Fourth World Evening.
28. Joseph Wresinski Centre: Archives, 'An interview with Mary Rabagliati for families' freedom', 1985.

Chapter 18

1. Joseph Wresinski Centre: Archives, 0138-XV56, morning meeting in Addington Square with M. Rabagliati about the history of ATD Fourth World in preparation for October 1983 Fourth World Evening.
2. Street Libraries are outdoor sessions for children in poverty to enjoy books and creative workshops.
3. Joseph Wresinski Centre: Archives, 1019-INT-Equipe-RelatExt-1977_1999-Inv, report by D. Wardi on her visit to ATD's international centre, May 1988.
4. Cherry Casey, 'The UK Has a Forced Adoption Problem', *Prospect Magazine*, 2022, https://www.prospectmagazine.co.uk/society-and-culture/the-uk-has-a-forced-adoption-problem
5. Simon Haworth, 'Hazily Defined and a Culture of Risk: How Can Social Workers Properly Approach Risks of Future Emotional Harm?', *Community Care*, 19 October 2018, https://www.communitycare.co.uk/2018/10/19/hazily-defined-and-a-culture-of-risk-how-can-social-workers-properly-approach-risks-of-future-emotional-harm/
6. Casey, 'UK Forced Adoption Problem'.
7. Patrick Butler, 'Government Lawful in Allowing 16- and 17-year-olds in Unregulated Care, Court Rules', *The Guardian*, 17 March 2022, https://www.theguardian.com/society/2022/mar/17/government-lawful-in-allowing-16--and-17-year-olds-in-unregulated-care-court-rules
8. ATD Fourth World, 'Understanding Poverty in All its Forms', 17 October 2019, https://atd-uk.org/projects-campaigns/understanding-poverty/.
9. 'We Can Speak for Ourselves', *Amnesty UK members' magazine*, Summer 2023, https://gripp.org.uk/wp-content/uploads/2023/05/JNL-217-Pov-and-HRUK-p14-21.pdf

Chapter 19

1. Letter from P. de St Croix to D. Skelton, 4 July 2018.
2. Royal Holloway, University of London, 'Beyond the Ballot', a MOOC course taught as part of the Citizens' Project, 2018, https://www.royalholloway.ac.uk/research-and-teaching/departments-and-schools/history/news/beyond-the-ballot/
3. Joseph Wresinski Centre: Archives, 0138-XV49, Fourth World Evening on the theme 'The Woman', 3 April 1975.
4. Joseph Wresinski Centre: Archives, 0138-XV49, Fourth World Evening on 'The Woman', 3 April 1975.
5. Joseph Wresinski Centre: Archives, 1068-INT-ForetNoire-1981_2001-Inv, transcript of Black Forest Group, 19 and 20 December 1980.

6. Joseph Wresinski Centre: Archives, 1021-INT-ONU-RelatExt-AnneesInternationales-1975_2000-Inv, 'Social Work Education and Development', *Newsletter of the Economic and Social Commission for Asia and the Pacific* (Bangkok)16, July 1976.
7. Interview with H. Bossot Redegeld, 20 June 2018.
8. Joseph Wresinski Centre: Archives, 1021-INT-ONU-RelatExt-AnneesInternationales-1975_2000-Inv, letter drafted by M. Rabagliati to be signed by J. Wresinski, and addressed to Catholic Relief Services.
9. Joseph Wresinski Centre: Archives, 1021-INT-ONU-RelatExt-AnneesInternationales-1975_2000-Inv, letter from A. de Vos van Steenwijk, 'A toutes mes compagnes volontaires', June 1975, Mexico.
10. Joseph Wresinski Centre: Archives, 1030/43/02, Letter from M. Rabagliati to Hope Hay, 21 July 1975.
11. Joseph Wresinski Centre: Archives, 1021-INT-ONU-RelatExt-AnneesInternationales-1975_2000-Inv, letter from A. de Vos van Steenwijk, 'A toutes mes compagnes volontaires', June 1975, Mexico.
12. Joseph Wresinski Centre: Archives, 1021-INT-ONU-RelatExt-AnneesInternationales-1975_2000-Inv, report by A. de Vos van Steenwijk, 'Réunion sur Mexico – Année Internationale de la Femme', 2 August 1975.
13. Joseph Wresinski Centre: Archives, 1021-INT-ONU-RelatExt-AnneesInternationales-1975_2000-Inv, 'Women in the Fourth World', *Newsletter of the Women's Forum and the Standing Conferences of Women's Organisations*, series no. 4, Winter 1975-76.
14. Joseph Wresinski Centre: Archives, 0138-XV49, report by M. Rabagliati on 'The Abortion Law' discussion during a Fourth World Evening, 13 May 1976.
15. The Charter is available at https://www.atd-quartmonde.org/wp-content/uploads/2023/03/Charte-de-la-femme-du-Quart-Monde-1.pdf
16. Joseph Wresinski Centre: Archives, 1021-INT-ONU-RelatExt-AnneesInternationales-1975_2000-Inv, letter from M. Rabagliati to J. Wresinski from Copenhagen, 24 July 1980.
17. https://www.un.org/womenwatch/daw/cedaw/history.htm
18. Joseph Wresinski Centre: Archives, 1021-INT-ONU-RelatExt-AnneesInternationales-1975_2000-Inv, excerpts from a contribution made by M. Rabagliati to the panel on 'The Family' at the forum in Copenhagen for the Mid-Decade for Women, 22 July 1980.
19. Joseph Wresinski Centre: Archives, 1021-INT-ONU-RelatExt-AnneesInternationales-1975_2000-Inv, resolution ref. 29A/CON/94/C.1/L35, cited five years later in letter from Mary Rabagliati to Baroness Young of Farnworth, Minister of State for Foreign and Commonwealth Affairs, 27 June 1985.

20. Joseph Wresinski Centre: Archives, 1030/40/03/01, Letter from J. Wresinski to Louise Tappa, 1 July 1985.
21. Joseph Wresinski Centre: Archives, 1021-INT-ONU-RelatExt-AnneesInternationales-1975_2000-Inv, letter from M. Rabagliati to Baroness Young of Farnworth, Minister of State for Foreign and Commonwealth Affairs, 27 June 1985.
22. Joseph Wresinski Centre: Archives, 1021-INT-ONU-RelatExt-AnneesInternationales-1975_2000-Inv, letter from Baroness Young to M. Rabagliati, 5 July 1985.
23. Joseph Wresinski Centre: Archives, 1021-INT-ONU-RelatExt-AnneesInternationales-1975_2000-Inv, report by M. Rabagliati, "Conférence gouvernemental de l'ONU à Nairobi, Décennie de la Femme", July 1985.
24. Joseph Wresinski Centre: Archives, 1021-INT-ONU-RelatExt-AnneesInternationales-1975_2000-Inv, letter from M. Rabagliati to Mrs. J. Mixer of DHSS, undated but probably in December 1985.
25. Joseph Wresinski Centre: Archives, 1021-INT-ONU-RelatExt-AnneesInternationales-1975_2000-Inv, untitled draft of an article by M. Rabagliati for *Feuille de Route*, 2 August 1985.

Chapter 20

1. P. and E. Hamel, letter to D. Skelton, 10 April 2018.
2. Ruth Maclean, 'Democracy Teetering in African Countries Once Ruled by France', *New York Times*, 22 March 2024. [Available at: https://www.nytimes.com/2024/03/22/world/africa/democracy-senegal-africa-france.html?, accessed 24 March 2024]
3. Joseph Wresinski Centre: Archives, 1068/4/1.6, open letter from M. Rabagliati to senior Volunteer Corps members, 2 August 1983.
4. Joseph Wresinski Centre: Archives, 1068/4/1.6, open letter from M. Rabagliati to senior Volunteer Corps members, 2 August 1983.
5. Joseph Wresinski Centre: Archives, 1068-INT-ForetNoire-1981_2001-Inv, notes from Black Forest Group meeting, 19-20 August 1982.
6. Joseph Wresinski Centre: Archives, 1068/4/1.6, open letter from M. Rabagliati to senior Volunteer Corps members, 2 August 1983.
7. Interview of J. Beyeler by D. Skelton, 17-18 April 2018.
8. Joseph Wresinski Centre: Archives, 0375-7, letter from M. Rabagliati to J. Wresinski from New York, 23 March 1966.
9. http://overcomingpoverty.org/
10. Joseph Wresinski Centre: Archives, 1068/13/1.3, Black Forest Group meeting, 1 February 1992.
11. Joseph Wresinski Centre: Archives, 1030/03/01.
12. Joseph Wresinski Centre: Archives, 1030/06, Note by M. Rabagliati, 5 June 1986.

13. Interview of Duncan Charles Pringle Rabagliati (a great-great-grandson of Giacomo Gaetano Francesco Rabagliati and Caroline Kinnison) by D. Skelton, 27 March 2018.
14. Kelso Mail 7 June 1827; The Scotsman 5 December 1827.
15. 'Pen Portrait No. 20. ACF Rabagliati', *Yorkshire Notes and Queries*, November 1905, and Obituary, Andrea Rabagliati M.D. F.R.C.S., 20 December 1930, British Medical Journal.
16. Letter from Margaret Rabagliati Wood to D. Skelton, 10 September 2018.
17. Interview of M. Rabagliati Wood by D. Skelton, 18 September 2018.
18. Letter from A. Rabagliati to D. Skelton, 1 February 2019.
19. Letter from M. Rabagliati Wood to D. Skelton, 27 January 2019.
20. Interview of Julia Moss by D. Skelton 6 April 2018.
21. Joseph Wresinski Centre: Archives, CJW-0028/039-052V, M. Rabagliati, 'What Voluntariat will we be in Africa?', article in ATD's internal 'Dossiers de Pierrelaye', May 1983.
22. Joseph Wresinski Centre: Archives, CJW-0028/039-052V, M. Rabagliati, 'What Voluntariat will we be in Africa?'
23. Joseph Wresinski Centre: Archives, CJW-0028/039-052V, M. Rabagliati, 'What Voluntariat will we be in Africa?'
24. Joseph Wresinski Centre: Archives, 1030/22, Letter from N. and D. Kikaya to J. Wresinski, 2 April 1984.
25. Letter from S. Devins to D. Skelton, 23 March 2018.
26. Joseph Wresinski Centre: Archives, 1030/02/01, presentation by S. Devins to the board of directors of ATD Fourth World, 20 October 1990.

Chapter 21

1. Interview of J. Grandi by D. Skelton, 15 March 2018.
2. M. Rabagliati, 24 April 1985, 'The Story of a Commitment at the Heart of the Poorest of the Poor', from the personal archives of J. Grandi. A shorter and slightly edited version of the same story was published in French and is available at the Joseph Wresinski Centre: Archive, CJW-002/054-065VQM, 'Un engagement au coeur des plus pauvres', 'Dossiers de Pierrelaye', La Vie en Quart Monde, March/April 1985.
3. 'Air pollution is responsible for 6.7 million premature deaths every year', World Health Organisation. [Available at https://www.who.int/teams/environment-climate-change-and-health/air-quality-and-health/health-impacts/types-of-pollutants, accessed on 27 January 2024]
4. Interview of J. Grandi by D. Skelton, 15 March 2018.
5. Joseph Wresinski Centre: Archives, 1030/02/01, letter from M. Rabagliati to S. Devins, 25 March 1985.
6. Joseph Wresinski Centre: Archives, 1030/05.

7. Joseph Wresinski Centre: Archives, 1030/02/01, presentation by S. Devins to the board of directors of ATD Fourth World, 20 October 1990.
 8. Letter from S. Devins to D. Skelton, 1 May 2018.
 9. Interview of J. Beyeler by D. Skelton, 17-18 April 2018.
 10. Letter from F. Klein to D. Skelton, 2 May 2018.
 11. Letter from K. Hart to D. Skelton, August 2016.

Chapter 22

 1. The quotes from F. Didisheim in this chapter are combined from two sources: a report she wrote in 1963, and a tape-recorded message she mailed to M. Rabagliati in 1983.
 2. From notes dictated by B. Cornuau to Jean-Michel Defromont on 15 December 2010 for the preparation of his biography of her *J'ai cherché si c'était vrai* [I Went to Find out if it was True], (Paris, France: Editions Quart Monde, 2015)
 3. From notes dictated by B. Cornuau to Jean-Michel Defromont on 15 December 2010.
 4. Joseph Wresinski Centre: Archives, YH38, letter from M. Rabagliati to John de St Croix, 5 January 1964.
 5. Jona Rosenfeld, in dialogue with Jean-Michel Defromont, *From Exclusion to Reciprocity: 'Learning from Success'* (Lanham, MD: Hamilton Books, 2017), pp. 93-94.
 6. Joseph Wresinski Centre: Archives, 1030/15-2, report by Mary Rabagliati and Bernadette Cornuau, 'Visit to Israel', May 1989.
 7. Joseph Wresinski Centre: Archives, 1030/15-2, Dan Izenberg, 'French Social Workers Help the Ones Social Welfare Misses', *Jerusalem Post,* 17 May 1989.
 8. Joseph Wresinski Centre: Archives, 1030/15-2, letter from Mary, 2 June 1989.
 9. Joseph Wresinski Centre: Archives, 1030/15-2, letter from Mary, 10 May 1989.
 10. Joseph Wresinski Centre: Archives, 1030/15-2, Monday meeting in Méry-sur-Oise, 29 May 1989.

Chapter 23

 1. Joseph Wresinski Centre: Archives, 1030/40/03/01.
 2. N. Tweehuijsen, letter to D. Skelton, 3 April 2018.
 3. Letter from M. Gérardin to D. Skelton, 14 August 2018.
 4. Joseph Wresinski Centre: Archives, 1030/05, Letter from M. Rabagliati to M. Samura, 14 November 1988.
 5. Joseph Wresinski Centre: Archives, 0375-22, letter from M. Rabagliati to M. Gérardin, 30 October 1990.

6. Joseph Wresinski Centre: Archives, 0375-22, Letter from M. Rabagliati to M. Gérardin, 24 November 1990.
7. Joseph Wresinski Centre: Archives, 1068/4/1.6, open letter from M. Rabagliati to senior Volunteer Corps members, 2 August 1983.
8. Joseph Wresinski Centre: Archives, 1068/4/1.6, 'Ce que les familles attendent de notre Volontariat', speech by M. Rabagliati at ATD Fourth World's General Assembly of senior Volunteer Corps members, August 1983.
9. Joseph Wresinski Centre: Archives, 1068/4/1.6, 'Ce que les familles attendent de notre Volontariat', August 1983.

Chapter 24

1. Joseph Wresinski Centre: Archives, 1068/5/1.1.
2. Interview of J. Beyeler by D. Skelton, 17-18 April 2018.
3. Joseph Wresinski Centre: Archives, 1068-INT-ForetNoire-1981_2001-Inv, letter from J. Wresinski to M. Rabagliati, 9 December 1980.
4. Joseph Wresinski Centre: Archives, 0269-INT-FondsChronoMvt-1954_2005-DS, Interview of M. Rabagliati in November 1985 by a 'Hibernation' group of H. van Breen, A.-M. Caron, C. Egner, D. Robert, and J. Toussaint.
5. Joseph Wresinski Centre: Archives, 1068-INT-ForetNoire-1981_2001-Inv, transcript of 'Rencontre des anciens', Bierbronnen, Germany, 29 December 1980.
6. Joseph Wresinski Centre: Archives, 1068-INT-ForetNoire-1981_2001-Inv, transcript of 'Rencontre des anciens '.
7. Joseph Wresinski Centre: Archives, 0274-YH66, M. Rabagliati, 'Réflexions sur le thème proposé pour les Assises 1981', open letter 3.
8. Joseph Wresinski Centre: Archives, 0274-YH66, M. Rabagliati,'Réflexions sur le thème proposé pour les Assises 1981'.
9. Joseph Wresinski Centre: Archives, 1068-INT-ForetNoire-1981_2001-Inv, transcript of 'Rencontre de la Forêt Noire', Baillet, France, January 1982.
10. Joseph Wresinski Centre: Archives, 1068-INT-ForetNoire-1981_2001-Inv, transcript of 'Rencontre des anciens ', Bierbronnen, Germany, 29 December 1980.
11. Interview with H. Bossot-Redegeld, 20 June 2018.
12. Joseph Wresinski Centre: Archives, 1068-INT-ForetNoire-1981_2001-Inv, transcript, Black Forest Group, August 1982.
13. Joseph Wresinski Centre: Archives, 1068-INT-ForetNoire-1981_2001-Inv, transcript, Black Forest Group, 18 August 1984.
14. Interview of J. Beyeler by D. Skelton on 16 April 2018.

15. Joseph Wresinski Centre: Archives, CJW-0028/039-052V, M. Rabagliati, 'Revue de Presse', article in ATD's internal 'Dossiers de Pierrelaye', January 1987.
16. Joseph Wresinski Centre: Archives, 1068/9, transcript of Black Forest Group meeting, Paris, 3 January 1988.
17. Joseph Wresinski Centre: Archives, 1030/15/01, letter from M. Rabagliati to J. Grandi, 22 April 1988.
18. Joseph Wresinski Centre: Archives, 1019-INT-Equipe-RelatExt-1977_1999-Inv, report by Dina Wardi on her visit to ATD's international centre, May 1988.
19. Joseph Wresinski Centre: Archives, YC54, letter from J. Beyeler to G. Erpicum, summer 1988.
20. Joseph Wresinski Centre: Archives, YC54/0238, "Assises", August 1988.
21. Interview of J. Beyeler by D. Skelton, 17-18 April 2018.
22. Joseph Wresinski Centre: Archives, 1068/10/1.3, Black Forest Group meeting, 18 March 1989.
23. Letter from J. Beyeler to D. Skelton, 4 April 2025.
24. Joseph Wresinski Centre: Archives, 1068/10/1.3, Black Forest Group meeting, 18 March 1989.
25. Joseph Wresinski Centre: Archives, 0259-WC69, activity report by M. Rabagliati covering December 1989 to February 1990.
26. Joseph Wresinski Centre: Archives, 1068/13/1.3, Black Forest Group meeting, 1 February 1992.
27. Joseph Wresinski Centre: Archives, 1068/11.1.11, A. Modave's notes on a Black Forest Group meeting, 28 May 1990.
28. Joseph Wresinski Centre: Archives, 1068/12/1.7, Black Forest Group meeting, 27 February 1991.
29. Joseph Wresinski Centre: Archives, 1068/12/1.11, note from M. Rabagliati to the Black Forest Group, 6 April 1991.
30. Joseph Wresinski Centre: Archives, 1068/12/1.11, note from M. Rabagliati to the Black Forest Group, 6 April 1991.
31. Joseph Wresinski Centre: Archives, 1068/12/1.12, note from J. Beyeler to the Black Forest Group, 6 April 1991.
32. Joseph Wresinski Centre: Archives, 1068/12/1.12, note from J. Beyeler to the Black Forest Group, 6 April 1991.
33. Interview with Jeanpierre Beyeler on 18 April 2018 and letter from J. Beyeler to D. Skelton, 4 April 2025.

Chapter 25

1. Joseph Wresinski Centre: Archives, 0375-7, letter from J. Wresinski to Mary, 1965.

2. Joseph Wresinski Centre: Archives, 0330-XV87, speech by M. Rabagliati to the Faith and Light European Region Meeting in Llanelli, UK, 21 September 1978.
3. Sève, 'Mary, volontaire à ATD Quart Monde'.
4. Fox, *Watching the English*, pp. 484-87.
5. Letter from Colin Barham to D. Skelton, 18 August 2018.
6. Interview with A. Van Elderen, 7 March 2018.
7. Interview of S. Baker by D. Skelton, 22 June 2018.
8. Letter from S. Baker to D. Skelton, 27 August 2019
9. Wresinski, *Ecrits et paroles aux volontaires,* volume 1, p. 202, citing a meeting of volunteers on 8 October 1965.
10. Joseph Wresinski Centre: Archives, 0375-7, letter from M. Rabagliati to J. Wresinski from New York, 6 April 1966.
11. Joseph Wresinski Centre: Archives, 0303-XL50, letter from M. Rabagliati to Helene von Burg and Jeanpierre Beyeler, 3 March 1970.
12. Joseph Wresinski Centre: Archives, 0138-XV51,14 December 1978.
13. Joseph Wresinski Centre: Archives, 0330-XV87, speech by M. Rabagliati to the Faith and Light European Region Meeting in Llanelli, UK, 21 September 1978.

Chapter 26

1. Interview of J. Beyeler by D. Skelton, 16 April 2018.
2. Interview of H. Bossot-Redegeld by D. Skelton, 20 June 2018.
3. Archives of ATD Fourth World–Addington Square, letter from J. Wresinski to M. Rabagliati, 30 June 1982.
4. Archives of ATD Fourth World–Addington Square, letter from M. Rabagliati to Lilias Graham, 21 June 1982.
5. Archives of ATD Fourth World–Addington Square, notes by Lily McAuley, Eddie Moore, Lesley Moore, Tracey Roberts, Eilish Scott, and Michael Steele, 21-25 July 1982
6. Archives of ATD Fourth World–Addington Square, report by Eilish Scott, 'Trip to Rome to Meet the Pope', 25 August 1982.
7. Joseph Wresinski Centre: Archives, 1068-INT-ForetNoire-1981_2001-Inv, notes from Black Forest Group meeting, 19-20 August 1982.
8. Joseph Wresinski Centre: Archives, CJW-0028/039-052V, Rabagliati, 'What Voluntariat will we be in Africa?'
9. Joseph Wresinski Centre: Archives, 0110/26, 'Note sur les réflexions de … à propos du projet d'une congrégation religieuse', 18 October 1984.
10. Joseph Wresinski Centre: Archives, 0110/26, 'Note sur les réflexions de … à propos du projet d'une congrégation religieuse', 18 October 1984.
11. Interview of J. Beyeler by D. Skelton, 16 April 2018.
12. Interview of J. Beyeler by D. Skelton, 17-18 April 2018.

13. Joseph Wresinski Centre: Archives, 1068/9, minutes of Black Forest Group meeting, 10 May 1988.
14. Joseph Wresinski Centre: Archives, 1068/9/1.18, letter from B. Cornuau to the Black Forest Group, 29 May 1988.
15. Joseph Wresinski Centre: Archives, 1068/9/1.18, 'Réflexions de Mary sur les différentes discussions, lectures de lettres concernant la dimension spirituelle dans le Mouvement', 31 May 1988.
16. Joseph Wresinski Centre: Archives, 1AVP027 - E – Q9, audiotape, undated.
17. Letter from J. Beyeler to D. Skelton, 7 April 2025.
18. Joseph Wresinski Centre: Archives, 0375-22, letter from M. Rabagliati to Michèle Gérardin, 3 November 1988.
19. Joseph Wresinski Centre: Archives, 1030/02/02.
20. Joseph Wresinski Centre: Archives, 1068/11/1.17, 'Compte rendu de la réunion du groupe de la Forêt Noire', 19 September 1990.
21. Interview with A. Van Elderen, 7 March 2018.
22. Interview of J. Beyeler by D. Skelton, 17-18 April 2018.
23. Sève, 'Mary, volontaire à ATD Quart Monde'.

Chapter 27

1. Michèle Grenot, *Le souci des plus pauvres: Dufourny, la Révolution française et la démocratie* (Rennes: Presses universitaires de Rennes, 2014), p. 432.
2. Coste, 'Mary la Volontaire', *Télé 7 Jours*, March 1964.
3. 'Guildford Girl (22) Helping the "Lame Ducks" of Paris'. The article is unsigned and although three clippings of it survive, none include the exact date or the name of the publication.
4. Joseph Wresinski Centre: Archives, 'A Holiday for the Homeless', *Daily Telegraph and Morning Post*, 21 March 1964.
5. Joseph Wresinski Centre: Archives, Interview with M. Rabagliati by 'Hibernation' group, 1989.
6. Joseph Wresinski Centre: Archives, speech by M. Rabagliati to a general assembly of allies of ATD Fourth World, 1 November 1989.
7. Joseph Wresinski Centre: Archives, Interview with M. Rabagliati by E. Boespflug, 2 September 1976.
8. Joseph Wresinski Centre: Archives, report by M. Rabagliati, 1 March 1967.
9. Letter from U. Jomini to D. Skelton, 11 April 2018.
10. Interview with A. Van Elderen, 7 March 2018.
11. Interview of S. Baker by D. Skelton, 22 June 2018.
12. Joseph Wresinski Centre: Archives, 0375-22, letter from Mimi Parnell to Stuart Williams, 21 November 1992.

13. Joseph Wresinski Centre: Archives, 0775/05/2F11-2, Planning session, 15 January 1982.
14. Joseph Wresinski Centre: Archives, CJW-0028/039-052V, M. Rabagliati, 'Devant l'existence interdite d'une famille', article in ATD's internal 'Dossiers de Pierrelaye', February 1984.
15. Interview with A. Van Elderen, 7 March 2018.
16. Pauline, in collaboration with Anneke Van Elderen, Isabelle Williams, and Mary Rabagliati, *Pauline: Families of Courage* (London: ATD Fourth World UK, 1984).
17. Circular letter from S. Williams sent out to university social work tutors, April 1985. His letter cites Bob Holman's review in *Community Care* on 17 January 1985 and Elizabeth Irvine's review in *Social Work Today* on 5 November 1984.
18. International Movement ATD Fourth World, *Fourth World Chronicle of Human Rights* (Pierrelaye, France: Fourth World Publications, 1989).
19. Letter from M. Rabagliati to D. Skelton, 18 June 1990.
20. Joseph Wresinski Centre: Archives, 0375-22, letters from M. Rabagliati to Michèle Gérardin in Haiti, 12 February 1988 and 11 January 1990.
21. Joseph Wresinski Centre: Archives, 1068/11/1.16, Black Forest Group meeting, 14 September 1990.
22. Joseph Wresinski Centre: Archives, 1068/11/1.21, Black Forest Group meeting, 28 November 1990.
23. Joseph Wresinski Centre: Archives, 1068/12/1.1, Black Forest Group meeting, 9-11 January 1991, and 1068/12/1.28, 9 November 1991.
24. Obituary by S. Williams, 'Mary Rabagliati', *The Independent*, 17 November 1992, pp. 12.
25. Joseph Wresinski Centre: Archives, 0238-CINT-SecGeneral-1988_1993-Inv, letter read at a Monday morning meeting in ATD's international centre in Méry-sur-Oise, France, 27 January 1991.
26. Joseph Wresinski Centre: Archives, 0375-22, eulogy delivered by Mary Totham following M. Rabagliati's death, November 1992.
27. Joseph Wresinski Centre: Archives, 0375-22, Letter from M. Rabagliati to Michèle Gérardin, 5 March 1990.
28. Sève, 'Mary, volontaire à ATD Quart Monde'.
29. Letter from C. Vesey to D. Skelton, 28 Jan 2019.
30. Interview of E. Brand by D. Skelton, 12 Nov. 2024.
31. Interview of S. Devins by D. Skelton, 22 Oct. 2024.

Index

abortion, 208–9
Acevedo, Mariette, 125
Adoption and Children Act (2002), 195
Adriaensens, Ghislaine, 137
Africa, ATD Fourth World in, 215–17
air pollution, and premature deaths, 239
Alexandra (South African township), 93
American Civil Liberties Union, 78
Amnesty International, 199–200
Aparicio, Mathilde, 37, 40, 314–15
apartheid, South Africa, 92–103
Appalachia, USA, 87–8
ATD Fourth World:
  30th anniversary, 283;
  'Black Forest Group,' 277–92, 305–6;
  'Children of Our Time' exhibition (1979), 180–3;
  delegation to Pope John Paul II, 302–4;
  'Fourth World Evening' discussions, 188–90, 193;
  'Fourth World Women's Charter,' 205, 209;
  at Frimhurst Family Centre, 162–3;
  in Madagascar, 248;
  mission statement, 54;
  name, 10;
  participates in World Conference on Women (1975), 204;
  Pierrelaye training centre, 135–8, 167;
  publications, 321–4;
  and religion, 293–312;
  in Senegal, 215–16;
  in Sierra Leone, 241–50;
  in Switzerland, 164;
  UK branch, 14–15, 144–5, 153, 154, 170–1;
  UNESCO seminar, 69;
  US branch, 89;
  Volunteer Corps, 63–6, 81, 123–4, 164, 217–19, 274–6
Aurières, Marie-France, 146–7, 164
Ayassamy, Babette, 300–1, 303

Bailey, Patricia, 200
Baillet-en-France, 17
Baker, Stephen, 165–6, 189, 295–6, 320
Barghouti, Mustafa, 258
Barham, Colin, 166–8, 295
Bazaine, Jean René, 44, 296, 297
Bedouins, in Israel, 265–6
Ben Rhydding Women's Unionist Association, 33
Bennett, Fran, 165, 170, 184, 186
Beyeler, Jeanpierre, 151, 164, 221, 243, 277, 282–3, 285, 287, 290–2, 305, 307, 309

birth control, 122–3, 138–9, 208–9
Black Power Movement, 86
Black Sash (anti-apartheid movement), 92, 94, 104
Boone, Dick, 80
Bottomley, Baroness Virginia, 174–7
Bottomley, Sir Peter, 174–7, 188, 327
Bourgein, Margaret, 22–4, 54–5
Brand, Eugen, 289, 291, 330
Braque, Georges, 44
Bright, Helen, 32
Burg, Hélène von, 151, 164
Button, Amanda, 197, 199, 200

Chaplin, Charlie, 296
Chapman, Reggie, 183–4
Chávez, César, 83–4
Chequers, Buckinghamshire, 24
Child Poverty Action Group (UK), 179–80
children, taken into care, 130–4, 195–200
Christian Fellowship Trust (CFT), 92, 96
Churchill, Winston, 21, 24
Citizens' Crusade Against Poverty, 80
civil rights movement, 14, 82, 105
Cleaver, Eldridge, 88
Cloward, Richard, 69
Cola, Lenore, 310
Cornuau, Bernadette, 251–5, 258–9, 261, 263, 293, 306, 309

Denmark, World Conference on Women (1980), 209–11
Desire Housing Projects, New Orleans, 82
Devins, Susie, 232, 241–2, 279, 288, 331
Didisheim, Francine, 251–3
Dufourny de Villers, Louis Pierre, Les Cahiers du Quatrième Ordre, 314
Dumayet, Françoise, 316
Duquesne, Lucien, An End to Injustice (1984), 192

Elderen, Anneke van, 13, 19, 35, 185, 187, 188–9, 271, 295, 309, 320, 321–2
Emmaüs International, 37
Erpicum, Gabrielle, 45, 89, 135, 164, 289
European Trade Fair, Strasbourg, 318

Faithfull, Lucy, Baroness, 182
Fanelli, Vincent, 71–2
Fawcett, Millicent, 32
feminism, 115
Ferrand, Claude, 289
Fleming, Ian, Goldfinger, 33–4
Ford Foundation, 14, 69
Fox, Kate, Watching the English, 294
Friedan, Betty, 205
Frimhurst Family Centre, 143–69
Frimhurst Journal, 156, 168

Gainsford, Margaret, 145, 146
Gaitskell, Helen, 227
Gaza, 263–4
Gérardin, Michèle, 272–3, 308
Giscard d'Estaing, Anémone, 207
Giving Poverty a Voice programme, 168
Goodman, Grace, 109–11, 145–8, 154, 163
Grandi, Judith, 235–40, 283
Guildford Technical College, 29

Hamel, Elisa, 215–16, 230–4
Hamel, Philippe, 215–16, 230–4, 235, 247–8, 249
Hart, Karen A., 247, 271–2, 330
Haworth, Dr Simon, 195–6, 200
Huerta, Dolores, 83
human rights, and poverty, 58, 190–2
Human Rights Festival, Brussels (1982), 190–2

International Year of the Child (1979), 179, 188
International Youth Year (1985), 241

Index

Israel:
  Mary's first visit to, 251–67;
  Mary's second visit to (1989), 258–67

Jahrling, Bernard, 37–8, 40, 167–8
Jarman, Julie, 27–8
Jelinek, Donald, 78
John Paul II, Pope, 302–4, 308
Jomini, François, 245–7
Jomini, Ursula, 137, 186, 295, 319–20
Joseph Wresinski Centre of Archives and Research, 17
journalists and the media, 313–17

Kalisa, Martin, 103–4
Kassé, Saco, 308
Kikaya, Neccy and David, 232
King, Coretta Scott, 283
Klein, Fabienne, 245–7, 271
Kotze, Rev Theo, 98
Kronenfeld, Daniel, 72, 89

Labbens, Jean, 124
Lacey, Marc, 316
Lambert, Dr Michael, 146
Lazarus, Alley, 104
León, Cándido de, 73–4
Lescour, Jean-Pierre, 99, 103
Lesotho, 99–103
Lister, Ruth, 180
Luckhoff, Lucille, 104

Madagascar, 248
Maréchal, Paul, 11, 12
Mason, Christopher, 13–14, 57
Mauriac, François, 135
McLaren, Agnes, 32
McLaren, Duncan, 20
McLaren, Priscilla Bright, 20, 31–2
Medical Committee for Human Rights, 78
Mexico City, World Conference on Women (1975), 204–8
Miller, Professor S.M., 69, 76, 86, 89
Miró, Joan, 44

Missouri, racial segregation, 86–7
Mlambo, Nombeko, 97
Mobilization for Youth (MFY), 69–78
Moira House School, Eastbourne, 26–7
Mosley, Oswald, 110
Moss, Julia, 227
Mount Tabor, 254
Muigai, Salome, 223–5, 228–30, 283
Musallam, Father Manuel, 262–3

Naidoo, Phyllis, 100
Nairobi, World Conference on Women (1985), 211–13
National Conference of Catholic Charities (US), 82–3
National Farm Workers, California, 83–5
Naudé, Beyers, 92–3, 102
Naudé, Ilse, 92–3
Ndebele, Mpho, 101–2
New York, Mobilization for Youth (MFY), 69–78
NGOs (non-governmental organisations), 215
Noisy-le-Grand emergency housing camp, 6–7, 10, 37–42, 54–7;
  women's centre, 43–52, 60

Ohlin, Lloyd, 69

Palestine, Mary's visits to, 251–67
Pathway Films, documentary on Frimhurst, 168
Pierre, Abbé, 37
Pierrelaye training centre, 135–8, 167
Prospect Magazine, 195

Rabagliati, Alexander Coultate ('Sandy'), 19, 20–3, 226–7
Rabagliati, Catrine, 26, 31, 33
Rabagliati, Euan, 34
Rabagliati, Francis, 22, 227
Rabagliati, Helen (née McLaren), 32–3
Rabagliati, Julia, 19–20, 226–7

Rabagliati, Mary:
  advocacy with UK politicians, 173–8;
  arrested in Alabama, 78;
  article in Women's Forum newsletter (UK), 208;
  and ATD Fourth World in Africa, 217, 221–5, 232;
  ATD publications, 321–4;
  ATD trip to South Africa and Lesotho (1983), 98–103;
  attends UN World Conferences on Women, 204–14;
  and birth control, 122–3, 138–9, 208–9;
  in the 'Black Forest Group,' 277–92;
  cancer diagnosis, 271–2;
  contributes to UK Children OK? pamphlet, 179–80;
  creation of ATD archive, 54;
  death (1992), 326–7;
  distrust of social workers, 72–3;
  education, 25–30;
  family background, 18–25, 31–4, 225–8;
  at Frimhurst Family Centre, 143–69;
  and importance of joy, 57–8;
  interview in La Croix, 328–9;
  at the London School of Economics, 164;
  mistrust of welfare benefits, 80;
  in Noisy-le-Grand, 6–7, 10, 12–13, 35–52;
  in Palestine and Israel, 251–67;
  personal characteristics, 3, 4, 13, 184–7, 330–1;
  profiled in media reports, 316–17;
  and public speaking, 318–21;
  purchases 48 Addington Square for ATD Fourth World, 171–2;
  on racism and poverty, 106–11;
  and religion, 302–12;
  report writing and research, 59–63;
  research in Birmingham, 121–2;
  secretarial work, 30;
  in Sierra Leone, 235–50;
  study trip to South Africa (1973), 92–6;
  travels round US with Wresinski, 78–91;
  TV interview (1974), 152;
  in the USA, 14;
  works for MFY in New York, 69–78
Rabagliati, Sandra (née Rhoda Bourgein), 19–27, 30–1, 63
racial segregation (US), 77–8, 82, 89–90
racism:
  and poverty, 106–11;
  in the UK, 107–11
Ramose, Mogobe, 97
Redegeld, Huguette Bossot, 35, 54, 56, 89, 143, 186, 204–8, 281, 302
religious beliefs, and ATD Fourth World, 293–312
Roberts, Moraene, 311
Rosenfeld, Dr Jona, 257–60;
  Emergence from Extreme Poverty, 259
Rosenfeld, Ruti, 259, 264
Royal Tunbridge Wells, Kent, 25
Rucker, Mary, 115–16
Russell, Gina, 313–14
Russell, Kit, 164

Salaman, Juliet, 28
Samura, Rev Michael, 240–1, 273, 283
Seinnave, Brigitte, 98–103, 170
Selma, Alabama, 78
Senegal, ATD Fourth World in, 215–16
Sheriff, Gladys Jusu, 238
Sidinga Uthando Self-Help Group, South Africa, 103
Sierra Leone, 235–50; Boys' Society, 240–4
Smyth, Dame Ethel, 146
Soames, Mary, Baroness, 182
social workers, 72–3, 193–200, 259–60
Sorbonne University, 30

Index

South Africa, apartheid, 92–103
Soweto uprising (1976), 101
Speakers' Corner, Hyde Park, 15, 16, 187, 319–20
St Catherine's Home for Cancer, 33
St Croix, Paul de, 13, 27, 30–1, 184, 203
St Monica's Home for unmarried mothers, 33
Stanley, Jo, 33
Steenwijk, Alwine de Vos van, 204–8, 307
Steindl-Rast, David, 104
Stone, Judith, 27, 179
Swann, Mona, 28

Tardieu, Geneviève and Bruno, 219
Terry, Peggy, 88
Thatcher, Margaret, 174
Titmuss, Richard, 164
Totham, Mary, 327
Truth, Sojourner, 205
Tunnard, Jo, 180
Tweehuijsen, Niek, 271

UNESCO, 69, 180, 272, 283, 322
UNICEF, 247–9
United Nations:
  conference on poverty (1972), 257;
  World Conferences on Women, 15, 102, 204–13;
  World Day for Overcoming Poverty, 15, 17

violence, and poverty, 117–20

War on Poverty, 14, 69, 76, 88
Wardi, Dina, 193–4, 259, 285, 308
Weissman, Harold, Community Development in the Mobilization for Youth Experience, 90
Weldt, Erika van, 277, 302

welfare benefits, 80
Westminster Abbey, 'Children of Our Time' exhibition (1979), 182
Williams, Isabelle, 170, 172–3
Williams, Stuart, 170, 171, 184
women:
  and birth control, 122–3;
  disappointment in feminist activism, 204–5;
  losing child custody, 130–4;
  and violence, 115–20
Wood, Margaret Rabagliati, 19, 31, 34
World Day for Overcoming Poverty, 15–16, 283, 311
World Health Organisation, 239
Wresinski, Father Joseph:
  ATD mission statement, 54;
  and the ATD Volunteer Corps, 63–6;
  attends first World Conference on Women (1975), 204, 205;
  and birth control, 123, 138–9;
  and the 'Black Forest Group,' 277–8;
  childhood poverty, 18;
  death, 277, 283–5, 287;
  friendship with Grace Goodman, 146;
  on male anger, 117–18;
  in Noisy-le-Grand, 3–4, 6, 14, 36–7, 39–42;
  on the place of religion in ATD Fourth World, 302, 305;
  travels round US with Mary Rabagliati, 78–91;
  at the UN conference on poverty (1972), 257;
  Extreme Poverty and Social and Economic Insecurity, 284;
  The Wresinski Report (1987), 259

Yanka-Kanu, Mustapha, 240, 283
Young, Janet, Baroness, 212–13